To
My mother, for teaching me how.
My father, for being my biggest fan and daily editor.
Christine, for believing in me.
Pepper, for keeping me grounded.

All of the operators of *Black Flag One*,
both living and feasting in the halls of Valhalla.
Keith, Brandon, Zach, and Scotty-Boom-Boom,
for being giants among men.

The VA, for having the resources and knowledge
when I needed them most.

A very special dedication to
M-J from the YouTube channel "Reading This Life."
Without you Moe, this would never have happened.

VALHALLA BOYS

VALHALLA BOYS

Marine Recon Sniper in Iraq

BRENNAN MORTON

CASEMATE

Pennsylvania & Yorkshire

Published in the United States of America and Great Britain in 2025 by
CASEMATE PUBLISHERS
1950 Lawrence Road, Havertown, PA 19083
and
47 Church Street, Barnsley, S70 2AS, UK

Hardback Edition: ISBN 978-1-63624-481-5
Digital Edition: ISBN 978-1-63624-482-2

A CIP record for this book is available from the British Library

Printed and bound in the United Kingdom by CPI Group (UK) Ltd, Croydon, CR0 4YY

Typeset in India by Lapiz Digital Services, Chennai.

For a complete list of Casemate titles, please contact:

CASEMATE PUBLISHERS (US)
Telephone (610) 853-9131
Fax (610) 853-9146
Email: casemate@casematepublishers.com
www.casematepublishers.com

CASEMATE PUBLISHERS (UK)
Telephone (0)1226 734350
Email: casemate@casemateuk.com
www.casemateuk.com

A previous edition of this work was published by the author under the title *Dying for Strangers*.

Cover artwork by Dragan Paunovic.

All photographs from the author's collection unless otherwise indicated.

The views expressed in this publication are those of the author and do not necessarily reflect the official policy or position of the Department of Defense or the U.S. government. The public release clearance of this publication by the Department of Defense does not imply Department of Defense endorsement or factual accuracy of the material.

Contents

"Be polite, be professional, but have a plan to kill everyone you meet."
—James Mattis

Preface

The first draft of this book was written in fitful chunks whenever I could not sleep, which seemed much too often, given the dark rucksacks under my eyes. My therapist at Veterans Affairs (VA) had me writing about certain moments, over and over, to try to get beyond them. Only a month out of the service, and it was as if the floodgates had suddenly opened and everything I had been walling off broke free. Those were not good times and the content, as well as the writing, reflected that turmoil.

I had squinted at the screen through tears, smashing away at the keyboard, while listening to my two editors, self-loathing and anger, neither of whom conducted themselves professionally during the process, though I must give credit where credit is due. They certainly knew how to keep me motivated.

And so, the words flowed, and the stories congealed into, well, into something. The stories were morose and without hope, a literary toilet of despair, ever swirling down, down, down. That is the polite version, anyway.

But it did help, and I owe my life to my VA therapist.

A good friend, who did not serve, read them recently and said, "Why don't you go back and give the stories a little of the love you seem to have gotten back. You have more stories than just these sad, terrifying ones."

It is hard to admit when something you created, that you poured your soul into, is flawed. But it was. So, I tried to strip away some of the angst and emotional tarnish, like trying to clean residue from the *Mona Lisa*, though in this case I only found a stick-figure version of dogs playing poker underneath. Still, it felt good. It felt like letting go, like finally exhaling, as I watched the burning-ship pyre of my past sail out into the darkness on its way to Valhalla.

Still, it is not pretty.

These are not your grandfather's letters from the front, censored and spilling over with optimistic glory about conquering the Nazis. This is about the childhood left behind and, as in the end of everyone's story, this is about death.

This is about Peter Pan's Lost Boys going to war.

This is the dirty, bloody truth of it.

All names have been changed, as has the timeline of some events.

CHAPTER I

A Joker Born to Kill

In first grade, I was given a thin phonics book made of coarse gray paper, that smelled faintly of old burnt socks, and asked to draw a cat coming out of a box wearing a bow. It was a simple assignment, with only three requirements: include a cat, a box, and a bow in your picture. I was overjoyed as I gazed at the gray rectangle I had been offered to render my visual masterpiece inside. I worked diligently for days on the assignment, working delicious crayons down to nubs, trying to express the grand vision threatening the boundaries of my tiny mind. Finished, I oh-so carefully ripped the thick page from its poor binding, still leaving ragged edges despite the perforations, and gave my masterpiece one more satisfied smile before the teacher snaked her way around our desks to collect it.

It featured no fewer than five tanks, four airplanes (or what passed for the general idea of one), two jeeps, and a legion of kittens in brown and green fatigues, fiercely gripped in the art of war, with streaks of red insinuating bullet trajectories, as well as entrance and exit wounds in some of the less lucky kittens. It was a sprawling visual depiction of my most favorite subject. "War" was printed in big, bold letters across the top of the picture and, as it was scooped up and stacked with the others of the class, I sighed triumphantly.

It was perfect.

It received an "unsatisfactory" mark as I had, so wrapped up in the details of viscera and impact craters, forgotten to put a bow on the kitten. There was also a note above the tank the principal kitten was coming out of. It read, "Is this really a box?" It was more of a rectangle.

Not being the brightest boy, I still beamed. Someone looked at it! I did not fail. The teacher simply had not understood the social commentary I was trying to express. Or, rather, I had failed and was too simple to realize it, which seems an even finer thing. My ignorance was blissful.

As far back as I could remember, war and the military had held a fascination usually reserved for the loveliness of the opposite sex in most young boys. Army–Navy surplus stores were like Mecca, Disneyland, and Dollywood all wrapped up into one. I had old fatigues kept together by my mother's deft hand with needle and thread, and myriad unit patches that meant very little to me at the time except in that they were a military unit. My friends and I ran around the deep woods with plastic replica guns yelling "bang" at each other. If plastic replicas could not be had, we would find a stick with a vague semblance and yell "bang" even louder to make up for its visual shortcomings. We would play War from dawn until dusk, slumping motionless on the decaying leaves and damp pine needles when we were shot dead, only to jump up and counterattack when the moment seemed ripe.

If only it were so easy to get everyone back up after.

When it became too dark to play in the woods without getting lost or impaled, I would go inside and play with my three-inch "G.I. Joe" action figures, of which I had hundreds at the high-water mark in my G.I. Joe recruiting. Enlistment bonuses ran as high as whatever I could scrounge from my piggybank and beg for holidays. In the quiet battlefield of my room the War never ended, only skirmishes won or lost, and always down to the final man, whichever figure curried the most favor at that moment.*

For many years, "Soldier" was the only thing I aspired to be. It was seemingly the greatest, most noble profession. With its sharp uniforms and access to firearms at virtually any time, it seemed like the simplest choice in the world. Even when my voice cracked, my hair grew past my frail, bony shoulders, and I sneered at everything society had to offer, I still felt that pull. When a girl finally touched me, I suddenly stopped sneering at society and cut my hair, but I still felt that undertow clawing at my ankles, eating away the sandy foundation I stood upon. It was always there, sitting in the back of my head. That scratch, no matter how I tried to replicate combat, could not be itched. It only grew.

Despite all of this, I do not know if I would have signed the dotted line if an actual "war" had not broken out. In my defense, college did have a lot more women, choice in my schedule, and the ability to leave my bed unmade.

The truth is that Hemingway, Heller, and Vonnegut had more to do with me swearing the oath to defend my country than any other factor or persons in my life. They had written extensively about the brutish senselessness of war in lurid detail, spent entire novels warning anyone who would listen, about the dark place in a man's soul that war seemed to water and nourish until it blossomed, crushing anything beautiful underneath its unbearable weight. War, they wrote, showed the true depths of humanity, however heroic or terrible.

I believe my literary idols would turn in their graves if they knew their writings had created the desire to go off to war in one of their readers.

---

* It was never "Gung-ho," despite his service branch. I think Hasbro really missed the mark with that figurine. To a small boy there was something unnerving about a muscular man who looked like he would be more comfortable at a rave than in combat.

It was not only my literary heroes whose damning of war became a siren song, growing my curiosity even further. Before burning Atlanta to the ground, General Sherman wrote a letter to the mayor of the city, urging him to evacuate all citizens before the assault began in earnest.

"War is cruelty, and you cannot refine it," he wrote candidly in his appeal, hoping his vast knowledge on the subject would lead to fewer civilian casualties. Sherman then went on to address the Michigan Military Academy five years later and concluded, "You don't know the horrible aspects of war. I've been through two wars, and I know. I've seen cities and homes in ashes. I've seen thousands of men lying on the ground, their dead faces looking up at the skies. I tell you, war is hell!"

Though the weapons and tactics have changed drastically since the first homo sapiens took up the sharpened stick and the jagged rock against each other, the unrefined brutality of war has been immutable over millennia. War is one of the universal threads that weaves through all of history, connecting every human being who has experienced it. Every account recorded has been rife with horror and despair, sometimes punctuated by moments of redemption, but not often. For any single account of war as a glorious deed, there are thousands of dead men who never left the field to have the chance to write their rebuttal.

But secondhand accounts were all they were—the words of other men who had experienced something so provocative it changed the course of their lives and the very nature of their being. They were someone else's experiences, and I could not abide that.

Proxy never satisfied me in the least. It only grew my desire further. I wanted to walk through this hell and see it for myself, firsthand, with the Roman poet Virgil as my tour guide. I wanted to experience the stygian nightmare and explore my own soul there in the darkness. Despite every warning and sound piece of advice, I wanted to throw myself into the despair of combat and find out who I truly was. After a lifetime of pretend and plastic facsimile, I needed to know, to experience what I had only imagined and read about from the safety of everyday life.

But how do you tell friends and loved ones you want to find out what it is to put yourself directly in harm's way, to stand as close to your own death as possible?

How do you explain you want to know what it feels like, or if you even have the courage, to get into the trench or firing line and pit yourself against a mortal foe, whose sole occupation is to snuff out your beautiful flame, to crush under their boot the unique snowflake you think you are?

How do you express your deepest fear, that you just might be a pathetic coward, fearing, when the moment to perform arrives, you are found wanting?

I needed to know.

After a youth spent pretending I was courageous under fire, I needed to find out the answer to the question that had gnawed at me for nearly twenty years. September

11 happened like a sign from the gods to me; it swept away any doubt as to my future. Here, suddenly, was a real "war."

I was needed. I finished college, traveled the country for a few months in case I never got the chance again, made my peace with the consequences, and signed my name on the dotted line.

What is the old cliché? Careful what you wish for.

CHAPTER 2

Melted Down and Remolded

Immersion was the name of the game. They would take away our nasty civilian language—so full of "want," "can't," and "think"—while simultaneously stripping us of our sense of individualism. No more "me," "my," and "I." They would be replaced with a highly disciplined and deliberate culture of "we."

I fear and bleed, cower and whimper.

I am a liability.

Together, we are invincible, willing to charge machine-gun nests without hesitation, howling the cry of war.

We are immortal.

The individual must be broken, crushed under the boot heel, to give rise to thoughts only of a fire team, a squad, a platoon, a company, and the greater good of "we."

Boot camp was a game, a highly sophisticated game that has evolved over thousands of years of war and warrior cultures, but the turning of lambs into wolves was still just a game. As a lamb, the trick was to realize there was no winning. The house always wins; to rage against that idea was only to invite further attention and correction.

Brick was a standard-issue 18-year-old male of the squad bay: straight out of high school, strong from the enormous chip on his shoulder, but burdened by an unfounded arrogance that elicited disdain in every authority figure he turned his smug grin upon. Brick believed he was different, that he was an unbreakable spirit, despite the evidence of millennia of military training to the contrary. Everyone capitulates, or at least smiles through their teeth and pretends to.

Not Brick. Brick wore his defiance like a badge of honor, flaunting it whenever he could find the chance. But what he believed were little victories against the system were only droplets of blood in the water, serving as a beacon to the toothy grins of the sharks charged with his shaping. Brick could not see the shadows gathering in the dark water beneath him, as he was too busy smirking and sticking his chin out to the world above the waves. The sergeants grinned their awful smiles and bided their time.

When Brick's moment came, no one was ready for it. As we stood in our underwear on the line for morning inspection, three unfamiliar sergeant instructors burst into the squad bay like a fierce winter storm, howling and snapping their frothing jaws at every terrified face as they rushed toward Brick like an avalanche. Gods help him, Brick tilted up his chin and gave his most smug sneer to the banshees.

We were made to stand "on line" and watch the first 10 minutes while the three tan, muscular instructors surrounded Brick and screamed at him without pause, his face spattered with flecks of their warm, thick spit as they went absolutely berserk. Their questions were rhetorical, and the insults were designed to cut to the absolute core of a man. After 10 minutes and the pitch of their fury not dropping, Brick's grin slowly began to crumble under the sheer weight of their verbal assault.

We were ordered to get our socks on; five, four, three, two, one—back on line. Business as usual.

Brick did not move, as his own personal hell warmed to a roaring boil.

We were ordered to put on our shirts and running shorts in turn. Five, four, three, two, one—back on line.

The obscene screaming only seemed to rise to a crescendo.

We were ordered to put on our shoes (no, not shoes, "go-fasters"). Five, four, three, two, one, back on line, and still the three men howled mere inches from Brick's quivering face. "Left face, fall out to the training fields" and, just like that, Brick was left unexpectedly behind to reap what he had sown.

An hour later, we returned from our physical training to find Brick exactly where we had left him, standing at attention in his underwear, still surrounded by the three slobbering instructors hopping up and down like witch doctors, with their fingers and noses uncomfortably close to Brick's face. The only thing that had changed was one of the sergeants had begun to lose his voice, as the veins on his neck bulged and throbbed with each punctuated syllable. There was no trace of Brick's grin and his quivering chin bobbed ever deeper toward his chest with each shallow exhale.

The platoon showered and dressed. We kept our eyes straight ahead and tried our best to ignore the three screaming elephants in the room, lest we garner their attention and join Brick. Their immaculately tailored uniforms, tight, sinewy muscles, and wild, bulging eyes brooked no defiance, and the idea of foolishly inviting such men into our personal space knotted the stomach and filled the bladder to bursting point. Given a choice, most of the platoon would have rather grappled with a feral dog than have those three monsters' full attention.

When we were given the order to fall out to the parade grounds without Brick, there was an extra lively kick to our step. "No man left behind," that is, unless that man is being severely berated and you do not wish to join him. In that case, be brisk in your abandonment and always make it look snappy and crisp.

While the rest of the platoon trained all day to our normal battle rhythm, Brick was given private "instruction" in the squad bay by the three instructors, who took turns after the initial two hours of group effort. While two of the instructors would be off enjoying a leisurely lunch and a shower, Brick was never given a single moment of reprieve. If he had to go to the bathroom, he would have to try pissing with one of their wild faces in his, screaming that Brick must be sad over how he had been issued a pistol, when every other man carried a nice, long rifle, or an AT-4* in the instructor's case.

Where the squad bay was outfitted to house 80 lambs when we first began boot camp, by halfway only 50 remained. The empty bunk beds had been pushed up together at the back of the squad bay in what we referred to as the "dead zone." It became a place of fear and punishment, a dark place where superstition bested reason, and even the learned men would avoid looking into the shadows for deep, primitive reasons that could not be explained.

Brick was escorted into the dead zone before lights out, tucked away as far back as he could be, out of direct sight from the rest of the platoon, but still right where we could not ignore his audible plight. At lights out, a fresh instructor relieved the current and, like the harpies of Greek mythology, Brick was never left to himself to enjoy a moment of serenity in an already unstable and terrifying world. His fresh instructor silently leered at him from only inches away, staring down eagerly into his face as Brick laid at the position of attention on his rack. There would be no games from lights out to lights on, as the sergeant instructors were very cognizant of their limits and the standing orders, that each would-be warrior would not be deprived of sleep. By the letter of the order, Brick was allowed to lay in his rack and given the opportunity to "sleep"; whether or not he exercised that right was his own choice.

Come "Lights, lights, lights," Brick did not look like he had exercised his right even for a moment. His head drooped and, when a fresh, bright-eyed instructor relieved the night watch, the games began anew. While Brick seemed to have lost the spark of his defiance from the day before, the oncoming sergeant instructor seemed only more eager and overflowing with vigor. The tan demon grinned and growled orders, as Brick failed repeatedly to dress in an appropriate manner and speed. Over and over, Brick put his socks on as fast as he could, only to fail again and again. After half an hour, Brick was almost fully dressed save his blouse. He failed to retrieve it, put it on, and be back on line in time. The sergeant instructor smiled wickedly.

"Strip. We start all over from the beginning again," he growled.

After an hour, Brick was ready to start his second day of instruction.

The task for the day was easy enough. Brick was ordered to take apart every bunk bed "rack" in the dead zone. Each rack comprised four pieces fitted together by sheer force of will and elbow grease. There was not a single tool needed to do the job save two hands, sweat, and possibly blood magic. When we arrived back in the squad bay that afternoon from training, Brick had just finished taking the last rack

---

* An unguided antitank rocket the length and width of a human leg.

apart. His clothing was completely soaked through with sweat and his eyes lolled drunkenly as he stepped onto the line, mumbling that he had finished. The sergeant instructor lazily glanced at all the pieces laid out on the floor.

"Excellent. Now put them back together," he growled.

And Brick did.

And took them all apart.

And put them all back together.

By the end of the third day of Brick's own private hell, he looked punch drunk. His eyes would shut for a moment and then suddenly spring open with a sense of alarm reserved only for prey on a stormy night where only sight could save. He stood on line looking down at his dinner, which had been brought back in a small Styrofoam container. There was a heaping pile of white rice and a rubbery piece of chicken.

The smallest of Brick's three personal sergeant instructors stood next to him with a toothy sneer on his sharp, angular face, staring holes into Brick's drooping head. The sergeant instructor's overly tanned skin was stretched unnaturally tight across his high cheek bones, giving the look of a leather mask from which his two beady eyes glared out from behind, as he pointed his hairless, sinewy arm down towards the meal at Brick's feet.

"Hungry?" the sergeant instructor asked. Brick looked up with the last bit of defiance he could muster and stuck out his shaking chin. The sergeant instructor grinned a most awful grin, as if Brick had granted him his most secret wish. "Well, dig in. Oh, wait, I almost forgot."

The sergeant instructor held out his balled fist toward Brick and the grin became something of pure evil, something so touched by malice that to see it was to almost be driven mad, with the lips pulled impossibly wide exposing too-white teeth and too much of his pink gums.

"I almost forgot," the sergeant instructor repeated turning his fist over, slowly unraveling his thick, meaty fingers like a venomous snake uncoiling, and presenting a pair of metallic tweezers. "I want you to count every grain of rice. Every grain. You will pick it up from the left side of the container, count it, and then put it in the empty side. When you have moved every piece of rice to the right side of the container and can tell me exactly how many pieces, you may eat."

Brick sat cross-legged, moving pieces of rice from one side of the container into the other side, counting to himself. When his luck held, he could grab two pieces of rice in one pinch, doubling his production speed. To his credit, Brick almost finished the task within thirty minutes. With only a small pile of rice left to count, Brick seemed to pick up speed.

The sergeant instructor squatted on his thin, birdlike legs until the knees of his trousers seemed ready to split from the pressure, his buttocks hovering only an inch from the ground. With only a few grains of rice left unaccounted for, the instructor reached out and grabbed the half of the container stacked high with the already counted pile and flicked his narrow wrist. The container folded back on top of itself, dumping the counted rice back on top of the chicken and last few uncounted pieces. The sergeant instructor slowly opened the top, laying it delicately open and empty again.

"Clumsy me. Begin again."

Brick's shoulders shivered as he closed his eyes. They shivered and then they quaked. They quaked and then they shook, growing in intensity with each moment that passed. Suddenly, Brick let out a low moan that expressed such utter defeat and sorrow that every man in the squad bay felt his heart tighten at the sound. The moan was followed by racking sobs so violent it looked as if Brick was being electrocuted with his every breath. The sergeant instructor looked on impassively while Brick cried harder than I had ever seen someone cry before.

After five minutes of letting Brick ugly cry, the sergeant instructor spoke.

"Get up," he growled. Brick did, though he looked like a marionette with half his strings cut as he lurched into something resembling the position of attention. "Now, rejoin your platoon and eat."

The sergeant instructor held out a fork. Brick took it meekly, scooped up his food tray, and shambled over to his normal place on line. The sergeant instructor did not say another word, just turned and stormed out of the squad bay with a purposeful stride.

The next day, Brick was a new man and suddenly glowed with potential. He was quickly made a squad leader and seemed to be the ideal warrior. Brick was honored with carrying the company flag at graduation and earned a Purple Heart overseas while serving with his special operations unit.

The house always wins.

CHAPTER 3

Whipping Boy

I was never an alpha male, nor did anything about my physical person speak of violence—either overt or that veiled, smoldering aggression that sometimes burns behind some rare people's eyes. In grade school, I was small and uncoordinated, which didn't instill fear into the hearts of my enemies (namely anyone physically bigger than me, which, unfortunately at the time, was everyone). I avoided physical confrontations at all costs for the outcome was already known to me.

Until the day I signed up for the military, I had only been in two fights in my entire life. Neither ended with me holding up a gold-plated belt, grinning victoriously to the roars of the crowd.

My first fight was something out of a grade-school nightmare. After years of being picked on as the smallest boy in my class, I finally decided to stand up to one of the bullies. We squared off and, before I knew it, the reptilian side of my brain threw a punch with everything my thin, frail body could muster. I was as completely surprised I had it in me as everyone else was.

I watched with pride as my fist arched toward his face, only to realize with mounting horror that I had incorrectly judged the distance from my knobby shoulder to his nose. My twig arm snapped to full extension, with a vast canyon of an inch left between my knuckles and the bully's face. Without knowing what else to do, I leaned forward at the waist and ever-so-gently mashed his cheek with my knuckles, hoping that if a mere stone could kill Goliath, then perhaps a light tap from a small fist could best a bully.

It did not. I got my ass kicked. Again.

As for the second fight, I did not even know I was in it, or had lost it, until I woke up covered in its crimson aftermath, which was pouring in great torrents from my mouth. I deserved every drop of blood spilled and more. I had begun running my small, vicious mouth to a much bigger boy who had nothing to lose. He had endured a painful childhood that constantly kept his fists in tight, white-knuckled balls. In his defense, he had tried to turn the other cheek and walk away from my verbal assault. Confusing his self-control for weakness, I followed only a step behind, a stupid little dog still yapping ferociously and nipping at his heels. I was in mid-slander when he pivoted and twisted his shoulders around faster than my mind could comprehend.

What beautiful, bright colorful lights, I thought.

I woke up on the ground, my bottom lip almost completely chewed through. My braces had sawed it into thin ribbons of flesh and left it a bloody, dangling, barely attached flap. I tried to stand, coughed up blood, and wavered before falling back onto my narrow shoulder blades with my eyes turned to the sky. The boy should have put the boots to me but, to his credit, he did not. I had said awful, horrific things about him. He should have folded me up with his sneaker in my gut and broken my nose. Instead, he walked away.

I sincerely hope that boy is doing well in life. He is a better man than me.

I joined the military with all the violence of a kitten wearing a bow sleeping peacefully in a box of yarn. Whereas others seemed to bring with them a duffle bag full of pain and deep-rooted angst, just waiting to be sprung on the enemy like some kind of awful secret weapon, I brought a lifetime of happy, middle-class memories that made me feel warm and smile whenever I thought of them.

A lot of the other recruits seemed to exist in a perpetual state of anger and violence, with tiny vacations of distrusted happiness.

I was a delighted tourist wandering around with a camera slung from my neck, wearing high black socks with my leather sandals.

Still, the military did not need to file any chip from my shoulder to get me to follow. Brick defied the system and was broken on the wheel. I loved the system and threw myself into every order with mindless zeal. Brick oozed violence in his defiance and short temper, while I had good penmanship and excellent bookkeeping abilities. Once they tamed Brick, he would be a readymade warrior, bloodthirsty and itching to close with the enemy. My violence had to be stoked and worked like a great forge, starting as a faint glow but, through pressure and pain, grown into a white-hot flame.

It took three days to break Brick and control his vast inferno. It took six weeks before they stoked my spark into something that could even boil a cup of tea.

Teras must have wandered into the wrong doorway at some rural mall out in the sticks, stumbling into some far flung recruiting office while looking for the bathroom, or the Orange Julius stand. That sly recruiter must have grinned ear to ear as Teras stood gaping, chewing on the thin piece of straw between his teeth, and lethargically brushing off his overalls while looking around in puzzlement.

"Congratulations, son, you just won a free trip, compliments of the You-Sssss-Guverrr-meant," the recruiter must have said through his broad smile.

"I did?" Teras probably replied in his monotone drawl, his excitement showing in one slightly upturned brow.

"Yessir, yessir, all expenses paid, just sign right here my boy, sign right here."
And sign he did.

Teras was the strangest bird I could have ever imagined standing on line in basic training. His spine bent him into a disturbing shape that pushed his head far out in front of his body. The instructor sergeants repeatedly asked if he had ever been diagnosed with any spinal issues, such as kyphosis; after a long pause, Teras would reply he had never been to the doctor. The sergeants would then scream and curse the recruiting medic who had put their stamp of approval on Teras, to which Teras would not react in the least. He would stare impassively, almost as if hibernating behind his gray, lusterless eyes, which would only enrage the sergeants more. They would order him to do push-ups and other various exercises, which he would comply with, but always at a leisurely pace that would send the sergeants off the deep end. No matter how much faster they would try to get him to go, he would simply not go any faster, as if their wants meant nothing to him.

Teras was not defiant like Brick, for defiance stems from strong emotion.

Teras was simply a rock, an inanimate object that ideas shattered upon and never penetrated.

Despite the sergeants' best efforts, Teras was not improving after weeks of futile attempts. Moreover, he was dragging the rest of the platoon down with his constant failures to make simple timelines, for which we were all punished, and then forever playing catch-up with our training-day schedule. It was a vicious cycle; Teras was a rock chained to the leg and drowning the rest of the platoon.

The idea must have hit the sergeants like a bolt from the heavens for they burst from their own private sleeping quarters into the squad bay with feral grins and laughing like madmen. Their bodies quaked with unbridled excitement as they turned their wide, twitching eyes upon Teras.

"You," growled one, pointing at Teras. "Grab your shit—you're moving up to the guide's rack."

I inhaled sharply, glaring down at the red, felt armband that said "Guide" on my arm. My heart sank. I had a new bunkmate. I had so enjoyed bunking alone.

"And you," the sergeant said, pointing at me. "Each time Teras messes up or does something stupid, you will suffer. Get it? He is your problem now. Fix him."

I did not quite understand what he meant.

My problem? How was he my problem? Surely the sergeant was mistaken or confused. I decided to write a very strongly worded letter in my thoughts that night, never daring to put any such words down on paper.

Within thirty seconds, Teras had failed to move his blankets and spotless rifle fast enough for the sergeants' liking and I found myself on my face doing push-ups until my arms gave out. I was being punished while they made Teras watch what his failure to follow simple directions had caused. Teras looked on inertly, the rock he was, his face not registering any emotion as he watched me suffer for his mistake.

"Does it bother you, Teras? Does it bother you that he suffers because you are slow, because you cannot follow simple directions? Does it bother you that men will die because of you?" the sergeants screamed inches from his face.

But Teras was not bothered, not in the least. He watched me scream and writhe like he was watching an animal at the zoo, with whom he had no interaction with beyond his own viewing from afar. My endless suffering, and presumably even my death, seemed to wake no emotion in him save boredom.

He was still waiting for that free trip he was promised.

But while the sergeants made Teras watch me, they made me watch him as well. I was not allowed to take my eyes off him while I suffered. Wide-eyed, I was not allowed to shut out the image of his apathy as my muscles burned. His very being began to pain me more and more with each instance of our own private *Clockwork Orange* training sessions. And oh, my droogs, know that the tiny glow in my belly, that almost imperceptible spark of hate, it began to grow, fanned by his disgusting detachment from what he had caused, that seething ultraviolence.

Day in and day out, I poured sweat and bled from the knees, elbows, and hands whenever Teras would not play the game. Everything he did, every fiber in his body, went against the grain of our training, of becoming a warrior. But worse, while others constantly struggled with the training but wept silently and pushed on, trying their hardest to adapt and become something more, something better, Teras simply did not care. He would not try harder and at times I swear he would even slow down out of spite, though that might be giving him too much credit. Teras would idly watch me suffer for his sins and I would feel the hate growing in me just a little bit more with each sluggish blink of his gray eyes.

It wasn't fair! It wasn't fair! I did everything right! I should not be punished!

Later I would learn it was fair. The sergeant instructors were preparing us for the moment when our personal mistakes would not lead to simple "physical instruction," but would get brothers killed; when a moment of laxity would not affect just ourselves, but the warriors to the left and the right of us. Teras failed and, through his failure, his "brothers" suffered. I suffered because I could not fix him, could not keep him toeing the line when I was given the sacred right to lead him.

We both failed; I died a thousand sweaty deaths for it.

My hate grew and festered. Even when not being punished I would stare at Teras and seethe. My lips would curl into a feral snarl and I would growl soundlessly. From the cracks in the blinds of their private quarters overlooking the squad bay, the sergeant instructors must have watched and smiled. They waited patiently for my churning insides to finally erupt and drown Pompeii in molten fire. It may have taken time, but time they had and erupt it did.

One beautiful Southern day, Teras dropped his rifle.

"This is my rifle. There are many like it, but this one is mine," said the rifleman's creed we repeated over and over daily as we cleaned and oiled our rifles.

"My rifle is my best friend. It is my life. I must master it as I must master my life."

The sharp, metallic report of Teras's rifle initially striking the floor stopped our world from turning. The continued rattle, as it bounced around on the concrete floor of the squad bay, was deafening in the utter silence of disbelief. Every muscle in the squad bay locked up and held every man fast, no matter how awkward or unbalanced their position. The hallowed trust between man and weapon had been shattered and heads were going to roll.

"My rifle, without me, is useless. Without my rifle, I am useless."

I had never before witnessed such an explosion of emotion as when the sergeant instructors realized what had happened and instantly shed their mortal forms, replaced by wrathful gods set on mindless slaughter. Racks were toppled and footlockers were flipped into the air, spilling their contents, as the sergeants tore their way toward Teras, leaving behind them a wake of destruction and trembling bodies. For all the terrifying fanfare, Teras did not look in the least bit perturbed by the coming storm. He simply did not understand.

This is my rifle—

… and I just dropped it carelessly.

As they neared, the sergeants split up. Sergeant Buck, an African American Adonis, with round, flaring nostrils and enormous ebony arms, eclipsed Teras, getting as physically close as two human beings could without actually physically touching. He roared in Teras's stone face loud enough that those closest to us winced with each syllable. Sergeant Tank, a pale yang to Buck's dark yin, sidestepped Teras at the last second and barreled toward me, his wide, corded back swelling with each enraged breath he took, until it looked as if his immaculate uniform would split, from his inhumanly wide shoulders to his narrow dancer's hips, and sprout 15-foot-tall demon wings. It took my brain too long to comprehend.

Surely Teras would be alone in this calamity, I thought.

And then Sergeant Tank was upon me, drowning out all other thoughts but pain, a howling tempest of righteous fury as he instructed me in the ways of physical exertion to ensure compliance. There was a new ferocity suddenly. Where each time before the sergeants would stand, arms folded across their massive chests, and give me new exercises in icy detachment, as if reading off a recipe over the phone, there was now a frenzied passion in Sergeant Tank that had him on his hands and knees beside me, grinning and seething in my ear.

"You hate him, don't you?" he whispered, as he quaked in violent rapture. "You hate everything about him."

I did not answer. I could not disagree; I just believed I was being tricked into answering and would be further punished for my lack of "brotherhood."

But I did hate him. With each minute that passed, with Sergeant Buck howling at the impassive mockery of a human being that was Teras, my hate grew, fed by Sergeant Tank whispering the things my fury wanted to hear.

"He is weak." *He is.*

"He is disgusting." *So very disgusting.*

"He will get men killed." *He will kill every last one of us.*

"You hate him." *With every fiber in my body.*

Teras "stood," hunched forward, his head bobbing in front of his crooked body like a bored cartoon vulture, watching me suffer for his sins. He let his eyes droop and shut for a moment, as if he would drift off to sleep from the sheer monotony, as my veins carried ever more burning acid to my shaking muscles. Sergeant Tank looked at my face, then looked at Teras, the weak, disgusting rock who would kill us all, and then Sergeant Tank grinned, the semblance of cruel joy I imagine a wolf would make right before snapping its jaws on a windpipe.

"You hate him, don't you?" he whispered quietly. A confidant, a friend.

"I hate him. I hate him, I hate him," I blubbered, my wind stolen from me and unable to give birth to the proper scream I had hoped. What was a howl in my mind was born into the world as a quivering mewl. However pathetic, it satisfied Sergeant Tank.

Without a word Sergeant Tank stood, beckoned Sergeant Buck, who was all but hoarse, and together they strode off toward their private chamber. I lay in a puddle of my own fluids, that I would like to imagine was only sweat, and stared at Teras, my limbs shaking with exhaustion. I caught his gray, lifeless eyes for a moment, a delicate juncture that could bind us in the bonds of brotherhood and friendship forever with a simple gesture of concern—Teras sighed loudly, blasé, and looked away—or destroy my faith in humanity utterly.

I broke. The violence and hate buried deep finally spilled forth in great torrents of bright, fiery magma.

From my prone position on the ground, I pressed off in a ballistic push-up just enough to get my legs, already pumping, underneath me. I was falling forward, my legs churning to delay the fall just long enough. I did not need to go far.

I planted my left foot and made one last lunge forward, my right fist cocked at my ribs. As I fell forward, I drove all of my hate and fury into my swinging fist. I wanted to see Teras's eyes go wide, to see him react to what was about to happen. He did not.

Instead, he simply flew backward, vacated from his previous spot by all my rage made manifest. His crooked body landed limply between the racks. I caught my balance and stood, watching Teras wheeze and writhe, trying to catch the breath I had knocked out of him.

This was what I imagined someone dying looked like, their eyes rolled back, clutching at their wound, shaking in fits. My rage spent, I was suddenly left with the urge to cry, vomit, and piss myself simultaneously. I wanted to scream, "You did this!", but I knew saying it would not make it true. Nothing could take back or change what I had done.

I did this.

This recruit was fucked.

I would face non-judicial punishment. The military court and the endless parade of witnesses to my sudden unprovoked assault would keep the trial short. I felt sick and my knees warned of giving out on me. I reached out and held onto the rack while I watched Teras twitch and try to take in short, choppy breaths, like a fish flopping on the bottom of a boat.

"What's going on here?" Sergeant Buck growled, stepping out into the squad bay. I did not move, could not move, only continued to stare down at Teras. Sergeant Buck strode up beside me and put his enormous hands on his muscular hips. "Get up, Teras. We don't lay down until lights out. Back on line."

I dragged myself back onto the line, a gnawing feeling that I had left something there between the racks, something vital and important. But there was another feeling, that nothing was actually lost, only replaced. Where once I had found fear and cowardice, I now found a smoldering fury. I did not think it was a fair trade, but it was too late to go back on the blood barter now.

It was much too late, dear Faust.

We were swept up in our training for the rest of the day so there was no time to dwell, only endure, and think of the next meal, the next meal, the next meal. Like animals we all lived thinking of the next meal and the physical comfort such nourishment might bring. I was blissfully lost in the demands of survival.

It was not until that night, when the senior sergeant stepped into the squad bay and made a straight line for me, that I realized how much trouble I was in. His tan face was tight in thought, brooding, as if the world rested upon his shoulders. I wanted to fall to my knees, stick out my wrists for shackling, and beg mercy, though I had discovered this was not a place of mercy, of disgusting weakness. The irony did not escape me.

"Gentlemen, it is with a sad heart that I must inform you that one of your men will no longer be joining you in training. Teras came to me this evening and told me quite a tale."

Fuck. I began to step forward, my guilt already weighing my head so that my chin dipped low.

"It seems, gentlemen, that Teras was not cut from the same cloth as the rest of you. He begged me to stop his training and let him out of my military. Begged me. Seems I could not get his orders processed fast enough, and the captain was all too happy to sign off on his release, given the repeated reports we have made about his inability to adjust and conform to our high standards."

"There is an empty bunk tonight, gentlemen, because someone was too weak. Think on that, gentlemen, while you lay in the rack. Would any of you fight so little to keep your place among us? Do any of you wish to leave?"

"No, Sir," we screamed as one.

"I didn't think so," he grinned. "Carry on, guide. Carry on."

CHAPTER 4

Tin Soldier

There was an addictive numbness in the process of becoming a warrior. All memories of our past lives and individual personalities were bled from our veins, only to be replaced by a viscous dread and overwhelming sense of devotion that bordered on religious fanaticism. It was an opiate, administered hourly in Two Minutes Hate,* where we were whipped into a frenzy as we were told how, thousands of miles away, the enemy was training day and night to increase his ability to kill us. The enemy was clever and heartless, we were told, so we must be even more clever, even more heartless in our delivery of death to those who would harm us and those we loved.

The more they screamed and enraged us with the talk of our loved ones being in danger, the more we became zealots. Some, the scared and weak, never gave themselves to the fervor, but most of us enthusiastically embraced our new being. We thirsted for order. We hungered for cohesion and precision.

In our basic training, I was placed as the leader of our platoon for the simple reason I had established early on, that I would obey all commands without the normal resistance of a young boy being assimilated, and I did so with a zealous delight that unnerved some of the other recruits. I wanted to be changed. I embraced it, enjoying the simplicity of the system I found myself immersed in. I was pliable, they knew. Every time they looked at Teras's empty bunk they would stare at me for a moment, smiling.

We had been cleaning the squad bay when our senior drill sergeant stepped onto the floor, with his feet splayed just perfectly outside his shoulders and his hands gripping his hips menacingly, surveying the flock of docile civilian sheep he had been charged with turning into bloodthirsty wolves. I stepped in front of him and reported the platoon's disposition while he glared at me. Suddenly, he looked down at his feet and saw a bug crawling across the floor between us. Enraged that his

---

* A reference to the practice referred to in George Orwell's *1984*, in which the citizens of Oceania indulge in "A hideous ecstasy of fear and vindictiveness."

squad bay could host such a filthy creature, he snapped one arm perfectly straight, his quivering finger pointing at the bug with such venom that I thought the veins on his forehead might pop with how engorged they became.

"You, vacuum," he growled. Without thought I bent down, picked up the bug without even checking its nomenclature, and swallowed it whole before coming back to the position of attention. The senior's eyes went wide with proud disbelief. He had been expecting my resistance to his joke and my terrible punishment that would follow, a fine respite from the tedium of watching young men cleaning the squad bay.

He leaned in. "You will go far," he purred before sidestepping me and addressing the entire platoon.

"That is why he is your leader," he screamed, boastfully. "If I told him to jump out that window right this instant, he would do so without question. The rest of you disgusting creatures could learn something from him."

I would have, without question. I was caught up in the mad fervor of becoming a warrior. A small, quiet boy for most of my life, weakness had been my most bosom companion since I could remember, so often confirmed by the grade-school bullies I could not defend myself against. But, suddenly, I was finding I was far stronger than I could have imagined. I could tap into the savagery of the monster hiding inside me to overcome my fears and hesitations. I found I could become a vessel and let its cold, unfeeling essence fill me.

Like any good team-building retreat, our warrior training was filled with contests of martial prowess and the spoils that went along with winning. By some fluke, our platoon had won the first companywide competition of drill, marching in perfect unison and obeying commands instantly, moving together in lockstep like a flock of birds in flight. Our sergeants were pleased. Their bragging rights would last all the way until the final marching competition, where the movements were vastly more difficult.

I could not march to a steady rhythm if my life depended on it, which, for as much as we practiced, I began to fear it might. Five or six steps into a straight line and I was already off cadence, stomping blithefully at random intervals to the horror of my sergeants or breaking off in a new direction, as I did on several occasions during practice. I was incorrigibly terrible and spent most of our time allotted to marching practice doing calisthenics as punishment for my absentmindedness. I found the calisthenics infinitely more pleasurable, though I never let on. Better an hour doing push-ups, pull-ups, and mountain climbers until my arms felt as if they would fall off, than one second spent trying to keep rhythm.

The final marching competition loomed on the horizon, only two days away. I woke up perfectly fit for duty, stepping on line with vigor and my clean-shaven chin held high. At the appropriate time, I requested to see a medic.

"Why do you need to see a medic?" my senior sergeant growled.

"Because this recruit feels unbalanced, Sir, and may not be able to compete on Friday if it's as serious as this recruit fears." He grinned in understanding, his pride shining through on his tan, weathered face.

"Very well, go see the medic. Report to me on how long you will be unable to perform physical duties as soon as you return."

During my medical exam I experienced sudden bouts of nausea, vertigo, labored breathing, numbness, blurred vision, and a severe pain in my liver. The enlisted medics stroked their chins, obviously confused by my myriad symptoms, and conferred for a moment.

"When is final drill?" the chief medic asked, stepping out of his office. He had obviously been listening to my symptoms through his open door and took interest in such a severe case as mine.

"Friday, Sir."

"So would you agree that you have an ear infection until Saturday morning?"

"Yes, Sir, I think that is exactly what I have, Sir."

"And you'll be feeling miraculously better Saturday morning?"

"Tremendously better, Sir."

"That's good to hear. Here is your light-duty chit. I have made a specific note for no marching of any kind, but you can still take part in very light calisthenics. I imagine we will not be seeing you again."

"No, Sir."

"Excellent. Report back to your senior."

It seemed I was not the first to visit the medics only days before a drill competition. My senior sergeant took me into the gear closet upon my return so we could have a private word, screaming at me that I had botched up the inventory of disinfectant bottles as cover. And because I had.

"That's good work," he said dropping his voice into a low growl as he shut the door behind us. "Now, there are three more who look like they are also sick."

"This recruit will ensure that they see a medic right away, Sir," I replied.

"You'll go far, son."

The next morning two more boys from our platoon saw their way to the medic station with strange and amusing symptoms. Both were told they had a mild head cold and that it would be cured Saturday morning. Saturday morning, it seemed, was when anyone could expect to feel well again. Their chits also read for no marching of any kind but that they could take part in light calisthenics. The sergeants' definition of "light" was slightly more heavy-handed than the dictionary definition, but we had done our duty to our platoon, ensuring the best chance of mission success through our own selflessness.

The day before the final competition, the entire company was marched into an enormous grass field to be taught hand-to-hand combat, or just enough of it to start and then swiftly lose any bar fight. Hundreds of bodies blocked and counterattacked in perfect synchronicity, a veritable aerobics class of martial combat. Again and again, we threw our fists wildly into the vacant space in front of us, twisting our hips to get our full weight behind the punch. We screamed loudly with each punch, kick, and knee to the imaginary groins of our enemies.

"All right, we are now going to practice arm-bars. Pair up with the man next to you," the combat sergeant instructed, flexing his arms the size of Christmas hams and sneering as everyone scrambled to get a partner. Hell would find those who paired up last.

I felt a hand on my shoulder and turned to find my senior sergeant staring me dead in the eye. His face was stern and his eyes became small slits as he whispered through his teeth.

"Bruhmer still wants to march. He does not realize he is sick. Convince him." The senior sergeant let his sentence die between his tightly clenched teeth.

"Understood, Sir."

My senior leaned in, his nose pressed against mine, and stared directly into my quivering eyes. The sudden proximity to his fury made my legs weak and my bladder suddenly feel on the verge of letting go.

"He. Does. Not. March," he growled, flecks of warm spit spattering my lips and cheeks.

"Yes, Sir."

I cut through the throng of bodies desperately trying to pair up and stepped up beside Bruhmer and his already chosen partner.

"I'm with Bruhmer," I said, my voice low and full of the authority invested by the senior sergeant to the platoon guide. Bruhmer's partner nodded his understanding and disappeared into the maelstrom, hoping to not be last in a partnership. He was last and, along with the other stragglers, was marched off for an extra dose of physical training to promote future haste to obey a given order.

We were shown the proper technique for grabbing and maintaining pressure on the fragile wrist to subdue and, should the need arise, incapacitate our enemy. We practiced the move slowly at first, step by step at a learning pace. Again. And again. And again. And then again until it started to become muscle memory.

"Now, let's do it at combat speed and see what you have learned."

I squared off with Bruhmer and let him go first, presenting my wrist in a slow, awkward punch. He grabbed, pulled, positioned his other hand, and applied the proper torque. My wrist lit up with pain, and instinctively my knees bent to reduce the pressure. He released and, foolishly, I threw yet another slow, ineffective punch that he turned into a blinding flash of white light in my wrist. So incompetent were my first two punches that I decided to throw 18 more, all of which ended with me down on my knees trying not to show the pain on my face as he applied pressure.

"Switch," the combat sergeant barked.

Bruhmer was 140 pounds soaking wet. His gaunt, birdlike body gave the impression of a marionette with a head carved much bigger than normal for comic relief. His enormous Adam's apple bobbed constantly as he stared out at the world from behind his huge, terrified eyes.

He punched, beginning the dance, and I caught his wrist.

"Bruhmer, you are sick. You need to go to the medics following this," I growled, my dry and cracked lips drawn up into the twisted vestiges of a feral smile. Bruhmer stared at me, his brow dipping in utter confusion.

"I feel fine," he whispered quietly, as if we were trading midnight secrets at sleepover camp.

"No, Bruhmer, you don't. You are dizzy. You need to go to the medics." I emphasized my point by applying slightly more pressure on his thin, balsa-wood wrist. He grunted and his brow only tightened as his confusion grew.

"But I'm not sick," he whispered, genuinely confused. I shook my head.

"Bruhmer. You are not going to march tomorrow. You are going to pretend to be sick to get a light-duty chit. Do you understand?"

A terrible look of understanding swept his long, thin face, and his Adam's apple bobbed uncontrollably.

"But I like marching," he squealed. My lips pulled apart further and I bared my crooked teeth menacingly.

"You will not march tomorrow—is that understood?" I growled, applying further pressure to his wrist. His knees buckled and he quivered trying to stay standing.

"No, I want to march," he whined.

"I don't care what you want, Bruhmer. Say you're sick."

"No," Bruhmer wheezed. "I am going to march."

"Is there no way to convince you, Bruhmer?" I asked. He stared up at me defiantly, his decision made. He would march regardless of the fact he could not tell his left foot from his right. He would march in his truly awful fashion and the platoon would lose, sentencing us to weeks of utter derision from our sergeants for having lost their bragging rights.

"I am not sick," he said boldly.

"Okay," I replied.

I promptly pulled my body weight down and back with as much force as I could muster and heard the distinct snapping of a dried branch as his wrist shifted unnaturally just above my clasped hands. It took a moment for Bruhmer to register the pain. He looked down at his wrist for a moment before I let his hand slip from mine. He fell to his knees and clutched at his wrist with his still-operational hand.

"Medic," I screamed, coming to attention as low, guttural sobs wracked Bruhmer's kneeling body.

The medics hustled over to where I stood at attention. My senior sergeant followed closely behind and stood over Bruhmer as the medics examined his wrist.

"Bad?" my senior inquired.

"Nah. Probably just a cast for a bit."

"Good. Hear that, Bruhmer? Just a cast. I will make sure you can finish your training with the platoon. All of the physical requirements are completed, so I will make sure you graduate with us."

"Yes, Sir," Bruhmer sobbed, and he was led off the field by the medics.

My senior sergeant did not even look at me but turned on his heels and started back toward the rear of the formation where the other drill sergeants stood watching their chattel practice. I stood at attention and stared off into space awaiting orders.

"Follow," he barked over his shoulder, pausing only for a moment.

"Yes, Sir," I yelled, and I fell into step behind him. He stopped and conferred with the senior from another platoon in our company. They talked at leisure in low tones, nodding and smirking as if I was not standing directly behind them. Finally, after a minute of what sounded like bartering, my senior nodded his head.

"Very good," he said, and then turned to address me. "You, follow Sergeant Duvals. He is in need of you."

I followed Sergeant Duvals behind the back of the formation until I was among drawn faces I had never seen before, all practicing their arm-bars. We stopped abruptly and Sergeant Duvals turned to face me.

"Davies is sick. Understand?"

"Yes, Sir," I said, a knot forming in my stomach.

Suddenly, I did understand.

Sergeant Duvals marched me through the formation of his platoon until I stood beside two men performing their arm-bars without any passion or attempt at understanding the steps. They were simply going through the motions but trying not to draw attention to their lackluster performance.

"Humphreys, back of the formation," Sergeant Duvals barked, and one of the men sped off to the back of the field like a jackrabbit being coursed by greyhounds. "Davies, this is your new partner. Arm-bars practice, as you were."

Davies looked at me as if I were an extraterrestrial, his eyes shining out from behind his wide, doughy cheeks like a man confronted with an unknown entity in an old, abandoned house. He stood for a moment in shock and then suddenly regained his composure for fear of being singled out by the combat instructor to be sent off for extra physical training, a prospect which was known to him by the looks of it.

Davies held his thick sausage fingers in front of him, waiting to receive my slow punch. I shook my head and kept my hands down at my side. He nodded fearfully, his breathing beginning to quicken as he felt the eyes of the sergeants searching the formation for the weak or uncooperative.

I smiled and held my hands up instead, shaking them lightly in a show of readiness. Davies sighed and threw a slow, unenthusiastic punch into my awaiting grasp. With a sudden downward jerk of my body, Davies's knees buckled, and he fell forward into a kneeling position.

"You are not going to march tomorrow," I seethed.

"I heard what you did. I heard him," Davies whimpered.

"I am going to let you go. You are going to fall down and say you twisted your knee when I pulled you forward. Be convincing."

"Thank you," Davies whispered and threw himself down at my feet, grabbing his knee and blubbering how much it hurt. The medics rolled their eyes upon seeing me standing at the position of attention in front of the second training casualty of the day. Before they could inquire, my senior sergeant scooped me up and hustled me away, back to the sanctuary of my own platoon. He did not say a word to me and pushed me into my familiar position in our order of march.

"Platoon, forward march, double time," he barked, and got us the hell out of there.

I will always wonder what favor was owed by Duvals for my terrible service.

Our platoon won the final marching competition, performing a feat that had not been done in years they told us, the same platoon winning both initial and final drill. Our senior was awarded an enormous trophy which he proudly displayed in our squad bay, his name engraved on the beautiful gold plate at the base along with those few who had accomplished such a feat before him. He threw us a party where we were each allowed an entire eight-ounce ration of Gatorade, the height of decadence in the midst of our training.

The three of us who had become mysteriously ill so close to final drill were all awarded meritorious promotions. I was awarded honor graduate of the platoon. The real reason we were rewarded was not because of our illness; the "illness" was just a symptom of our devotion.

As he promised, the senior sergeant kept Bruhmer in the platoon despite the cast on his wrist. Shortly after his return from his medical appointment, Bruhmer cornered me in the gear closet as I pretended to oversee inventory and the painting of our platoon flag. I turned to face him, my body tightening when I realized I was trapped with the only exit blocked.

"I get it now," Bruhmer said, suddenly holding up his cast. "I should have been sick. I'm sorry." I slowly nodded my acceptance, still wary of an ambush.

Without another word, he turned around and rejoined the platoon.

CHAPTER 5

Blood Sport

We were given many orders in our training: wake up, eat now, clean this, march here, clean this, sweat there, clean this, clean this, sleep now. All were carried out without the least bit of dissension or deliberation, only the hurried worry of knowing there was no carrot for success, only the stick for our failures. No order evoked any emotion beyond self-pity or hunger, as we endlessly concentrated on the next meal as a rallying point for our courage.

Early one morning, when the dew still clung to the sharp grasses and you could still smell the rich, loamy scent of the earth before the sun baked it away as it climbed, we were marched double time out into a field. We were formed up around a small wooden stage roughly four feet off the ground and four feet wide on its sides. Painted on one of the smooth sides was the slogan, "Pain is weakness leaving the body." I stifled a laugh. Wouldn't weakness and quitting be pain leaving the body as well? Isn't that why people are weak, because it's less painful? But I withheld my question, assured the answer given would be the same explanation as always: a lot of "weakness" leaving my body.

Perched on top of the stage was a demigod who made our instructor sergeants look downright scrawny and emaciated. His tanned muscles danced and rippled as he flexed his folded arms with nervous energy in a black T-shirt two sizes too small for his frame. His square, thick-jawed head slowly swiveled side to side, like a machine-gun crew meticulously traversing to seek out new targets. He stared at each of our upturned faces, his disgust obvious.

"Today, you will learn perhaps one of the most important and lifesaving actions for a warrior," he growled. "Today you will learn how to fix bayonets."

My heart dropped down into my stomach and I felt the sudden swimming sense of vertigo.

Most important? Lifesaving? When I had pictured combat, I had always envisioned an enemy quite far away, shooting ineffectively as I shot him through the impersonal sights of my rifle before moving on to my next target. Wielding our advanced weaponry with a bayonet dangling off the end, as if we were cavemen with a sharpened piece of flint on the end of a stick trying to take down a mammoth, had never been part of the fantasy.

Suddenly, and for the first time since signing my name to the dotted line, I realized I was going to die. It was not a foregone conclusion, but the necessity of being shown how to use a crude spear somehow suggested the odds were far greater than I had imagined them to be. I could not stop picturing that somewhere, in some forsaken place we would be sent, there was a man sharpening his *shamshir*, just waiting to run that curved sword through the chest of some American warrior.

The moment the sergeant took the bayonet and snapped it home on the end of the rifle, it became real. We all jumped when it suddenly snapped into place. These were not costumes and we were not playing warrior out in the backyard anymore. This was happening. As I looked around, I was buried under the awful thought that some of us on the field were going to die, and soon.

A disgusting, secret piece of me whispered, "Just not me. Take one of them. Just not me." I did not know it then, but later I would beg the gods for my own death if it meant my brothers could be spared. But not yet; right then, I still wished everyone else to die if it would save my own skin.

We were shown how to run at a full charge and stick the bayonet into a man, twisting as we pulled it back to dislodge the blade from bone and sinew, and then charge on to the next dummy made of wood and discarded tires. Sometimes, despite our best efforts, the point would get stuck in the weather-beaten wood underneath the scraps of tire and we would pull and twist, as we screamed our battle cries, trying desperately to free the blade from the corpse of our enemy. Each yank twisted my own stomach a little bit more.

We stabbed and stabbed until it became just another order.

The rubber dummies never fought back, never instilled the fear of death enough to cripple a man and dull his senses. Any man could drive a blade into rubber and wood, screaming viciously and victoriously when no one was screaming back. Any man could win an unfair fight. There was only one way to test our mettle against a real enemy—in the heat of martial combat against a living, breathing combatant.

They ran us to a strangely placed bridge at the end of the field. It was a bridge that appeared from, and went to, absolutely nowhere. It was a simple wooden deck eight feet wide and ten feet long that rose two feet off the surface of a lake of tiny rubber shavings; these shavings would cushion the fall of even the heaviest of men. There was no tactical advantage to the bridge—one could simply walk around it—but damned if we were not tasked with holding that bridgehead at all costs as if it were Anzio.

Helmets and pugil sticks were issued. We finally figured out what the mouth guards that we'd carried with us at all times were for, and slipped them into our grinning mouths. We bounced up and down eagerly. All of our pent-up angst and energy would finally have catharsis.

"The rules are simple, gentleman," the sergeant announced from the edge of the bridge. "One man will start at that end of the bridge while the other man starts at the opposite end. On my 'go' you will close with the enemy and either deliver a killing blow or knock him off the bridge completely. The fight will not stop until one of those two requirements is met. Do you understand?"

"Sir, yes, Sir," we screamed in unison.

The sergeant's instruction had been simple. Plant your lead foot, drive the tip of the pugil stick forward as if it was a bayonet, and reach with your entire body to ensure maximum range. The first three matches within our platoon, however, quickly devolved into two men pushing against each other's sticks or swinging wildly, as if kayaking blind whenever there was a break in the pushing. Our senior sergeant, watching from the periphery, shook his head and scoffed.

Clanter was called to the far end of the bridge and he lumbered to his place. He was a hulking slab of meat who rarely spoke; when he did it was with a soft, falsetto voice that embarrassed him terribly. He spoke exclusively about the fine wife and beautiful infant he had left back home to join up and earn that steady paycheck his family deserved.

When Clanter stepped up on the bridge, his opponent, a full seven inches and fifty pounds smaller, actually grinned awkwardly in his mouth guard, so little was Clanter's menace. On "Go," the wiry bastard sprinted forward, took three hop-steps as he closed, planted, and jabbed Clanter square in the stomach, knocking him back and then onto his butt without a breath left in his body. Clanter quietly left the bridge and took his place in formation until he was called up again, to lose just as quickly. The third time he at least tried to block before losing, however ineffectively.

Some of us showed promise, winning most, if not all, of our matches. Senior sergeant took note and eyed us warily, judging our "martial" worth as we stood at attention, staring off into the distance, as he walked up and down our ranks. We were nothing but racehorses to him at that moment.

"We're ready," he growled. Sergeant Buck nodded and sprinted off, leaving us under the senior sergeant's scrutiny. His face softened and he began joking with some of our men, assuming his role as the conspiratorial good cop. Most of the men, recent high school graduates who had never been away from home before, were so taken in by the ruse that they may have chosen him over their own fathers if the choice were put to them. While they feared Sergeant Tank and Sergeant Buck, they loved the senior sergeant with all their hearts. They would have killed for the man, even died for him.

"Gentleman," he said, signaling us in for a school circle where the first rank moved close and sat, the second rank took a knee, and the third rank stood, all leaning in eager for knowledge and praise. "We have been challenged by another platoon. That nassst-tee Bravo Platoon saw us training right now, saw us weak and failing, and thought they would challenge us to show how strong they are."

Senior looked around the half circle of faces quivering with genuine outrage and shook his head frowning, a father disappointed in his heirs.

"I don't know about you, gentlemen, but I cannot abide such an affront to this platoon's fighting spirit. I am sick to my stomach thinking that we are thought of as weak, that we are thought of as the lesser. Doggone, but that makes me angry. Does that make you angry?"

"Sir, yes, Sir," we screamed in unison, genuinely angry.

"Good, that's good. Because in about one minute that nasty Bravo Platoon is gonna march up to the other side of this bridge and we are going to fight them for it. Make no mistake, gentlemen, this is not a game. Failure to defeat that nasty doggone Bravo Platoon will result in, well, let's just say I won't be able to hold back Sergeant Tank and Sergeant Buck tonight. They hate losing, and I don't wanna imagine how bad it will get in the squad bay when I am not there to save you tonight, I really don't," the senior sergeant said, shaking his head. He let that thought swim around in the humid air for a moment. Then he leaned in and lowered his voice conspiratorially, master of oration that he was.

"But I tell you what, if any of you can bring me back one of their mouthpieces, well, I will give you a thirty-second call to whoever you want. Don't let me down."

Fear drove most of us: the fear of failing, the fear of disappointing the men around us, and most of all the fear of what would happen back in the squad bay should Senior turn the other sergeants loose. The fear made us shake and have to piss, but the fear made us strong and agile. The right amount of fear can make a man into a fighting machine because, hell, what choice does he really have but to fight.

The platoons were lined up in order from smallest man to largest, and then the first in line were sent against each other, then the seconds faced off, then thirds. There was no clear winner as the lines dwindled. Some struck merciless victories for our platoon, while the next man in our line was beaten in the blink of an eye. We remained silent, but always followed our senior out of the corner of our eyes. Every grimace made us shudder, every smile sent us to rapture.

I stepped up to the bridge and exhaled. I was yet unbeaten and I planned on keeping my perfect record. There were few moments that one could take pride in during training; I was going to be damned if I let this one slip through my fingers through sheer laziness. They had told us the simple formula for victory. It was only a matter of applying it, and doing so a blink faster than our opponents.

On "go" I dashed forward, planted my lead foot just inside range, and leaned forward, twisting into my opponent, thrusting my stick forward as fast as I could. He was late, just beginning to wind up for a large, arcing sweep like a baseball player as I stepped into range. Quickly, I touched his chest with the tip of my stick and then darted back out of range before he had even finished redirecting his haymaker. I looked to the combat instructor, who nodded and raised his arm toward our platoon's end of the bridge.

Still undefeated. To be honest though, I do not know if my thrust would have even broken skin for its power dwindled at such an end range. It may have taken off a button or even torn a pocket corner, but little more. I would have made one hell of a combat tailor.

The next few bouts were a wash. The odds had not yet tipped in either platoon's favor and senior was beginning to show his agitation, growling underneath his breath while pacing back and forth behind the combat instructor.

Clanter stepped up on the bridge and Senior rolled his head toward the heavens with his eyes closed, already chalking up the loss to Bravo Platoon. When he opened his eyes, he focused his attention on the next man in line behind Clanter, our last man and our last hope of pulling off the win. He was a huge, brutish-looking boy with a tall, flat forehead, but senior slowly shook his head in resignation. It was a façade; the boy was more molded out of marshmallow than hewn from wood, and would most likely take three shots to the face before he even realized he was supposed to be fighting back. With two known quantities left, our obvious loss did not sit well with senior, who turned away from the bridge and glared at those that had already finished, on what suddenly felt like death row.

It was the loud footfalls that made senior turn back around. The footsteps shook the bridge as Clanter made his charge, howling his poor opponent's death song as he ran. The veins bulged on Clanter's arms as he clutched his pugil stick, his huge frame closing the distance impossibly fast, a Viking berserker of legend making his final stand.

His opponent, a frost giant only a moment before but suddenly a trembling boy, held his stick up vertically in an effort to hide behind it.

Clanter's first powerful blow knocked his opponent spinning sideways to the edge of the bridge, his pugil stick lowered and all but forgotten as he teetered, trying to keep his balance on the precipice. To lose by combat was embarrassing enough, but to be forced off the 8-foot-wide bridge was unacceptable. The trembling boy turned his full attention to arresting his momentum and remaining on the bridge, but Clanter would not be ignored. He stepped in close, bent his knees, and dipped his front shoulder. With all his might, Clanter drove his body upward, just as his opponent caught his balance and was turning to present a defense, his pugil stick still held low, more of an implement of balance than a proper weapon.

Clanter drove his full body weight into his vicious uppercut, catching the boy under the loose helmet, snapping his head back. The power of the blow took the boy airborne off the edge of the bridge, his body already limp as it trailed after his lolling head.

But Clanter was not going to be robbed of his true prize.

Clanter did not arrest his drive but used it to follow the vanquished into Niflheim. He leapt off the bridge, shadowing his opponent, his pugil stick still held high above his head where the uppercut had finished. Clanter screamed as he followed the limp body toward the ground, a blood-curdling yell that was as much pain as it was triumph. The flaccid body, the soft, rubbery ground, and Clanter's brutal overhead blow all made contact at the same time, coming to rest with Clanter straddling the defenseless form with his pugil stick planted firmly in his opponent's guts like a flag.

Still screaming, Clanter threw his now-bent pugil stick aside and tore the chin strap from his opponent's helmet. He yanked the mesh mask up enough to expose the boy's nose and partially open mouth. While everyone watched in complete awe and confusion, Clanter reached into the boy's mouth and tore out the black mouth guard, holding it up as high as he could and screaming in triumph.

No one in our platoon cheered. No one needed to. The look of absolute horror on Bravo Platoon's faces as Clanter walked up to senior, presented the mouth guard as if it was the Holy Grail, and then silently took his place back in formation, was beyond a simple victory, beyond the gauche cheers of the crowd. It was a work of art, and no one cheers in museums or galleries. They simply smile and love, their eyes twinkling.

Bravo Platoon bowed out of the last bout due to our strict timelines, all training having to stop as the medics tended to Bravo's fallen until he was revived. Though rattled and mentally scarred, he had no lasting physical injuries. Senior could not have been more thrilled. Our last fight was assumed to be a "win" despite our last fighter being a declawed blind kitten with epilepsy. Senior called "right face" and we double timed away from the bridge, our platoon's legend growing with each sergeant instructor that told the tale.

The mouth guard went on our platoon's trophy table, and Senior sent the other sergeants away for the night, giving us a moment of "respite," as he told us rousing tales of Medal of Honor recipients and brave men who had given their lives for their brothers, the men whose place we would take on the wall to protect our country. He took Clanter away for a few minutes, only to return with Clanter smiling, tears streaking down his face. He had gotten his call home to his fine wife and beautiful infant.

Before retiring to his private quarters, Senior faced the platoon and smiled.

"I am proud of you, gentlemen. You did what it took to win. That is all that matters in war. I am very proud," he said and then disappeared behind his door.

No one has ever slept better than Clanter did that night.

A week later, we were marched out into the woods for our final bayonet combat exercise. We stacked our rifles in the campfire pyramid formation we had been taught and formed up in front of a miniature coliseum to be issued pugil sticks. The sight of the roofless structure alone was enough to set our knees to shaking. The "Octagon" was a 20-foot-tall wooden gladiatorial arena, the graying wood covered in a thin layer of moss, born of the constant humidity and cool shade of the giant willows that surrounded it. Camouflage netting was our heaven and boot-churned mulch was our earth, but hell lay between.

While the sergeant instructors were allowed direct doorways to enter and windows to spectate from, as well as an upper viewing deck along the rim of the arena, the gladiators themselves started from long, blind hallways that zigzagged twice before spilling out onto the killing floor, so that no opponents could see each other prior to combat. While kneeling before the entrance to the gladiators' hallway, all you could see was the first jagged turn, but you could feel all of your secret fears and insecurities waiting for you just around the corner.

The seniors from multiple platoons gathered on the upper viewing deck, where they could see both gladiators before they entered the arena and then wage their bets accordingly. I have absolutely no doubt they placed wagers on each fight, or at least on the final outcome of the platoons' war. They were likely bets of non-monetary value; pride and favors were capital of far more import than any coin that could have changed hands among them. Whatever the wager, the seniors lost their cool, calm demeanor atop that arena and howled for blood whenever the combatants met in the mulch.

We were lined up in order of size as we had been on the bridge. No man knew the outcome of the battles before him, as those who fought were herded into a new formation out of earshot from those silently waiting at the gladiators entrance hallway. When the warrior in front of me trotted down the hallway and around the first bend, I stepped to the entrance and faced the combat sergeant from our battle on the bridge. He had been assigned as our platoon's arena liaison.

"When I say, announce your name and your weight loudly," he said, snapping my head around inside my helmet with his giant hands, checking the safety straps, and then peering into my mouth to check for my mouth guard. "Move fast, close, and don't hesitate, Doe."

He knew my name. I felt elation, which was quickly followed by nagging doubt. *Why would he know my name? He had not said anyone else's name.*

"Announce," the combat sergeant said, holding his hand across the entrance as if I were so eager I would sprint out into combat before my time.

"Doe, one hundred and fifty-five," I shrieked, my high-pitched voice shrill and trembling, like a miniature steamship announcing its intent to leave the dock.

"Basque, one hundred and fifty-eight," came the faint reply on the humid morning breeze. The combat instructor who'd been waiting inside the walls of the arena to be the referee began the countdown.

"Five."

Oh, shit.

"Four."

Breathe.

"Three."
Breathe, stupid.
"Two."
OH, SHIT.
"One."
I think I just peed a little.
"Go."

My emaciated body, a full 30 pounds thinner than when I had stepped into the squad bay for the first time, lurched forward with little grace but a loping gait that carried me into the arena a second before my opponent. The arena was slightly bigger on the inside than I had imagined it would be when looking at it from the outside, and the mulch was deep enough to make finding footing more difficult than it had been on the hard-packed gravel that lined the hallway. It served its purpose, however, as the seniors bayed for blood from their perch, tyrant emperors all.

Basque was six inches shorter than me and wore his weight heavier on his frame, while I was all gangly long limbs. Like the awkward bird I looked like, my head sticking forward into the world on a too-long and too-thin neck, I hopped forward toward my opponent. I hoped the sight of a gawky skeleton dancing toward him might frighten him into lowering his guard. It did not. If anything, he brought the pugil stick up higher to guard his face.

His mistake.

I had at least six inches of reach on Basque, my thin, drinking-straw-size arms stabbing out at the exact moment I thought I was in range. I could make up for any jab that fell short with a slight lean forward. I did not aim for his head or chest as he expected. I jabbed the tip into his lower abdomen within the last half inch of my reach. The tip may have tickled him into submission if given enough time. It was barely a touch, but it was a touch, nonetheless. The combat sergeant flipped his arm up toward my hallway, signaling a win for our platoon. I could hear my senior stomping back and forth across the viewing deck, mocking those who had bet against him and his awkward avian-looking guide.

I had won and remained undefeated.

I was so proud. I stood at the front of the platoon formation lost in my reverie. I had never won anything physical before, avoiding sports to be free of the shadow of an older brother, who held state records and was as athletic as they came. I would remain undefeated and leave training a new …

Why are we being lined back up?

Senior had come down from his perch to personally reorder us in front of the arena entrance. Gone was the sensible order of weight, pitting men of equal stone against each other. Instead, Senior seemed to have a very specific order in mind that defied any categorization I could determine. All I knew was, suddenly, after being in the middle of the pack, I was at the very end of the line.

I was the last man in the stack.

Senior, grinning, sprinted back up to rejoin the other seniors. His counterpart did the same. They met on the railing of the observation deck, each confident their platoon would be victorious given the ability to stack the deck.

One by one the men of our stack called out their name and weight, disappeared down the hallway, and joined in glorious combat, the end of which was signaled by the spectators cheering wildly. The rest of the men in the stack jostled nervously, wondering what Senior had thought of them, as victors or as useless chattel to be sacrificed to a more skilled opponent. The cheers gave no clue as we waited.

Finally, the man in front of me disappeared down the hallway and I was all alone with the combat instructor, who terrified me by doing the last thing I expected. He smiled. Warmly.

"All right, Doe, this is it," he said, checking my safety straps and mouth guard with a strange tenderness that came either from pity for my coming slaughter or, far harder to believe, genuine goodwill. We waited in silence as the last fight went on for what felt like hours before finally ending in an uproar. Finally, breaking the silence and ripping me from its safety, he nodded.

"Now."

"Doe, one hundred and fifty-five," I screeched. The reply was instant; my blood froze.

"Desni, two hundred and twenty-two."

Worse, the combat sergeant suddenly chuckled. I was suddenly petrified at the thought of facing whatever Goliath they had put me up against. At least David did not have to close with his enemy, cleverly staying back at sling range should he have to turn tail and run. The combat sergeant suddenly grabbed my shoulder with one enormous hand and slammed his palm across my helmet with the other, in what I imagined was supposed to be a comforting, masculine show of camaraderie. I did my best not to say "ow" out loud.

"Run. He'll be slow. Run fast as you can and catch him before he even knows what hit him. You can beat him, Doe."

All I heard was "run fast" and the sound of my own shallow breaths, as my body began the evacuation process with a loud gurgle in my stomach.

On "go," I took off as fast as I could run, kicking up dirt behind me as I tore through the hallway to meet my hulking opponent in the arena and strike before he had time to get set. I tore out into the mulch; to my surprise the arena was empty.

Oh, that dumb bastard, I thought with a grin.

I sped up, aimed straight for my opponent's hallway. Win at any cost. There was no chivalry here, no sense of gentlemen meeting on the lawn for a highly ritualized duel. This was combat and I did not want to meet my opponent on an equal footing where I could lose. I wanted to fight dirty and win.

I entered my opponent's hallway and kept my focus on the last turn as I slowed, ready to plant my foot. After a heartbeat I saw the leading edge of his pugil stick, then the left arm and shoulder. I planted my lead foot and threw my entire weight behind my jab, aimed directly at where his head would hopefully be if my timing was right.

The enormous juggernaut never saw it coming. Desni's head snapped back as my pugil stick slammed into his face shield, with my full body weight behind it. The direction his enormous girth was going in suddenly changed and he stumbled back against the hallway wall, stopping him from toppling over fully.

I won! I wanted to tear my helmet off and scream at the top of my lungs. *I was undefeated. I was the champion. I was ...*

There was no cheering, no deafening roars of approval from the balcony. Besides Desni's breathing, which was becoming more ragged and furious with each gigantic inhale, the arena was eerily silent.

The combat sergeant I had passed in the middle of the arena stood in the hallway behind me and signaled for both of us to follow. He walked us out into the arena and all three of us faced the seniors. Suddenly, he raised his hand toward my hallway, and I could see my senior's mouth grow into a smug smile that he would wear for the next week at least.

I had won! Ha! I was undefeated.

UNDEFEATED!

I looked up so I could watch them cheer, so I could watch as I was hailed as ...

Fuck. I could see it in their faces, they had wanted blood and I had not delivered. I had failed to give them the fight they had wanted.

But Desni would.

Another senior nodded at the combat sergeant and he quickly stepped out from between Desni and me as he chuckled.

"Go."

I did not even have time to open my mouth to ask, "What do you mean 'go'?"

Desni slammed into me, a speeding freight train carrying cars full of nothing but muscle and absolute hate for my face-jabbing, ambushing existence. I could not even lift my stick up into the guard, as Desni slammed it aside with each horrific blow. I had remembered the arena being rather large but suddenly it seemed too small, too confined, as Desni drove the wind from me and threw me into the wall, hard enough that I bounced right back into his next terrible swing.

And the next. And the next. And the next.

Now the seniors were cheering, frothing at the mouths as they watched Desni pummel me with every powerful swing of his pugil stick. The seniors jumped up and down, slamming their meaty hands against the railing as they cried out for my "death." Desni, the sting of his pride still fresh, was only too happy to oblige.

I would love to say I held my own, but I did not. I do not know if I was even holding my own pugil stick at the end, though I would assume it hung limply at my thighs or lay on the ground, given that when Desni's pugil stick swung around in one last haymaker, there was nothing to slow it down save my weak, soft body, which, to its credit, did stop the stick completely.

I fell sideways to my knees and then toppled onto my stomach. The cacophony of hate and anger grew to new heights from the viewing deck as the combat sergeant led Desni back toward his hallway. The seniors had gotten their sport after all.

Finally, I got up and brushed myself off. Limping back to my formation, I realized the lesson they had wanted me to learn.

No one leaves training undefeated. The house always wins.

CHAPTER 6

The Giggle Game

Midway through our training we were blessed with the addition of a brand-new instructor sergeant, glowing hot and still steaming from whatever demonic schooling they received before being unleashed upon the recruits. There was no fanfare, no big welcome-aboard announcement with heartfelt introductions; one moment there were two demons and then suddenly there were three.

We had been judged by the gods and found wanting.

Sergeant Bills was almost a carbon copy of our current sergeants, physically different only in his being a hand shorter, but otherwise with the same oversized arms, same sardonic scowl, and same towering rage when the erratic switch flipped. The exact same, only in a smaller package. He would have gone over well in Japan.

Whereas we had been intimidated only by fear up to that point, Sergeant Bills loved to play one specific game with us that was worse than all the others we had experienced to that point. It preyed on our true weakness. He made us laugh.

Therewithin lay the insidious nature of his game. We wanted to laugh. More than anything else in the world, more than sex, more than food, more than anything, we just wanted to laugh and feel human again. Humans, it seems, can survive almost anything so long as we do not lose hope and the ability to laugh; to look at the brighter side of almost any situation is an enormous part of that. Black or gallows humor is a staple of any occupation that deals with suffering or death. Ask any police officer. Or fireman. Or nurse. The ability to laugh occasionally and let off some of the deadly pressure building up inside is paramount to thriving in the human experience.

And the bastard knew it.

Every night before lights out, we would stand on line in our bleached-white underwear to be physically inspected for rashes, sores, or any other possible physical ailments that might impede our training. This was far more important than we originally thought. One recruit hid a red, angry looking scratch on his right wrist somehow and the next morning he woke to find an inky black line starting at his wrist, running up his forearm and bicep, and stopping just short of his shoulder. He was rushed away to the hospital and did not return to training. We were brought on line for a special announcement about the utter seriousness of nightly inspections for just that reason. A couple of more hours, we were told, and the infection would have reached his heart and spread to his entire body.

A week later, a recruit had what looked like a large pimple on his elbow and, not wanting to get sent off to medical, he tried popping it in the shower after physical training. A white ball the size of a large marble popped out from between his fingers as he squeezed and the smell of dead flesh that wafted out of the impossibly large hole it left behind made the rest of us clutch our knees and wretch until our eyes watered. He too was immediately whisked away to disappear into the gray limbo of medical.

On Sergeant Bills's night to hold inspection, he would start at one end of the squad bay, with me following two steps behind with a clipboard to record any anomalies that required immediate attention, or that were to be checked on in the morning. Any recruit with dirty fingernails was recorded. Any recruit with unwashed ears was recorded. Any deviance from the hygienic standard was met with swift reprisal, usually in the form of fire watch in the middle of the night. It was strange knowing that our squad bay, maybe the security of our country in the future tense, was being protected at night by the dirtiest of us.

Satisfied that all recruits were thoroughly judged, and offenders sent off to the showers to correct themselves, Sergeant Bills would begin his game.

While laughter is a basic human necessity outside of training, it was considered a cardinal sin in the squad bay, punishable in the most creative of ways. Sergeant Bills would walk to the beginning of the squad bay again and then re-inspect every recruit, while we waited for those who had been reprimanded to clean themselves and be reassessed.

And then the game would start.

Sergeant Bills would walk in front of a random recruit, never the same twice, and slowly turn to face them. With the blank face of an executioner, Sergeant Bills would deliver the most poignant and accurate joke one could imagine, a verbal shotgun slug from point blank. His visage would not give the slightest hint of humor but his jokes, despite the deadpan delivery, were mortifyingly hilarious.

At the delivery of his one joke for the night the game would begin. Sergeant Bills would not move as he stared, deadpan, at the recruit, letting the joke settle and be absorbed. The rest of us would begin shaking, trying to avoid making eye contact with each other. Any person who has ever tried to stop themselves from laughing knows that trying to hold it in only makes the laughter inside grow. Seeing the other recruits shake as they held their breath, trying not to be the one to laugh, would only make the situation worse. In the silence you could hear the sharp, rapid-fire inhales as we tried to stifle our laughter. Failure to do so would see us tortured when sleep was so close. All it would take was one small laugh and the roof would come tumbling down on our heads.

One evening, Sergeant Bills stopped short in front of Recruit Wiggly. The sergeant performed a slow, but perfect, right face, heels snapping together loudly in the silence of a half-empty squad bay. Wiggly had come quite far from his first day on line but still his breasts and stomach hung in heavy slabs off the front of his short, blockish frame. Sergeant Bills did not move or say a word and Wiggly began to tremble. Tiny diamonds of perspiration broke out across Wiggly's blushing forehead as he tried to stare through the instructor sergeant to the promised land of milk and cookies beyond. The silence grew like a cancer, causing ticks and tremors in all of the recruits as the anticipation of the night's joke festered and triggered some suicidal gene to activate as we found ourselves suddenly trying very hard not to smile.

When the agony of anticipation had ripened and borne fruit, signaled by shaking chests and white knuckles, Sergeant Bills struck. He lifted his left arm, palm up and elbow straight, at a pace deliberate enough not to startle the terrified Wiggly. When his arm was almost parallel, Sergeant Bills placed his calloused pink palm underneath Wiggly's right breast and lifted it an inch. The pale white flesh interwoven with light blue veins just underneath the surface quivered upon that massive palm, as Sergeant Bills continued to look Wiggly dead in the eyes.

Sergeant Bills then began to lift and bounce the breast in his palm, as if trying to figure the weight of such an item. Sweat dripped off Wiggly's chin in a waterfall where the rivers that ran down his bright red cheeks met.

"So what are you?" Sergeant Bills drawled. He inhaled and then cocked his head slightly sideways as if trying to figure out a difficult problem. "A C-cup?"

I jammed the pen I was holding deep into the flesh of my forearm, not enough to puncture the skin but close enough that my eyes closed to blot out the pain. It was all I could do to delay the laugh climbing swiftly up the inside of my ribcage like a trapped animal suddenly sensing freedom. I pushed harder as I felt the battle being lost. It was worth bleeding for.

I would not laugh.

I would not laugh.

I woul ...

Laughter peeled from the far end of the squad bay and, just like that, every defense every recruit had created to keep the laughter from seeing the light failed. For three full glorious seconds we shrieked and snorted like madmen, hands finding knees as we attempted to remain on our feet. Three beautiful seconds where finally we felt something again. A moment to treasure. A moment to revel in our humanity.

But only for a fleeting moment, like the time it takes for a "Bouncing Betty" mine to activate and spring up in the air before detonating.

After three seconds, Sergeant Bills sprung and detonated. Foot lockers went flying, racks were overturned, all to the soundtrack of his guttural roaring.

Once again, we had lost the giggle game.

CHAPTER 7

Mason

Deere was a physical specimen in every way a young man could be. He had been a high school sports legend in his home state and was a three-sport savant. He was handsome and his six-pack abs, large, muscular arms, and chiseled chest were worthy of envy. He looked like a superhero.

But that is not why the rest of us could not bear showering with him. No man wanted to shower next to Deere because he was the most well-endowed man any of us had ever seen, almost to the point of being unbelievable.

Being of a pale, northernmost European heritage, I never wanted to even stand near him when naked. If we were Lincoln Logs, Deere would be a great four-notch beam for building long walls, while I could barely help make the chimney with my one-notch stub. I avoided him whenever possible and, if it was not possible, we all made sure to give him a wide berth in the shower, in case something caught his attention and he turned quickly, which would most likely result in his court-martial for assaulting half a platoon in one swing.

But the gods do have a sense of humor. While they had seen fit to give Deere all the physical attributes that would ensure his seed was spread far, and what I can only imagine as painfully wide, they seemingly did so at the expense of diverting his blood supply to what was in his pants rather than in his brain.

Deere could do one thing with absolute precision. He could march in perfect rhythm and perform complex drill moves like he was machined in Switzerland. Much to my relief, after seeing me trying and failing miserably to walk in a straight line for more than four feet, Senior ordered that Deere be "drill guide" of our platoon. Any time the platoon had to march anywhere under observation, I slipped the "Guide" armband off and gladly handed it over to Deere, taking my place on the inside of the formation, somewhat hidden from view where my "happy feet" would not draw too much attention. Deere would puff out his chest and become a complete asshole, not quite realizing his position was literally ceremonial and very conditional. Every time we got back to the squad bay, and I would walk up to Deere to take back the armband, his face would crinkle up into a wounded look and he would ask why he was being fired. Again.

Just like yesterday.

And the day before.

At the recruiting office, after they have held your hand and calmed your nerves enough for you to sign on the dotted line, the next thing on the to-do list is to pick your M.O.S., or what they could have simply called a J.O.B.

Some go in knowing exactly what job they want.

"I want to be a Navy Seal! People will have to respect me," despite the fact they cannot swim or walk without getting winded.

Some go in knowing exactly what is important in life.

"I want whatever has the highest sign-on bonus!" not questioning why the military has to bribe people into those jobs.

And some go in to do the craziest thing imaginable.

"I will be whatever you tell me to be," or Open Contract as it is known.

Open Contract is exactly like the sign-on bonus system, where the military fills all of the positions no one wants, only they do not pay a single extra cent. It is a lottery of lesser evils.

Not surprisingly, Deere was an Open Contract, though he still did not quite understand what that meant until the day all two of the Open Contracts in the platoon were ordered to march over to attend the "Lottery." Random luck had nothing to do with the outcome. The most essential jobs no one picked at the recruiting station would be filled first, and then everything would be backfilled from there.

While they were gone, the platoon had nothing on the schedule for another few hours so we were graciously given the time to scrub every last inch of the squad bay. Again. We stripped down to our PT clothes, shorts and T-shirts, and sloshed buckets of water scented with Aqua Velva around until the smell made us want to retch.

One of the perks of being guide was the absolute nepotism I could command the platoon with sometimes. I assigned the best and brightest to cleaning the showers while the rest got the squad bay. I joined the shower crew and, while the instructor sergeants hawked the men in the big bay, those of us in the shower could whisper and feel some sense of humanity as we scrubbed.

Deere was sent to join the shower-cleaning crew upon his return. He entered the enormous gang shower with a dour look smeared across his face. He sighed and began scrubbing as the rest of us stopped completely and stared.

"Well?" Jenkins whispered, breaking the long silence.

"Well, what?" Deere whispered.

"Well, what the fuck did you get?" Jenkins hissed. Deere looked up and sighed heavily again, his massive shoulders rising and sinking as his face dropped into an even more morose look.

"I don't want to tell you. It's the dumbest job ever." Blood in the water. Now Deere had our full attention and Jenkins smirked as he leaned on his mop.

"Come on, Deere, give us a hint," Jenkins whispered. Deere looked around the shower as if looking for a sergeant and then leaned his mop up against the wall. He faced us and then began to mime his job in what was the world's strangest time and place for charades.

Deere reached down, picked up an imaginary handful of something, stood up, and slapped it against another imaginary object, his face getting longer with every second he thought about it. He then reached down with the other hand, grabbed another imaginary object, stood, placed this object with slightly more care, then repeated the entire process.

"What the fuck is he doing?" Thompson the First whispered, shaking his head in confusion. His twin brother, The Second, shrugged. The rest of us leaned our heads forward and squinted, as if that would help solve the mystery of Deere's terrible miming.

"Come on, guys," Deere whined, genuinely upset as if we were toying with him. He reached down, scooped, splat, reached down, grabbed, and placed again.

And again.

And again, each time with growing vigor, his movements becoming grander and more overblown.

"Seriously, I have no clue what the fuck you are trying to tell us," Jenkins said, raising his eyebrows in confusion.

"You guys are assholes," Deere spat, stopping his miming mid-splat. "You know what I am and you're just messing with me, so I feel worse."

"No, we really have no idea what you are," I whispered.

"I am some kind of builder," Deere said, his face flushing red. He reached down into his imaginary bucket and scooped up a handful of whatever it was, holding it up for our inspection.

"Nope, still don't get it," Jenkins said.

"I'm a mason-guy-thing. It's mortar, you idiots," Deere hissed, shoving his imaginary handful of cement mixture out toward us.

"Holy shit," Thompson the Second said, shaking his head, the only one yet to understand.

"What the fuck are you talking about, Deere?" Jenkins hissed.

"I'm a builder. I build brick walls," Deere said, rising to Jenkins's ire.

"You're an engineer?" I whispered. Thompson the Second moaned and covered his face with his hands, trying to stifle his laugh.

"I build walls, you guys. I work with mortar," Deere said loudly.

"No, no, no," I said, already beginning to laugh as I realized his error. Jenkins shook his head, still not understanding.

"I bring mortar to the masons," Deere screamed. "I'm a mortarman, you assholes!"

There was a long pause as the disbelief set in. Jenkins's jaw actually fell open before he collected himself enough for his rebuttal.

"Deere, you are so fucking stupid," Jenkins hissed.

"What?" Deere said, but no one replied as the sound of boots on the bathroom floor approached. We only shook our heads and waited for the sergeant to come to slay us for talking during cleaning.

CHAPTER 8

Scarface

Senior stepped out into the squad bay and stood like a proud father looking down the two ranks of his warriors facing each other from across an aisle, their bodies rigid and eyes staring straight ahead, the product of long weeks of disciplined training. A few more weeks and we would be sent to our next school: infantry, combat engineer, motor transport, or bean counting. We were down to the core group, the hardy wheat after all the chaff had been discarded and sent home with a pat on the back for a good attempt, or a dishonorable discharge.

"Gentleman, I have been informed that we will be receiving our drug-test results from when you first arrived in the next couple of days. Is there anything I need to know before we get the results? Anything I need to prepare the commanding officer [CO] for so we can perhaps head it off at the pass and keep you from getting court-martialed?"

Alans, a slight, enthusiastic man who looked barely a day over 15, raised his hand. Alans had been something of an ugly duckling in the platoon, transforming over the weeks of training from a nasty, sluggish hard case into one of the platoon's finest.

"Alans, what do I need to know?" Senior asked, not moving any closer and making Alans yell his responses down the entire length of the line.

"This recruit did coke before I, er, this recruit got here, Sir," Alans snapped off. Senior stared, blinking rapidly (what passed for his thinking face). Cocaine, or its metabolized form benzoylecgonine, is detectable in the urine for a relatively short amount of time, between 12 hours in light usage to 72 hours if the dose was very high or consumed with alcohol. Considering that the metabolite of THC stays in the urine stream for four to 10 days, the testing and detection of cocaine use is rather low by comparison. Senior knew the math as well.

"Well, when did you take it, Alans?" Senior asked. Alans looked suddenly embarrassed.

"This recruit got some at a party the weekend before I, er, I, this recruit shipped, Sir," Alans said, breaking out in a light sweat. Senior nodded and seemed satisfied, the math in Alans's favor.

"Then this recruit did it in the hotel the night before this recruit shipped, Sir," Alans added after half a minute. Senior's half smile began to vanish. He nodded and began recalculating his math.

"Then this recruit did it in the airport before I, this recruit, got on the plane," Alans added, putting his chin down and staring at his boots. Senior stared at him, his mind working furiously.

"And then on the plane on the way here, Sir," Alans added again. Senior's smile turned over into a grimace. Alans was shaking. Senior beat him to the punch.

"Then?"

"Then this recruit did whatever I had left of that True-True in the airport bathroom as soon as we landed here," Alans said, his voice quivering nervously. We had been herded almost directly off the plane and began in-processing at the airport, taking our drug tests within the hour.

"Oh," Senior replied. There may have been straight, uncut cocaine floating in the test cup, having fallen from Alans's flared nostrils. "I will inform the CO, see what we can do. Carry on, men."

Senior turned about face, shaking his head, and strode off toward the exit. All eyes were on Alans. He gave a nervous smile and shrugged his shoulders.

"What? I liked coke."

Alans did beat the drug test, however.

Two days later, while training, he jumped into what he believed was a very deep water obstacle. It was a shallow puddle and the sound of his shin snapping was as loud as a tree breaking in half during a strong gale. Before the drug test ever came in, Alans was given a medical discharge for his compound fracture.

CHAPTER 9

Apples and Oranges … and Pears

As guide of the platoon, I rarely ate what I felt was enough food. It was not that they did not dish out an utterly ridiculous heap each time we stood in the cafeteria line and held out our trays to be loaded with copious amounts of food to fuel our training. They did. The civilian contractors doling out our grub always had a sad look in their eyes and seemed conspiratorial as they heaped it on. We looked like we needed it—starving children desperately in need of a good meal and your sponsorship, for just pennies a day. Due to the physical rigors of training, paired with the constant stress state of the body, the weight melted off the bodies of every warrior in the platoon despite our being served three huge meals a day.

I just rarely got the chance to eat any of that food stacked on my tray. As guide and leader of the platoon, I would be served last, ensuring the men under me got everything they needed before looking to my own needs. The squad leaders under me were also served after the men they led, and so we were always at the back of the line, looking forward across the heads of our men at the almost endless tubs of steaming food, our mouths watering and our stomachs groaning audibly. But we knew exactly how the meal would end for us, usually just moments after it began.

There were rules for eating. One hand and one utensil only, other hand on your thigh. Sit up straight and don't make any eye contact with anyone else, and the gods help you if you try to make pleasant conversation with your neighbor. One drink only, to be gotten only after you have put your tray down, and to be carried with one hand, the other smartly at your side. If any of these rules were broken, the entire meal would come to a stop for everyone, and the entire platoon would pack up and leave. Those in the front of the line would get the most time to eat and the next man would have slightly less time, and so on and so forth down the line. The squad leaders and the guide would have few precious moments to pack enough food into our mouths until the inevitable fuck up by one of the platoon rocks and the subsequent termination of our mealtime.

For a long time after my tour of duty, civilians would be disgusted by the speed at which I could polish off my meals, my head down and shoveling food into my gaping maw, certain that someone might take it away from me if I was not fast enough.

Maslow only needs to show a skeptic a training platoon to prove his hierarchy of needs. Food and sleep were the most valuable commodities in our small world due to their scarcity. A million dollars in cash could be placed in the middle of the squad bay and be left unmolested for the entire training duration, but had a single Oreo or cheesesteak been left, it would have been gone the first moment the sergeants took their eyes off it. Constant hunger led to strange and rather pathetic-sounding crimes among the platoon.

In one horrible instance, the cafeteria had accidentally included cookies in our "fast lunch," a small white box usually comprising a sandwich, a piece of fruit, and two hardboiled eggs with accompanying single-serving packets of accoutrements. The sergeants were quick to confiscate the cookies and throw them in the dumpster out the back door of the squad bay.

That night the sergeants caught eight grown men in the dark stairwell of the back door of the squad bay shoving cookies in their mouths with looks usually reserved for heroin addicts plunging in the needle. Worse, the two men on fire watch who were supposed to be standing sentry had taken part, abandoning their posts. The rest of the platoon was awoken and stood on line in the middle of the night, watching eight men be asked the serious question.

"Who else stole the cookie from the cookie jar?"

The sergeants made sure every crumb of those cookies came back up, or at the very least the men would forever associate chocolate chips with searing muscle pain.

A week later, one particularly unlucky warrior was found with 20 candy bar wrappers cleverly shoved down inside the top of the hollow pipe that made up one of the bunk-bed legs, unable to be seen except from the ceiling. He may have gotten away clean had a sergeant not gone on a rampage and flipped the rack, suddenly seeing the top wrapper. Each wrapper pulled out was like a toenail being pulled from the unlucky warrior as he realized how much more trouble he was in with each subsequent find. He worked off every single one of those delicious calories within the hour.

What he did not say, and what has always bothered me since, was where he got 20 candy bars exactly. There was not a vending machine within our small universe and our mail was thoroughly checked. To his credit, he did not break and tell them where he had gotten them under hours of physical torture. He would have done well at SERE* survival school.

One particularly nasty, pathetic creature stole and ate the single MRE† we had been issued for the entire training day while he was supposed to be on gear guard. He

---

* SERE stands for "Survival, evasion, resistance, and escape."
† MRE stands for "Meal, ready to eat."

did not eat just one of the other recruits' MRE. He ate five. He would have gladly, and anonymously, watched the rest of us starve so he could "survive." Crumbs of lemon pound cake on his uniform betrayed him, the fat, nasty hobbitses.

During one week of training, most in the platoon were pressed into hard labor, breaking up into "work parties" assigned various tasks around the base. This was the week, we were told, all the platoon's crooked and messed-up teeth would be "straightened and fixed" compliments of the U.S. military, though "yanked" would have been a much more apt description. Six of our men lay in their racks on bedrest, their mouths swollen and their eyes staring off into the ether with the cloudy look of painkillers.

As scribe, as well as guide, it was my responsibility to make sure everyone knew where they were going and got there in a timely manner. I was given a large chalkboard to draw out the plan of the day, see the men were briefed, and send them on their merry way. When the working parties were away, I was left alone in the squad bay with six comatose men in their racks and nothing to do. The sergeants generally left me to myself so long as I looked busy cleaning or working on the platoon flag.

But each day that week, 40, unneeded fast lunches would be delivered to our empty squad bay and stacked in the corner—40 beautiful, gleaming white boxes stuffed full of delicious, calorie-laden food just sitting there all day until they were tossed out before dinnertime. Occasionally, one of the dental recoveries would ask for one and delicately chew on a hardboiled egg before passing back out, but for the most part it was just me and enough food to feed our phantom platoon.

I would sit cross-legged on the common space at the front of the squad bay and eat my single-serving lunch alone, staring up at the duty board to make sure I did not make any mistakes and send men to the wrong places. I would look over at the stack of fast lunches and daydream of food like I used to daydream of women.

Roast beef and bread dancing seductively together, pouring mustard down each other, while a harem of pears and apples slowly peeled back their skin to reveal their secret soft, wet insides.

My mouth watered and I would have been glad I was sitting if any possibility of an erection had not been completely deadened by sheer stress.

Sergeant Buck came out of his office and stood with his massive hands on his hips, his perfectly ironed uniform and mirror-shine shoes making him look something more than a mortal man. Without thinking through my decision, I stood up and snapped to the position of attention. Buck turned his flat, cold gaze in my direction.

"Sir, this recruit requests permission to have another box lunch, Sir," I said. "They are just going to waste, Sir, and this recruit is still hungry."

For the first time I saw a genuine emotion cross the sergeant's face: surprise. Sergeant Buck's eyes widened, and his head pulled back slightly, as if my words themselves were invading his personal space. He stood regarding me for a moment before he tilted his head slightly to the side. The small deviance from his normal posture was more unnerving than anything I had yet experienced. The next few moments made my skin itch and my feet sweat as he just stared, his eyes wide and his head slightly askew.

Oh, no.

Without a word he turned around and went back into his office. Despite his closing the door most of the way, I could hear him tell Sergeant Tank what I had just asked and them both laughing. It was not a chuckle. It was a deep, resonating boom from their great frames. They thought my request was very funny.

Oh, damn.

Both men emerged from the office and stood side by side, twin gods with their perfect, muscular bodies and malevolent stares. Sergeant Buck grinned.

"Permission granted. You can have more," he smirked. Sergeant Tank moved over to the pile of lunches and grabbed two boxes, then strode over in front of me to put them down, perfectly aligned.

Two, how wonderful, I thought. I was definitely hungry enough to eat two more fast lunches.

Sergeant Tank returned to the pile and aligned two more boxes next to the original two. Four. Four was a lot. Four was perhaps more than I wanted.

Two more boxes were set in the row, making six. Then two more were added to make eight—two perfect fire teams of fast lunches lined up in front of me for my inspection. My heart sank.

"Now, take out the first sandwich," Sergeant Buck ordered. I obeyed. "Consume." I obeyed.

"Take out the next sandwich." I obeyed.

"Consume." I obeyed.

Six small sandwiches later and I felt ill. Still, I ate. And ate. And ate. My stomach was fit to burst and I could hardly sit up. My every thought was of laying down and sleeping. Still, I ate until I had consumed the eighth sandwich. I clutched my stomach, rocking back and forth trying to compact it all and give whatever little relief I could find.

Sergeant Buck towered over me, grinning so smug I thought the corners of his mouth would touch his ears. It was his grin that irked me. It upset me that he'd won. I wanted to drive it from his face however I could, though I was quite sure given his stature and training that it would not be possible with violence.

"Had enough?"

Yes. Yes, I had. I could not have another bite.

"No, Sir," I replied. "It was the pear I really wanted."

I closed my eyes, hearing the words come out of my stupid mouth but not quite believing it was my voice. Sergeant Buck's eyes went wild, growing enormously and shaking as his anger welled.

"Oh. OH! It was the pears you wanted? Well, why did you not say so, Doe?" he howled. "You want pears! Get out every pear." I obeyed.

I could have stopped at any time. I could have begged off, tail between my legs. When I finally vomited and rolled onto my side after biting into the second pear, I smiled inwardly. I had won.

Sergeant Buck was not grinning any longer.

Let's call it a draw.

CHAPTER 10

The Road to Hell is Paved with Attrition

After basic training, we were sent to our appropriate combat schools. Those in the infantry were sent for 10 weeks to learn the secrets of our trade in destruction and killing. Those in the non-infantry jobs were sent for three weeks to learn just enough to know they never wanted to be anywhere near combat.

Halfway through infantry school, a school that seemed to primarily teach you how to wait in a cold hole of dark earth for endless amounts of time, a sergeant showed up to talk to anyone wishing to try out for the special operations community. When it was announced there was a talk outside for the "try outs," the instructors simply added that none of us would ever make it. It was said with complete conviction. Half of those eligible did not even bother to wander outside to listen, or even to just get some fresh air. The barracks always smelled of mushrooms and livestock. Livestock that bathed in Aqua Velva.

Eighty young warriors, only half of those eligible, packed onto bleachers to listen and daydream about the "promised land," the fabled special operations community. The number of applicants that even gained entry into the Holding Tank, the training platoon where warriors would await their chance to go to special operations school, was incredibly small, and smaller still was the number of those that made it through and actually graduated the training itself. But to the majority of the 80 warriors seated on the benches, statistics meant little.

Literally, I do not know if some seated there understood statistics.

The sergeant sauntered in front of the bleachers with none of the usual rigidity that comes with the higher ranks. He smirked and seemed completely relaxed in his surroundings. He looked like he would be completely relaxed anywhere and stood like he was just killing time at the mall waiting for his significant other to surface from looking at bras.

"I am Sergeant Mixter, and I'm here today to talk to you about the special operations community." His weathered face was sharp and pulled tight around the eyes as if in tremendous focus. There was a slight, smug grin at the corners of his mouth as if he knew a joke in which those of us seated on the bench were the punch line. He seemed to be staring right through us as he spoke.

"Most of you know who we are, so I won't take up much of your time. One thing I will say is this." He took a moment to survey the crowd. The grin increased. "Chicks dig spec ops guys."

A tremble of laughter swept through bleachers, but the sergeant's face did not reflect our mirth, holding only the strange, unnerving grin that suggested he would always have the last laugh.

"None of you will pass." Whatever laughter lingered suddenly died. The faces of the 80 warriors went slack and lost their youthful conceit as if Sergeant Mixter had gone down the line and individually slapped each one of us. Until that point in our training, we had only been told we, as warriors, were capable of anything and there was no enemy or obstacle we could not surmount. This belief in the "nothing is impossible" is a hallmark of warrior tradition, often hailed as the basis of its strength.

There was a sudden conflict of belief and fact. Something did not figure for the young warriors seated on the bleachers. We could do anything and yet there it was out in the open; all of us would fail the Indoc. Some furrowed their brows and ground their teeth in a mix of confusion and anger.

The gauntlet had been thrown down.

"Today is Tuesday. The Indoc will be held Friday morning at oh-five-hundred at the pool. Most of you have a lot of soul searching to do before then. Carry on, gentlemen."

And just like that, the sergeant had dissuaded almost thirty of the 80 warriors seated on the benches. Despite his relaxed posture, he walked away quickly, a man who was used to running rather than marching through life.

"What an asshole," someone murmured from the top of the bleachers. A wave of consent rushed through the warriors.

"Whatever. I'd rather be normal infantry."

"Bunch of cowboy jerk-offs, you ask me."

"Who wants to be special operations anyway?"

But a few on the bench held a different sentiment that they kept to themselves. It had been the driving force through much of their lives and had carried them far for the most part. It was personal, strictly unsaid, but a handful of warriors on the bleachers that day, like every set of warriors anywhere that such a speech has been given to, shared a thought that is universal to their personality type.

Fuck. Him.

Two simple words that would be murmured under their breaths every time someone at the Indoc, during their stay at the Holding Tank, and the special operations school itself, got in their faces and told them they were not good enough, they did not have what it takes, that they should just give up and quit. Those two words would carry a handful of warriors through some of the most difficult training the military had to offer.

In that simple phrase was the underlying basis of their true strength; they would not be undersold by anyone, ever. It was more than just a chip on their shoulder. It was the search for personal perfection and the line in the sand that was truly the furthest they could push themselves both mentally and physically. Very few had ever come close to such a line before; they would not accept it as truth until they knelt before it, bloodied in final defeat.

For the few who felt the tightening of their jaw during the speech, they were certainly not going to swallow this personal line because some old man had told them so.

Of the 150 warriors who had exceeded both the mental and physical requirements, which was the ability to run a first-class physical fitness test, only 48 packed onto the bus at four in the morning on the following Friday. The other 32 warriors who had sat for the speech remained in bed, looking up at the ceiling or the rack above them wondering whether they should have gotten on that bus and made the effort.

It was a decision that would secretly haunt them the rest of their days.

Could they have made it?

Would they have been among the few to have succeeded?

But they did not get out of bed that morning. They practiced their excuses until they sounded convincing enough for the other warriors to believe.

But they could never be convincing enough.

It was dark on the bus. No one talked, only stared out the window at the passing lights and prepared for whatever lay ahead. Rumors had spread that the Indoc consisted of everything from 50 pull-ups in 2 minutes to a half-marathon with a ruck carrying 50 pounds. Everyone had heard from a friend who knew a guy that had taken the Indoc and "gotten hurt." Everyone not taking the Indoc had spouted off their theories and inside knowledge during the two days of meals preceding.

Three warriors seated in the rear of the bus scoffed at the rumors and made bold predictions about their own success, a foregone conclusion in their minds. They boasted of their physical prowess and how they would be running the special operations community in a short amount of time. They talked endlessly in a desperate attempt to drown out the tiny voice in the back of their minds that whispered and repeated what the sergeant had said.

The sergeant was right. None of the three would make it. By the end, each would collapse in on themselves like a house of cards.

The warriors filed off the bus into a poorly lit changing room on the far side of a building containing only the changing room and a pool. They were met by a sergeant with a small, amiable face and thick, coke-bottle glasses. He looked like a favorite uncle or distant relative who is always missed at family gatherings. He just smiled, fresh and full of get-up-and-go, as the last of the warriors piled into the room.

The room smelled of chlorine, pungent mold, and fear. This only seemed to make the sergeant happier, his grin increasing with each body that piled in. He smiled and raked his piercing eyes across the line of downcast faces.

From the showers that led to the pool, the warriors could hear laughing and sporadic splashes. It sounded like a high school pool party, though with a noticeable lack of female voices in the boisterous chorus. The sergeant followed a few of the looks to the voices around the corner with an awful smirk and then addressed the warriors for the first time.

"Don't be so eager to get out there, eh." The favorite uncle smile became a terrible, knowing grin spanning from ear to ear. "Now take your boots off."

We obeyed with the slow, deliberate movements of men going to their execution. We untied our laces slowly and paid particular attention to our bootlace patterns for the first time, fingering them languidly, contemplating just what the best method was for lacing up boots.

Right over left?

Left over right?

Skip a loop? Stop three-quarters up?

Suddenly, the questions seemed paramount. Then we began removing our socks, adjusting the stitches to line up with the toes and heel; anything just to make the moment of serenity last a bit longer. Out on the pool deck, the howls grew louder as the news spread that the warriors trying out had arrived and were changing presently. It suddenly reminded the warriors of every prison film they had ever seen; worse, they understood their role beyond a shadow of doubt.

Fresh fish. Fresh fish. Come get it while it's fresh.

The serious ones, the ones with their heads in the right place, could feel the stretch of each sinewy muscle, hear their slow, deliberate breaths, and feel their heartbeat in every vein and artery. They heard the voice of every teacher, parent, or authority figure that had said they would never amount to anything, that said they should just do the world a favor and quit while they were behind.

You're nothing.

Fuck you.

You will just fail.

Fuck you.

Just quit. Quit like we know you will.

Fuck you.

The rest of us just wanted to piss our fatigues and run away.

"Get on the pool deck," Sergeant Cheshire said cheerfully, only loud enough to be heard by those closest to him, and then bounced out through the showers to the pool deck to join his brethren. The warriors hesitantly followed, save two. Two warriors made it no further than the changing room. They quietly sat themselves back down on the empty benches and began slipping their socks back on, paying little attention to the stitching alignment or their bootlace configuration. They slipped out the door as quietly as possible and boarded the bus for the second time that morning. They had no idea what they were going to tell those waiting for them back in the squad bay. They had quit too late to shrug it off and try to claim indifference.

The joyous shouting ceased the moment the first warrior in the pack stepped onto the pool deck. Only the dying echoes reverberating off the bleached-white walls gave any sign the stony-faced veterans standing on the side of the pool had uttered a sound at all. Their cold, flat gazes seemed to take the heat out of the humid room, and gooseflesh became the uniform of the day for the young warriors lining up against the wall.

"Oh, shit, look at that. Lost at least thirty since the speech," Sergeant Mixter chuckled, stepping out from behind the gear locker onto the pool deck. He was the only veteran wearing his camouflage utilities, the bottoms at least. The rest of the veterans were dressed in black "ranger panty" shorts and nothing else. Their lean, cut bodies stood out in stark contrast to the fragile warriors lined up against the wall. Even Sergeant Mixter, a solid 15 years older than most of the other veterans, had a barrel chest and powerful arms that stretched his T-shirt and hung impatiently at his sides, as if unused to such inactivity.

"Well, warriors, you're here and that's more than I can say for the rest of the lot that is hiding back in the barracks, pretending they did not want to be here. As you know, my name is Sergeant Mixter and I will be administering your Indoc this morning. These others who are assisting me are, for those who want it enough, your future Holding Tank instructors and, in some cases, future team leaders. Stick your hand out and sound off with your name."

One by one, the sergeant went down the line numbering the warriors' hands in thick, black permanent marker. The young warriors did their best to look nonchalant but came up short, looking exhausted rather than apathetic.

"Right, standby for your safety brief." Sergeant Mixter explained that at any time a warrior could quit and ring the bell that only in the last few screenings was forced to become figmental rather than physical due to murmurs of hazing. The newfound context of the bell was lost on a handful of warriors who were already looking around the pool deck to see just where they needed to move in order to ring the bell and stop the vicious stares of those running in the Indoc. The veterans had the cold, glassy eyes of sharks.

Fresh fish.

"All right, gents, the first event is the five-hundred-meter swim with camouflaged utilities. Get to the end of the pool."

There was a moment of confusion, of complete and utter panic, where the warriors shuffled about bumping into each other while only a few headed in the right direction.

"Now." It was not yelled. It could hardly be considered louder than normal conversational volume, but the sheer hatred the sergeant's snarl conveyed was more than enough to send the warriors fleeing opposite his direction, which, not by luck, was the direction he wanted them to go in the first place.

The 46 warriors lined the 25-foot-long poolside two and three deep, wondering how the relays would be set up.

Would they be relays of ten or would they just split those trying out in half?

"Go. Clock's started."

Go?

But who?

What relay is this?

Those behind the second rank who wanted it badly enough did not wait for an explanation. They simply leapt over the first rank or tried to at least. Suddenly, the first rank was exploding, some diving into the pool willingly while others were sent corkscrewing off the edge into the water by those behind them who were too impatient to fail because of someone else's indecision. Some tried to hold back, but eventually those in the back rank forced them into the pool. This was how the buffalo must have looked to the hunters who had run them stampeding off cliffs, those in the front suddenly aware of the edge while those in the back of the herd pushed ever forward to escape the danger corralling them.

Only the buffalo probably did not scream at such a high pitch or make embarrassing faces at the realization that "this was not for them."

It was not swimming in the classic sense of sleek, almost-naked bodies cutting gracefully through tranquil waters. For the first few panicked moments, it was task enough to simply find water among the tangle of fully dressed bodies and limbs. It was a churning sea of dark, digital-camouflaged warriors writhing and wriggling to free themselves of those around them, and break for the open water. Hands originally straightened into paddles suddenly curled into hooks as those with the will clawed their way over, under, and through the maelstrom.

Those of the first rank who had not hesitated were already paddling awkwardly in the open waters 20 meters down the pool. Those of the second rank who had not hesitated but were forced to fight their way to the open water were finding their way there quickly. And then there was the great tangle, some of whom had already quit but were simply trying to find the surface of the water before inhaling enough oxygen to announce their intentions.

Unrolled, the trousers and blouses were too long, the fabric clumsily draping down over bare hands and feet. The open breast pockets and cargo pockets caught water like racecar parachutes. Everything was working against those trying to swim. Still, they tried like hell, some putting every last ounce of effort into the swim.

Only, it was one of many events. They were burning themselves out too quickly.

Stopping forward momentum got warriors physically yanked from the pool by one of the veterans helping run the Indoc. Touching the bottom of the shallow end got warriors yanked. Looking as if you were about to drown got you yanked. Almost any "cheat" or safety concern got warriors yanked from the pool.

Wanting to get yanked did not get you yanked; they left the quitters to crawl out and find the bus themselves.

One warrior, a large, muscular boy of 18, jumped off the edge of the pool and immediately sunk to the bottom of the pool as if his perfectly chiseled body was actually made of stone. It was several seconds before one of the safety swimmers was able to notice him in the froth of thrashing bodies and dive in. Pulled to the edge of the pool, he was met by Sergeant Mixter.

"Can you even swim?" Sergeant Mixter snarled.

"No, Sergeant."

"Then why did you jump in?"

"Because I had to try, Sergeant. I had to try."

The sergeant grinned and pulled the boy up out of the pool with almost no effort. He slapped him on the back heartily.

"You got heart, kid, I'll give you that," Sergeant Mixter said with a laugh. The boy was elated by the compliment.

"Does that mean I passed, Sergeant?" the boy asked excitedly.

"Fuck no. Get back on the bus," the sergeant replied coldly, and he turned away to watch those still moving forward.

Those who finished the swim stood against the wall where they had before first entering the pool. They were not allowed to lean against the wall to rest any longer. There were large gaps in the numbers on their hands: 1, 5, 7, 8, 12—gaps all the way down to 46. Sergeant Cheshire walked up and down in front of the warriors, grinning his terrible grin and bobbing his head like a nervous bird.

"Hard, eh?" he asked a few of the warriors. They opened their mouths to answer, but his unnerving grin informed them it was a rhetorical question, even if they did not know what the word meant.

"The next event will be the twenty-five-foot crossover," Sergeant Mixter announced, looking at his clipboard.

"Yeah!" Sergeant Cheshire howled abruptly, his eyes wide and full of absolute, manic joy.

"He's crazy," one of the warriors against the wall whispered as Cheshire moved back toward the end of the pool, punching his fist into his palm. The other veterans were grinning as well, their tight, muscular stomachs shaking with contained laughter that only registered in their big, toothy smiles. They all knew something we did not.

"The crossover is very simple, gentlemen. When you are told to do so, you will step off the edge of the pool and pencil dive into the water, completely submerging.

Without pushing off the side of the pool, you will then do a complete flip and swim the 25 feet across the pool without your face breaking the surface of the water. If you find yourself on the surface, keep your face completely submerged in the water and you will be allowed to continue. If you make it to the other side of the pool, make sure to touch the side of the pool before surfacing. If you fail to touch the side of the pool before surfacing, you will be cut. When you surface, you will stick one arm up in the air and make the 'OK' sign with your hand. Failure to do so will get you cut. Are there any questions? Good, great. The following numbers step to the edge of the pool."

Sergeant Mixter proceeded to read off 10 of the remaining numbers. Those 10, those unlucky fated 10, stepped forward.

Fresh fish. Fresh fish.

"Prepare to cross over."

That term would come to haunt those warriors who passed the Indoc and made it to the Holding Tank. The majority of the long hours spent at the pool every morning would be devoted to crossovers. Crossovers would be used as training, with each warrior having to complete a certain number before being able to exit the pool. They would be used as warm-ups and cool-downs at the beginning and end of each day. They would be used as punishment for losing any of the many "games" played. The warriors would be made to keep doing them until everyone in the pool completed one together as a team. There was always one who failed, and then the failures only compounded.

But for right then the term meant nothing, only a simple command for a seemingly simple task. Get in the pool, swim underwater for a spell, then get out.

Simple enough.

It was mayhem for the first 10 warriors in the water. Two were instantly disqualified for touching the side of the pool with their feet in an underhanded attempt to propel themselves forward. One of the warriors pencil-dived too deep and the sudden pressure pushing against his ears and chest scared him enough that he scrambled to the surface as fast as his fabric-wrapped hands could work. He surfaced like a dog trapped in a garbage bag, howling mournfully as he desperately attempted to search out the side of the pool blindly. Those who continued to swim were flailing wildly, some doing the breaststroke, while others found new and creative ways to propel their heavy, cumbersome mass forward.

Two warriors broke out ahead of the rest, pumping like machines for the opposite side. They were three-quarters of the way across before one suddenly stopped mid-stroke, shook wildly beneath the surface for a moment, and then headed straight up toward the grinning faces awaiting him. When he surfaced his face was bright red and, by his gasp, it sounded like he had not taken a breath in minutes. The second of the two was two arm lengths from the edge of the pool but was rising toward the surface, still horizontal, at a rapid rate. He surfaced, his face still in the water, but the sudden sensation disoriented him. He faltered. He obeyed his instincts and picked his head up out of the water only an arm length away from the other side.

Three more dropped, staggered between a quarter-length and three-quarters of the way there. They all looked as if they had seen demons beneath the surface and could not gulp down enough oxygen once they surfaced. The two warriors who were left swimming moved slowly but deliberately. They covered the distance and seemed almost mad with delight when they surfaced, their hands held high while they sported the OK hand signal, their grins matching that of the veterans looking on.

"See that?" Cheshire said, pacing in front of the young warriors waiting for their turn. "Eight more down, yeah? They quit on themselves. They gave up. They told themselves they couldn't do it. I've seen guys who can stay under for two minutes. Stay deep and just relax, eh?"

None of those standing there knew whether to believe him; about the staying deep, about the two minutes, or about any of it. His Charles Manson stare did not beg believability. Still, the alternative did not seem all that great either.

"He is crazy," the warrior beside me moaned.

For all his apparent madness, Cheshire was honest. Those who trusted in his advice pencil dove as deep as they could and flipped as close to the bottom of the 13-foot-deep pool as possible.

It was quiet and peaceful. Only the occasional splashing of a failure above could be heard over the sound of your own heart thumping loudly in your ears. The pressure drives at your eardrums painfully but it is also compressing the oxygen in your lungs, making it feel like you have an almost unlimited supply as you glide along the bottom. You frog kick and pull with your arms at the same time, the utilities making it feel like a bad dream in which you cannot move fast enough to outrun the darkness gnashing its ferocious teeth at your heels, but you are moving forward all the same. You stroke and then, with your arms limp at your sides, you glide silently, watching the lane markers appear at the top of your field of view and then disappear under you like movie credits as you drift perpendicular to them. Somewhere far away there are men yelling, screaming at you incoherently. You do not know whether they are cheering for your success or your extinction.

That is another world, though. Here, you are safe. Here, at the bottom, you only need to stroke, glide, and count the lane markers passing beneath you.

Four. Stroke. Glide.

Five. Stroke. Glide.

Six. Stroke. Pain.

Your world explodes as you run full speed into the other side of the pool head down, looking at the bottom. You panic. You look around and there is nowhere to go but up. You push off the bottom of the pool like a rocket and you imagine yourself breaching the surface like a dolphin in triumph. But you barely manage the simple process of breathing and sticking your OK sign up at the same time.

Still, you made it.

Some did not.

The next event was the rifle retrieval. A rubber rifle was thrown to the bottom of the 13-foot pool and, from treading water on the surface, the warriors dove to the bottom, retrieved the rifle, and resurfaced. Upon resurfacing, the warriors held the rifle with both arms fully extended above their head and began to tread water with their shoulders above water for a relatively short amount of time. Most of the warriors who made it this far completed the task with relative ease, but some sank the moment they stopped using their free arm to tread water.

One warrior held the rifle completely dry for the proper amount of time suspended only inches above the water while from the wrists down he was fully submerged and kicking wildly. He was given a second attempt, more out of curiosity and laughter than a sense he might succeed. Try as he might, he could not kick hard enough to keep his head above the surface, much to the amusement of the veterans looking on.

Of the original 46, 27 were standing against the wall, which was becoming a very familiar and uncomfortable place. Numbers that should have been distant, such as 5 and 12, were standing next to each other. Each event had taken its toll until there were just over half of the exhausted warriors still standing nervous and cold along a concrete wall waiting to be told what to do next.

"You'll be happy to know that this is the last swimming event before the physical fitness test, gentlemen. Almost done. For some of you, this will be an easy event. For most of you, it will not."

This was a lie. It was not an easy event for any of the warriors.

"The last event is treading water for half an hour. Thirty minutes of treading water and you'll be done," Sergeant Mixter smirked. "When you are told, get in the pool and move to the center."

Cheshire let out what can only be described as a mammoth war whoop, a cry of savage joy and excitement in the face of ferocious battle meant to strike fear into the hearts of the enemy. It did just that.

"Get in the pool."

The buffalo stampeded off the cliff.

The warriors were treading water in the middle of the deep end watching Sergeant Mixter attentively, looking for any clues to his body language that might give away the dangers of the next event. It was not his body language that suddenly crushed every hope but the body of Cheshire, who stepped to the edge of the pool and pulled his shirt up and over his head, throwing it over the bench. He wasn't wearing his glasses. In fact, he was just shy of naked, wearing only his short black shorts.

The amiable face was a lie. The truth was in his manic eyes. His harmless, almost pleasant face was a diversion, it was suddenly and universally realized in the pool, as he raised his arms to stretch. He was like the fish that dangled its own flesh antenna like a worm out in front of its mouth to attract and disorient other foolish fish, which it then devoured when they became fixated on the harmless-looking worm. His body was that of a Greek statue. It was terrible in its sleekness, in its perfectly defined abdominal muscles and square pectorals. He had somehow and impossibly doubled in size by removing his clothes.

Worse still were the tattoos. There was a half smiley face, half skull on his chest that summed him up so nicely that even children too young to read could at least get a sense of the danger from the pictogram. On the back of his neck was a barcode, and it did not look misplaced or comical as it did in every other instantiation. It looked just as it should, horrifically natural on the body of such a predator. His naked eyes were piercing and caused panic as they fell upon the group, each warrior thinking that Cheshire was staring directly at him and him alone.

"Let's get wet, yeah?"

Fresh fish. Fresh fish.

Cheshire dove in effortlessly with almost no splash.

Shark in the water.

Suddenly, all the veterans dove in save two; Sergeant Mixter, ever smirking, and the spec ops medic (like a normal medic only stronger and faster with more endurance, and a level of combat medical training that would have made the doctors from *M*A*S*H* jealous). Sergeant Mixters began chumming the water.

"At any time you decide to quit, simply swim to the edge of the pool and sound off with your number. If you have a medical emergency, swim away from the circle and you will be helped to the side of the pool."

From out of nowhere a long, red-and-white snake of a lane marker materialized. Cheshire swam the head of the snake around the circle of young warriors until it was head to tail, the ouroboros, eating itself in a vicious circle. The warriors were quiet, waiting for the possibility of another hint.

"Whatever you do, don't leave the circle, eh," Cheshire whispered as he tightened the lane marker until all the remaining warriors were swimming on top of each other. Those who were unable to swim without their hands had been lucky to drop out at the rifle retrieval. In such close quarters, most of the warriors' hands were pinned down to their sides. Sergeant Mixters looked at his watch for a few seconds and then said, "Go."

It was not difficult at first, save the uncomfortable feeling of being so tightly wedged up against one another. There was a general feeling of calmness in the circle as the warriors paddled and kicked gently, trying to conserve as much energy as possible after having already heavily exerted themselves in the previous events.

A splash of water was all it took to shatter the tranquility and crush the feeling of calm into that of sheer terror. Cheshire watched the circle for a minute, his eyes darting from face to face in an effort to find the weak links. Hidden in the middle, at the heart of the circle, a weak link struggled to keep his head above the surface and the crushing shoulders. A look of absolute nirvana crossed Sergeant Cheshire's face, as if not just one Christmas morning but a whole lifetime of Christmas mornings had suddenly been gifted to him all at once. He cupped both his hands, palms out, in front of his chest and aimed carefully, shoving at the surface of the water. A massive sniper's shot of water flew into the circle. It hit with unnecessary accuracy. There was more than one claustrophobic warrior in the circle, and whether the splash hit them physically or not, the intent surely did.

There was a sudden, spastic disturbance in the circle, beginning in the middle but quickly spreading outward to the warriors gripped by the lane marker.

Imagine for a moment being stuck on a crowded elevator and suddenly one of the once-peaceful citizens standing quietly in the middle of the pack believes he has just burst spontaneously into flames. He screams and scrambles to get out but only ignites more of the crowd with his panic. Soon, most everyone in the elevator thinks they are burning alive. Everyone suddenly begins violently searching for an exit that does not exist.

Only the warriors believed they were drowning.

This was contact hysteria and only 2 minutes into the 30-minute test; the warriors began growling and using whatever means necessary to keep themselves afloat.

"Everyone just calm down," one of the warriors in the circle tried to reason, but his mouth was suddenly flooded with a sharp gush of water splashed in by one of the veterans circling the panicked tangle.

"Shut up. No talking."

The true nature of every young warrior in the circle suddenly came to bear. Some, seeing only 25 more minutes of sheer naked violence and fear, opted to dive down and swim out away from the circle, surfacing and finding their way onto the bus without ever looking back. Others tried to remain calm and keep to themselves. So long as each warrior stayed within what little space they were given, there should have been no problem.

But there was panic.

And there was fear.

Warriors who were otherwise quiet and courteous were now clawing viciously at anyone around them to be able to pull themselves slightly higher than the pack for a breath of that crisp, fresh air that seemed to drift overhead, just out of reach.

We were all suddenly transformed into Tantalus.

One of the braggers from the back of the bus began putting both hands on other warriors' shoulders and pushing them under, using their added buoyancy for his own moments of respite from the brawl. He personally "caused" three warriors to leave the circle. They would later call him out on the bus about the incident. He vehemently denied ever touching anyone, saying it was he who had been attacked.

He was shunned for the rest of training and one can only hope the story followed him to his unit.

After multiple attacks without reprisal, he forgot himself and absently put his hands on another warrior's shoulders to push down once more. The shoulders just happened to be those of Private Lemune.

Lemune looked like an enormous Irishman—fair-skinned with a shock of well-shaped red hair—but he was French. He was the quiet type, keeping to himself but always listening to everything going on around him. He was deceptively intelligent for his size and uncommonly brutal when provoked.

He did not take kindly to the braggart trying to drown him.

Lemune was like a Buddhist monk and turned to face the braggart, smirking. The braggart suddenly reeled from the powerful hidden blows that began to land just under the surface of the water. Vengeful but not wanting to get caught, Lemune kept his punches where the veterans could not see. They were a quarter of the intensity they would have been out of the water, but the blows made quick work of the braggart. He could not escape fast enough through the mayhem from the red shock of hair that moved after him like a shark's fin. The braggart spent the rest of the tread trying to stay well away from Lemune who, after a minute, went back to his tranquil float in a lazy river.

With each quitter, Cheshire pulled the rope tighter. With each tightening, the number of dropouts increased. Unintentionally, the group of warriors began to rotate, swirling around like a great drain below them had suddenly opened up. One warrior jerked to his left, pushing into the warrior next to him who tried to swim away, but only to push into the next warrior.

Everyone was trying to move away from each other and soon the warriors were churning the water of the entire pool into an enormous whirlpool. Even if they wanted to stop the turning, they could not, the whirlpool catching greater momentum with each stroke. Only the warriors in the center of the circle did not feel the violent pull, but they faced a far worse punishment. The water was dead calm in the middle of the circle and warriors began viciously fighting for their place in the center. When one warrior violently claimed the space, he would instantly be pushed and dunked by other warriors eager to take his spot.

The circle was down to 20 warriors swimming on top of each other in an orgy of panic and determination. With 10 minutes left to swim, the veterans took to sharking those in the circle, swimming beneath their kicking legs and suddenly yanking them to the bottom of the pool by their ankles. To those swimming next to a warrior who got yanked, it looked horrifically like the opening scene of *Jaws*, when the young woman was unexpectedly pulled down into the darkness for the last time. Every warrior braced himself for his turn to be sharked. The anticipation alone was devastating. Two more quit before they were even touched. Those who were sharked surfaced with a look of ecstasy, the deed experienced and survived.

With 5 minutes remaining, the veterans circling the tight group began shoveling water into the 18 faces left.

"What are you going to do if you find yourself in prop wash? What are you going to do if the breakers are not what you expected and your zodiac flips? How are you going to survive?" Cheshire asked casually as he accurately splashed the warriors in their bloodshot eyes and gasping mouths like a carnival game. "If you cannot handle this, gentlemen, you are going to be a liability to your team. You are going to get your team killed because you cannot get comfortable in the water. Remember the rule of three, gentlemen. You can survive three weeks without food. You can survive three days without water. And you can survive three minutes without oxygen."

The 18 left swimming would not quit. They had come too far and fought too hard to willingly leave the circle, not in five minutes, not in five hours. Some were willing to drown and chance being revived rather than leave the circle at its most terrible. They could all see the clock ticking away the last minute of the tread.

"One minute, guys," a warrior said. He was instantly silenced with a surge of chlorinated water aimed with pinpoint accuracy into his open mouth.

"Time," Sergeant Mixter said, and the word never sounded sweeter than it did to those still within the confines of the lane marker. "Go get changed for the physical preparedness test and be outside at the pull-up bars in ten minutes."

The 18 warriors pulled themselves from the pool, their bodies feeling as if they had gained 40 pounds. Some of their muscles began to spasm and twitch, their bodies running low on electrolytes.

"Make sure you stretch," Cheshire said, smiling in the locker room as the few warriors remaining began to change out of their wet utilities. Sergeant Mixter entered and put out a box of garbage bags to put their wet utilities in.

"You've made it through the worst. Now just a few pull-ups, sit-ups, and a little run."

Worse than the exhaustion strangling the warriors' muscles was the chlorine burning away their retinas and tear ducts, or at least feeling like it was. It hurt them to keep their eyes open and, given the ungodly hour at which they had woken, sleep was calling its siren song; their bodies naturally began to slow after such a workout.

"I usually run a three hundred PFT," the braggart who tried to drown Lemune said.* "So I'll probably just run a two hundred and eighty or something this time."

"I'll be happy to just run a two hundred and twenty-five," one of the other warriors replied, only half-joking. The rest of the warriors nodded in silent agreement. Two hundred and twenty-five points was the bare minimum to pass the Indoc. Most of the warriors who remained scored an average of 270 or higher during a normal fitness test. Suddenly, even their worst fitness-test score seemed like a triumph in the face of such mental and physical exhaustion.

* PFT stands for "Physical fitness test," for which 300 is a perfect score.

When the warriors moved to the pull-up bar outside of the pool building, Cheshire was doing wide-grip pull-ups, his tight body pumping up and down rhythmically like a machine. At 30 perfect pull-ups, he stopped, still hanging mid-pull, and stared at the warriors.

"Pull-ups! Yeah!" he yelled, dismounting the bar. Cheshire would later go on to demoralize the students of the Holding Tank weekly by promising an end to their training day if any single warrior could do more pull-ups than him. The warriors' champion would always go first, giving their absolute all for a chance at an early day. No matter what number the warrior reached, Cheshire would always complete one more perfect pull-up, slow and grinning the entire time. No student ever found out how many he could actually do before he left his position.

But that was later, for only a handful of those who were lining up at the bars.

"All the way up, all the way down, gentlemen," Sergeant Mixter said, gripping his clipboard. "You know how to do 'em."

The veterans were strict in their application of the acceptable pull-up.

Not locking the elbows out completely, no joy.

Chin not clearly above the bar, no joy.

Swinging the legs or pumping the knees up toward the bar, no joy.

They did not scream or yell at the warriors as they performed an unacceptable pull-up. They simply continued counting as if those pull-ups never existed. "One, two, three, four, four, five, six, seven, seven, seven, seven, eight, eight, eight, eight, nine, [long pause] nine total."

After a miserable showing on the pull-up bar, the warriors lined up for the sit-up portion of the PFT. They were thankful for the sit-ups. It was an easy way to score a high number of points, if not the 100 maximum points.

They were all disappointed with their sit-ups but, worse, they could calculate the run score necessary to achieve the required points to receive a first-class physical fitness test, a passing score for the Indoc.

And before the race had even started, some warriors had already determined they could not obtain the necessary points needed to pass the Indoc, having to run a sub-18-minute 3-mile run. Even on most of the warriors' best days, a 19-minute 3-mile run time was quite fast.

But it was not the best day. Far from.

It was the worst day and growing darker with every passing second.

At the starting line of the 3-mile course, every one of the 18 warriors left was making the same calculations, determining the run time needed, and making the decision whether they would make that time or not. Some had already announced the results to their body before they even stepped off on the run. They were readying themselves to go through the motions of "trying" without any of the effort necessary.

A few would jog and later complain of foot or leg cramps being the culprit, but most had come too far to quit, no matter how outrageous their times. They were willing to put everything they had on the line just to say they did their best at the end of the day. It would be a small consolation for those who did not make the necessary time.

"Go," Sergeant Mixter said quietly, starting his stopwatch. There was no fanfare or crowds lining the road, but all the warriors knew that it would be the most important race of their entire lives.

It was like a slow thaw in the warriors' legs. Their limbs were heavy and unresponsive to the demands being asked of them. The run was slow and painful for all. At the turn-around point, each warrior yelled out his number to ensure no one turned back early to shave a minute or two off their time. A veteran would reply with the time elapsed as the warriors turned around.

Some were pleasantly surprised.

Most were not.

Most were far behind their projected halfway time, and the second half was usually the slower of the two. Those in the front of the pack were a full minute beyond the halfway point and passing in the opposite direction those who had quit before the race had even started and were jogging. A handful of warriors broke away from the main body, pushing themselves as hard as they could. They would only get one chance and they would not let it slip through their fingers without a fight.

One such warrior was Lemune. He took long, powerful strides while his face had turned a deep crimson. Another warrior just ahead of Lemune was talking to himself, telling himself he could not quit, he could not give up, over and over again in thick, choked breaths. The two rounded a sharp bend together and there, up ahead, stood a veteran with a clipboard looking at his watch. Lemune continued to power on at the same pace, unable to give any more, while the other warrior used the last bit of his strength to sprint toward the all-powerful clipboard. Passing the clipboard in a sprint, the warrior finally slowed to take his first elated breath of a finished race.

The veteran laughed.

"I'm not the finish line. I'm just watching. The finish is up there."

The warrior looked up ahead another 300 meters. To his horror, he saw Sergeant Mixter standing at the real finish line with another clipboard and another watch. Lemune passed the warrior, who began to pace himself with the French giant.

"Better hurry," the veteran laughed after them, his job of breaking their morale complete. They both picked up their pace slightly, though it felt like they had just increased their speed tenfold. Lemune lumbered on while the warrior drafting him began to throw up, his body revolting after his exhausting sprint. For 300 meters, Lemune powered through the pain while the warrior behind him tried to follow through watery eyes, the bile pouring out of his mouth like a broken lawn sprinkler.

Neufound, a warrior who devotedly smoked three packs of cigarettes a day, finished the run first, and well ahead of the pack. Lemune and two others finished a minute behind, and then began a slow, steady trickle of warriors across the finish line for the next four minutes. They fell into a cool-down circle roaming the grassy field at the finish line trying to catch their breath, one warrior trying to regain his stomach lining. Unlike every other fitness test they had run, their times were not yelled out as they crossed the finish line. Instead, their times were written down silently next to their number until all the warriors had finished.

While the young warriors walked in their slow circle, the veterans stood behind Sergeant Mixter as he calculated the total scores, laughing and teasing each other about how their "horse" had placed. The 18 warriors continued to circle silently, the whole of their being bent on trying to capture some clue as to their standing. It was the most excruciating 10 minutes the warriors would ever experience, outside of combat.

Finally, Sergeant Mixter spoke.

"School circle around me," he said. The 18 warriors jogged as fast as their throbbing legs could muster. Circled around the sergeant, they bowed their heads and waited for the results.

"Five passed."

The bus ride back to infantry training was silent. Those who quit before the test had even begun sat beside those who tried but did not make it. No one knew what to say to each other. There were no words spoken. Envy and disappointment were rife. Those who had bragged the most were the quietest, silently trying to rationalize their failure compared to those few who had passed.

Of the five who passed, only Neufound and Brick were expected to, running 300-point tests frequently. Lemune was never expected to pass given his brutish size, which usually did not lend itself to endurance. Nor were the other two warriors—Wilmore, a muscular Kentucky boy who hardly spoke, and the puker—neither of whom were known for their athletic prowess in running.

This was the new, easier Indoc to bolster special operations numbers. Ten years earlier and most likely none of the five would have passed, with the exception of Neufound, who was still medically discharged from the Holding Tank after it was found he was partially color blind. Wilmore would break, quitting within a few days of the training in the Holding Tank. The terror of one more day of "training" drove him to go AWOL, running home to Kentucky to take his chances with deserting in times of war, a capital offence.

Three out of five made the teams.

Three out of five, out of 48, out of 80, out of 150.

For the record, I was the weakest link, passing by a single point.

I was the puker.

CHAPTER 11

Holding Tank

The moment the austere graduation from basic infantry school ended with a sharp "Dismissed," the five who had passed the screening were hurried into a long, white duty van. The rest of the infantrymen were being loaded into the cavernous maw of the enormous five-ton trucks, idling in perfect alignment with lowly privates holding unit placards like chauffeurs. There were sergeants and staff sergeants hollering everywhere, corralling the graduates into their proper transports, along with the sum of their belongings stuffed into a single duffle bag.

"Some of them will be in the Sandbox in less than a month," the sergeant at the steering wheel of the van whispered sullenly. "Poor bastards. They just had all the training they will get before being thrown into battle."

Private Acosta was a pillar in our training platoon and a human jukebox who crooned to us whenever we were standing by, which seemed to be more than half of our infantry training. We would shout out songs and he would close his eyes as he belted out a slow, soulful a cappella version, often better than the original. Three weeks after being packed onto the five-ton, Acosta would be dead, both boots barely in the sand for the first time before he was killed by an improvised explosive device.

The five of us remained silent.

"Right, I am Sergeant Kay and welcome to the Holding Tank," he continued as we pulled away. "Don't speak unless spoken to and, when we get back to the barracks, I will assign you a room. Dump your shit and be ready for formation."

As ordered, we ran into the empty rooms we had been assigned as soon as the van came to a stop, dropped our canvas bags carelessly, and ran back outside to join the small band of warriors already forming up in front of a pale, bookish man with substantial glasses that magnified his already unsettling glare.

"For those that do not remember me, I am Sergeant Cheshire, and I will be your head instructor while you are in the Holding Tank. Training starts at 0430 tomorrow morning with PT. Be in formation right here," he said, looking at the five of us who were trembling at the end of the formation. He grinned and then looked back to the rest of the small pack who stood barrel-chested and silent, veterans to the daily rhythm of the Holding Tank.

"And you idiots," Sergeant Cheshire smirked, taking a step in front of the veterans. "Which of you joined Private Johnson this weekend in some extracurricular activities with a nice civilian woman?"

None of the men moved, as they continued to stare straight ahead as if they had not heard the question.

"No? None of you?" Sergeant Cheshire laughed. "Johnson said there were five of you, but he didn't give any names. So, four of you are lying and I think that's just great."

Sergeant Cheshire paced up and down in front of the veterans of the Holding Tank with a gigantic smirk that would wilt flowers and curdle milk. His meek face was capable of the most terrible expressions of malevolent glee, and he turned his grin on four warriors standing at the end of the formation.

"So, none of you took part? Excellent. It won't bother any of you then that I only know this because Private Johnson is right this moment with the medic, because it turns out she wasn't just filled with insatiable desire, but she was also rife with the clap."

Suddenly, the four men standing at attention in front of Sergeant Cheshire shifted uncomfortably.

"Do you know what the clap is, gentlemen? Chlamydia is what you get from swinging your rifles without the safety on. It starts as a tickle when you piss, and before long you can't piss without crying. You start leaking a thick discharge, and you can't cum without it hurting so bad."

"I was there, Sergeant," one of the men said, stepping forward with his hand raised and shaking nervously.

"Oh, we have a winner. Anyone else? You'll just wait until you can't piss, huh?"

"Me too, Sergeant," another man said.

"Me too, Sergeant."

"It already tickles, Sergeant," the last of the four said, looking to his boots and shaking his head.

"You idiots get yourselves to the medic right now. He is waiting for you."

The four men fell out of formation and jogged off around the corner of the barracks. Sergeant Cheshire waited a moment and then let out a howl of laughter, his eyes wide and manic.

"Do any of you know what the medics do for the clap? No? Let me tell you. They are going to shove a very long, thick swab all the way up their urethra. It is one of the more painful things a man can bear, they tell me. They don't need to do this, but hell if it isn't a great deterrent. Be in formation at oh-four-thirty tomorrow morning, gentlemen. Welcome to the Holding Tank."

With a mischievous grin and a wink, he added, "Sleep well."

We unpacked our single, large green duffle bags into the austere barracks rooms that smelled of too much disinfectant and yet still somehow reeked of mushrooms and sweat. Though still only candidates, we were housed right in with the unit, our room assignments seemingly random and spread out across the barracks.

Infantry graduation had begun at 1000 hours that morning so we had been required to be up at 0200 to stand for our squad leader's inspection at 0300, and be in formation at 0400 to stand for our sergeant's inspection. It had been a long, terrifying day spent worrying about tomorrow morning's PT. We had heard rumors of hours' long, grueling PT designed to drop candidates each and every day, and we all planned on getting a good night's rest to be bright-eyed and bushy-tailed to make a good first impression.

The first knock at the door woke me from a fitful, worried sleep and I shot up to attention, the fear of bootcamp still lingering in my nervous system.

Get on line: Five. Four. Three. Two. One.

Even before I opened the door, I heard the howling outside, and the insistent knocking on the other doors of the "ropes," candidates in the Holding Tank.

Little pig, little pig, let me in.

I opened the door and three sleek, grinning men in their PT gear crowded the doorway.

"Sergeant Eckles's going-away party is happening. Follow."

Further down the catwalk, Lemune stepped out of his door and we shared a weak smile. The courtyard below was full of warriors only a few days back from deployment in various states of dress, from full utilities to only black silkies. One was sitting in an enormous wooden chair drinking a beer while the others stood around him, laughing and cheering.

It was a sendoff, and it was one of the most beautiful things I have ever seen to this day.

Men stood in a half-circle and passed a small but highly decorated and braided paddle around as they told their favorite stories about Sergeant Eckles. The warriors of the unit laughed and cried together, sharing their stories and trials, and occasionally one would shake a beer and spray Sergeant Eckles to punctuate a truly beautiful moment in the story.

"Only these two came out of their rooms," one of the warriors hollered from the back of the group and, as one, every eye turned towards Lemune and I. "Sad, but at least we got these two."

We were not offered a beer.

We were a tribute, a parting gift for Sergeant Eckles.

We could have stopped at any time, bowed out and slunk back to our rooms. Instead, Lemune and I, slimy, wet, and grinning ear to ear, limped back to our room at 0300 hours after cleaning up the trash left by the party.

PT did not go well the next morning, but the grins never left our faces.

We had found the promised land.

CHAPTER 12

The Pen or the Sword

Sun Tzu wrote that one should never completely surround their enemy with no chance to escape, for that enemy will fight to the death. Instead, one should always leave an opening, for that enemy will succumb to fear and the hope of surviving, routing when they should have stood their ground. The world may have changed much since those words were first born, but people have not.

In the Holding Tank, our training platoon before being sent to the Schoolhouse, it was repeated often that "this is a volunteer unit," we were free to leave at any time if we felt it was getting too hard and we could no longer stand the rigors of our training. This, above all the hardships and intense moments, may have been the single sentence that sent more warriors running with their tail between their legs than any physical pain.

During the height of every training exercise, when the muscles burned their worst or when the log seemed just too heavy to lift again, in that moment when we were close to our breaking point, that is when they would pose the simplest question.

"Do you want to quit?"

Not once, not twice, but over and over the question would be asked as the run got longer, or the log seemed to get heavier. As our mouths became sticky with dehydration and our thoughts began to narrow down to the singular pain of the moment, they would even do us the favor of shortening the question for our tiny minds to comprehend.

"Quit?"

It would seem intuitive that, after saying no once, each subsequent answer would be easier and easier, that the "No" of one moment would be born of the same grit and tenacity that would lead to the same "No" of each subsequent questioning. That is also like saying that if red comes up 50 times on roulette, then the next spin must be black. They are both fallacies and end in tears if not understood. Each instantiation of the question was like a brand-new, never-been-heard-before idea.

"Quit?"

"Not on my mother's life!"

"Quit now?"

"Hmm, that is an interesting point you suddenly bring up."

For some the question simply got heavier on their shoulders with each asking. They would say no 99 times but, on the hundredth time, in a sudden moment of weakness, they would give in to that little nagging voice and utter the worst two words a warrior could ever let slip.

"I quit."

And their world would become a bit smaller and a bit darker, as they were whisked away from the promised land and thrown at the boots of the hard men of the infantry, who would know them for what they were: quitters.

We were briefed that the Holding Tank would be running three days of patrols around the base to evaluate our land navigation, radio communication, and basic team-patrol skills. We were divided into five-man teams, issued our serialized gear from the armory, and given our individual team briefs on our missions, including our roles. Each team had certain roles: team leader, assistant team leader, radioman, pointman, and slackman, aka gear-carrier. Each role had very specific functions and, in a good team, each man would be an expert in his role and the role above him, as well as being able to perform every other role proficiently.

I was chosen as team leader for our exercise. The team leader is like the goalie in sports. If you do your job very well, everything goes right, and no one seems to give a shit. It is not until you let one pass by that your role is truly noticed. Every single mistake, despite who made it, lands squarely on the head of the team leader. The entire patrol from beginning to end is his sole responsibility.

We divided out the serialized gear to the appropriate role and sat around the scale relief map we had made in a sandbox, discussing the best ways to tackle our mission. Everyone threw out ideas and we debated the pros and cons of each. In the end we agreed on a game plan and the team set about filling their specific roles within that framework. We were smiling and optimistic, suddenly putting our training to use in a realistic scenario, complete with an opposing force of cadre actively looking for us.

For all of our cheerfulness, our mission itself seemed rather boring. We were to patrol a couple of miles, set up an observation point, and watch an unmistakable bend in a tank trail for enemy activity for three nights and two days. After a couple of sketches and measurements of the bend itself, we were to just watch and report, straightforward and easy.

Oh, how naive we were.

The fun began only six hours after boots hit the ground. After radioing in our measurements of the bend in the tank trail and setting in to our observation post, we were told over the radio that we were just "attacked" by a mixed enemy of overwhelming size, forcing us to displace and retreat to a previous rally point. We had to make it there within twenty minutes or we would miss our extract window. People may make fun of those who LARP (live-action role play), running around fields with fake swords battling each other, but it is hard to throw stones when you are tearing through the woods, in full retreat from the pretend enemy that does not even exist at all.

Surprisingly, we made our extract point with a few minutes to spare, having to move across some rather nasty terrain that left us breathless as we took a knee in a hasty defensive circle and tried to get our instructors on the radio. Trying to calm my breathing enough to be understood through an already tenuous communication system, I passed our new coordinates and our availability for extract. Our instructors seemed genuinely surprised we had made it as well, telling us to stand by and await further orders.

After a minute, the instructors got back on the hook and the news was not good.

What Sun Tzu did not mention was that the cleverest enemy, the enemy that should be most feared, is the pretend enemy being controlled by sadistic instructors. Our pretend enemy was suddenly wielding rocket-propelled grenade launchers and had just shot down our pretend helicopter extract, exact location of the crash and survivors unknown. But damned if we were not tasked with going and finding that pretend helicopter crash and recovering those pretend pilots, so their pretend families would not have to have a pretend burial service with pretend empty caskets.

No pretend men left behind.

Seven hours into our 56-hour patrol and we could already see the trajectory of this mission, and it certainly was not anywhere easy or restful. Our pretend helicopter crash had been turned into a hasty ambush by our enemy (their pretend camouflage was amazing), and we were once again making a fighting retreat. Over the next 40 hours our pretend enemy only got more devious, and I began to suspect we had a traitor in our midst, given our pretend enemy seemed to know exactly where we were or where we were going at all times. Damn, but they were good. At every turn we were outmanned and outgunned, only able to catch a couple hours rest here or there before our well-hidden position was stumbled upon, by yet another pretend goat herder, which was strange given we were deep in a swamp—but who knows the minds of pretend goat herders and their heat-seeking pretend goats.

As dusk crept through the canopy, casting long shadows across longer faces, we were buoyed by the thought that this was supposed to be our final night tromping around through the "catch me, fuck me" vines that made a hundred-meter journey last an hour. Every man was exhausted and our team spirit was starting to break down, everyone thinking they knew best and wanting to control our destiny. Confidence in each other had ebbed since our first bright-eyed huddle after jumping out of the insert truck.

It was *Lord of the Flies* and I wondered who would be called "Piggy" when we all looked so horribly thin.

We stopped for a comm check to give our current position and I cringed as I was told to stand by.

"FNG-One, FNG-One, be advised that the enemy is advancing from the west en masse, battalion-size forces moving toward your position on line. You are to proceed to extract at coordinates 12345-67890, arriving no later than 0300. Do you copy?"

I hate you.

"FNG-One copies."

"And if we catch you on the tank trails or in the open, you're dead men. Copy?"

"FNG-One copies, Viper Nest."

We formed a circle around our map, all sense of defensive measures abandoned. A battalion-sized enemy, especially a pretend one complete with laser rifles from the future, heat-seeking goats, and apparently a satellite system so advanced it could give away our position at all times, would simply roll over us with their exoskeleton flying battle suits or whatever sudden new technology they had acquired in the past 40 hours. Speed was going to get us through, if that was even a possibility.

And looking at the map, it was not. We had to move a decent distance on the map, but by having to avoid the tank trails and open fields of the landing zones speckled across the base, we were being funneled into some of the worst terrain the base had to offer. Six hours to get from one side of the base to the other side was pushing it when we were fresh and full of well-fed energy. Fake MRE cheese constipation and lack of sleep had not left us feeling as fresh as we could have hoped.

There was only forward, however. There was only try, whatever the outcome. We would make it, or we would not, but if we did not call in comm checks every hour with our position crawling ever closer to the extract, there were far worse fates than getting scratched across every inch of exposed skin by thorns and falling over every third step as we shambled toward our extract.

Three hours later and we were not even a third of the way. We made a hasty map check and shrugged our ruck-strap chewed shoulders. Fuck it, there was only forward.

We stood up but, as the point man took his first shaky step forward, I called a halt.

"Trodan, where is your rifle?" I asked, noticing his shaking hands. He looked down at his empty hands for a moment, turned his palms up as if the rifle might be hidden behind them, and then stared with a quizzical look on his face.

"I dunno," he said, his voice flat and unconcerned.

"What do you mean, you dunno?" I growled.

Lose a finger, lose an ear, but never, never lose a piece of serialized gear, especially one capable of killing other people if found by the wrong person. Losing a serialized weapon system was just about the top of the list of the things that would end a military career in a hurry, starting at the bottom but rolling up the chain of command like a reverse avalanche. Only a year earlier the entire military base had been locked down when a rifle had been lost; every unit contained within the base had been put in an incredibly long line and walked side by side across the training area it had occurred in. The rifle was found within a few hours, but shutting down an entire military base and stopping all training and activity to look for a lost rifle could only end one way—heads rolled.

"Where did you leave it?" I seethed, a stupid question given my first.

"I dunno," Trodan said again, his voice beginning to quiver.

"We are all fucking dead without that rifle. We need to find that rifle in the next hour before our next comm check. If we find it, we take this to our graves and we take whatever punishment we get for being late."

Everyone agreed, and Trodan thanked us profusely. We quickly abandoned any pretense of stealth and camouflage, turning on every flashlight and headlamp we had with us. Anyone in space could have seen our small team wandering around the woods casting our searchlights on what we hoped was our back trail. The problem was that we had been traveling in the dark, slowly moving in a monochromatic world to pick our path. Now, with the lights on, nothing looked the same. Even landmarks we knew we had passed only a short time earlier suddenly looked like an alien landscape in the harsh white light of our headlamps and Surefire flashlights, which seemed bright enough to start fires if we held it too long on one spot.

After 50 minutes of tromping down all of the vegetation for 5 feet on either side of what we thought was our back trail, we had still not found the rifle, which was unfortunately an excellent shade of black for blending into the shadows. We had not made it halfway to our last checkpoint and our chances of finding it had dropped to zero. We could only look forward to the loss of rank and being booted back to the regular infantry.

We would need a miracle.

Trodan leaned his haggard body against a dead tree stump, which could not bear his weight and snapped, sending him tumbling to the ground.

"Oh, my God, I found it," he said, having landed on it during his fall. We all perked up as Trodan stood, holding on to his rifle.

But it was not his rifle. It was a dead tree branch, and the sudden excitement of a pardon turned into a sharp knife in my guts.

Miracles were for fairytales.

"Give me the hook, Clems," I said, cringing, just imagining what Sergeant Cheshire would look like while receiving the terrible news. I had watched him on many occasions punch hard, solid objects repeatedly enough to make his knuckles bleed, as he spoke in his low, calm voice, as if he could barely restrain himself and needed the pain to keep his wrath at bay, long enough to reprimand us without physically hurting us. He was a terrifying mix of sadist and masochist, relishing whichever was available at that moment.

"Viper Nest, Viper Nest, this is FNG-One," I said crisply into the hook.

"This is Viper Nest, go ahead, FNG-One."

"Permission to speak in the clear," I said, an overwhelming urge to vomit making my knees tremble.

"Is everyone okay?" Cheshire replied quickly, genuine concern apparent in his voice.

"No one is injured. Trodan has lost his rifle."

There was a terrible pause.

"It would have been better for you if you were all very hurt." Fatherly concern had turned to dreadful malice.

"Understood. We have searched for the last hour. Awaiting orders."

"Search back to rally point 'Budweiser' and await the cadre," Cheshire said. "Immediate contact if you find it."

"Understood."

"Viper Nest out."

The team looked at me as I handed the radio handset back to Clems. It would be light in four hours. If we did not find the rifle on the march back, the entire cadre staff would be out looking with us. If by light we did not find the rifle, every spare man in the battalion, which we were not yet even brothers in, would be pulled out of bed and would hate us for the rest of our lives.

"We need to find that rifle," I said, unable to hide the quiver in my voice. "Secure your rifles in your packs so we can have our hands free. And tie them in there with four or five different dummy cords."

Rally point "Budweiser" arrived far faster than I had hoped. Every step closer made my body tremble a little more until I looked like a 90-year-old man walking under a heavy load. We stepped out into the small clearing we had used as a hasty harbor site, to catch an hour sleep and eat, and were greeted by Cheshire and most of the cadre, some of whom looked to have been awoken very recently.

"You are so dead," Cheshire hissed at me. I nodded, accepting my fate. "All right, we are going to get on line, shoulder to shoulder, and cover as much ground as we can in the next hour or two."

No one spoke. We only pointed our flashlights forward and moved with care, moving every bush and branch that could possibly hide a rifle underneath. We moved slowly, covering only 10 to 15 feet every minute. At the rate of travel, it would take us half a day to reach our last patrol point where we knew Trodan had been in possession of his rifle. We did not have half a day, only a couple of hours before this went high enough to ruin careers.

"You idiots," Sergeant Less hissed half an hour later. Every flashlight snapped toward his direction, where he stood shaking with rage while pointing at a dead tree.

The rifle was leaned up against the dark, decaying tree as if it had been placed with the utmost care. Sergeant Less scooped it up, turned 90 degrees sharply, and strode off through the woods toward the nearest tank trail. Like ghosts, the other cadre followed without a word until only Cheshire was left, grinning.

My body revolted into civil war. My brain, foolish gray matter it is, shouted in joy and began dancing in celebration of our find. My guts, far more attuned to reality, tightened and readied my body for the inevitable fight to ensue.

"Lucky we found it, eh?" Cheshire grinned. I said nothing. "You know what comes next, don't you?" I nodded. "Immediate escape and evasion to LZ Taurus and await your extract. You have thirty minutes to get there. It's not close. You better run the entire way. Now turn those flashlights off."

Cheshire slipped back into the shadows, and we plunged ourselves back into darkness, our night vision ruined. At least we did not have to look into each other's faces as we moved. We ran full pelt down the tank trail, a barely visible gray line in an otherwise black world, the gravel crunching under our boots as we brayed and gasped our way forward. Despite the searing pain in my lungs and legs, I found myself wishing the tank trail never ended, that we could continue to run forever. I could handle that pain. As always in life, it was the unknown pain that lay ahead that terrified me.

We fumbled into LZ Taurus three minutes late, three Humvees parked in a small horseshoe with the engines facing us, and slowed to a brisk walk. We were suddenly in no hurry. Not that our lateness mattered, not after the great failure we had already accomplished. When we trudged the last few feet up to Sergeant Cheshire, he did not even mention our tardiness. He just grinned and smashed his fist violently into the hood of the Humvee he was leaning back against.

"Drop your rucks, gentlemen."

The five of us got into something resembling a straight line facing him and slid our rucks off our backs. We were a sad-looking bunch. The physical fatigue of the movement and the stress of the past few hours, all coupled with the absolute fear of what was to come next, had left us gaunt, trembling husks that mocked the "indomitable human spirit" so often hailed in human-interest stories. A light breeze would have knocked us to our raw, chafed knees as our heads twitched with anxious glances like the prey we were. Cheshire just stared at us with his large, manic eyes, pounding his fist into the hood rhythmically as if he needed the pain to feel at least something, the corners of his eyes twitching slightly with each rap of his knuckles.

"Dead men, eh?" Cheshire said finally, breaking minutes of simply staring at us like we were pathetic animals in a zoo. "Dead. Men."

There was no fitting reply for such a statement. I opened my mouth to voice a plea, but for what? Mercy? There would be no quarter given. Trodan had almost single-handedly, or empty-handedly rather, lost Cheshire his job, and the punishment would have swept uphill like a wildfire. An explanation then? For all my pretty words, what could I possibly say that would justify the one unbreakable rule for warriors who live and die by the gun? It is paramount to have a gun in such an existence, so negligent loss was akin to a murder/suicide in the civilian world.

I closed my mouth and my eyes followed quickly after. I listened to the morning breeze whispering through the trees and the sound of my ragged breathing mingling with the labored breaths of the four condemned beside me. For a moment it was almost pleasant.

"This unit is not mandatory," Cheshire said, moving to one side and revealing a manila folder laying on the hood of the Humvee. He scooped the folder up and let it fall halfway open in one of his hands, plucking a single piece of paper from a stack of many and snapping it up in the air like magic for our inspection. "You can leave any time you want to, understand? So, I am going to make this very easy for you. If you stay, you will be thrashed right here until we are forced to stop because one of you goes down or liberty formation about twelve hours from now, whichever comes first. There will be no paperwork and you will not be brought up on any charges for NJP.* Suffer here, right now, worse than you ever have and, after, it will be as if it never happened."

The other cadre were beginning to get out of the Humvees, leering at us as they leaned lethargically against the vehicles like a pack of lions. They wanted to hear our decisions.

"Or, you can sign this paper I have in my hand right here. It states that you have quit the training and ask to be placed within a line company as soon as possible, which, given the early hour, could be by the end of the day. You will receive no physical punishment and you will be driven immediately back to your room right now to shower and go have breakfast before we start your out-processing. No pain, no tears."

Cheshire turned, laid out the first piece of paper on the hood, and then laid out four more beside it, placing a pen meticulously in the center of each page so that it would not roll down the slope of the hood. He took his time with the ritual, making sure everything was properly aligned and in its place before turning back to us.

"Now, each of you will decide," he said. He pointed a finger straight at my chest and grinned. "Pen or the sword?"

"Sword," I replied. It was not a hard decision, not really a decision at all. The promised land was still within reach.

"Pen," Trodan replied before Cheshire's finger had even come to rest on him. I looked over, completely shocked, but before I could open my mouth to try to convince Trodan he was making a mistake, Cheshire cut me off.

---

* Non-judicial punishment.

"Quiet. He made his choice. Even if you convince him, he is tainted goods now understand. I still wouldn't keep him even if you changed his mind. Once a quitter, always a quitter. Now, where were we? You, pen or the sword?"

In the end, two boys chose the pen and three men chose the sword. We watched the two quitters sign their papers and crawl into the back of the Humvee, their faces flush with the embarrassment of slinking away while they left us to suffer. When their Humvee rolled out of the field and disappeared down the tank trail, Cheshire addressed the three of us left.

"I am proud of you. You chose the hard path, the path of suffering. They will forever live with the shame of their decision. They will make up stories, pretend that they got hurt most like, and everyone will pretend to believe them, maybe. But, in the end, they will know what they chose here, and it will haunt them. So, know that I am proud of you for taking the sword, gentlemen."

"But also know that my pride won't stay my wrath and make you suffer any less. I am going to try to kill at least one of you with calisthenics right here, right now," he said, slipping out of his blouse and rolling his neck around as he prepared to join us.

Cheshire was true to his word. I had never suffered worse nor would I ever. Every inch of our flesh seemed to have touched every inch of dirt of that LZ as we crawled, ran, carried, and rolled for hours. Still, no matter what they did to us, they could not wipe the secret smiles from our faces. We had passed a crucible few ever have the chance to meet so openly, one that would echo down through our lives forever. We had been given a gift of self-knowledge that would guide us along our path.

We had chosen the sword.

CHAPTER 13

The Schoolhouse

Compared to the Holding Tank, the Schoolhouse was gentlemen's training. We were not treated like lowly untouchables, but rather like aspiring applicants. In theory, the chaff had been separated from the wheat and what was delivered to the small compound, nestled out of sight on a beach gently lapped by the Atlantic, had been winnowed and found acceptable for the next phase. Unlike the random chaos and punishment of the Holding Tank, the training at the Schoolhouse had clearly defined rules and expectations. Fail those simple guidelines, you go home. No games, no undeserved suffering simply to see if you would break. We were treated like grown men.

The Schoolhouse was classroom academia punctuated by strenuous physical exertion. Between the difficulty of the two there was no need for games to drum candidates out. Our numbers dwindled just as quickly as they had in the Holding Tank.

Weekly we were to be tested on our endurance, physically as well as mentally. Long swims with diving fins while tethered to another candidate or weighted ruck runs would be conducted on Friday mornings. Instructors would always conduct the training with us. They would be our baseline. Stay with them, finishing when they finished, and you received 100 points for the test. For each minute behind, you lost one point. Failure was 79 points.

We all nodded and grinned during the explanation of the expectations on day one. Easy day. We were physical specimens, our tight bodies forged in the searing heat of the Holding Tank. How hard could it be to stay with the instructor "rabbits"? Twenty minutes seemed a generous cushion.

On Day Five, we formed two ranks outside the compound just as the bottom of the black veil of night began to smolder pink. We stood relaxed with our rucks and rifles, joking and trying not to let anyone notice our shaking hands. We had formed ranks without thought of our position in the formation as no one seemed to have any idea where we would be taken. When the safety vehicle that would follow us everywhere pulled up across the street and the cadre packed their gear into the back, our commander in charge of training, Captain Caveman, appeared out of the classroom door. His enormous frame bounded out to the front of the formation, all of us having to look up into his stoic, chiseled face. He did not put his rifle down but cradled it gently in his massive arms like a baby.

"Gentlemen, I will not be your rabbit today, but I do like to take part in the first ruck run just to get an idea of the men I am in charge of. I will be running with you, same loadout and gear. I do have one extra piece of gear, my trusty bullhorn, in case any of you need motivation, but this looks like a strong group. Still, let's see. Staff Sergeant Coven, you have the command. Carry out the training of the day."

Staff Sergeant Coven appeared from the shadows with his own full load out, same as us, and took his place in front of us. We shifted eagerly. He was a small man and constantly half-smiled like he was remembering a joke from the night before. He did not look so tough.

"Right face. Double time," he smiled.

We barely had time to register the command. We all turned to our right and before we had made it five steps, Coven was already opening up a commanding lead on our first two in formation.

"This is not a formation run, gentleman," Captain Caveman chided from the darkness behind. "You would do well to start running at your ability."

Chaos blossomed as 30 men tried to free themselves of the tight pack and maneuver to the front. We watched the chem-light on the back of Coven's pack get smaller and smaller as we ran down the side of the road to catch up.

"How is he so fast?" someone gasped.

"He can't keep that up forever," someone replied hopefully.

But he could. We found out on Week Six that he could actually hold a much faster pace, but he was taking it easy on us as he lead us out onto the soft sand of the beach for a mile, before turning onto one of the tank trails that lead into the dark forest. What was once a formation became a long line of men strung out across a mile of serpentine sand trails interrupted by sudden hills.

No matter how bad the situation, no matter how bleak and impossible things get, shit can always get worse. Suddenly, piercing the silence at the back of the pack was the siren of a bull horn followed by the deep booming voice of Captain Caveman.

"Quit. Get in the truck. Quit."

His suggestion alone was not terrible. It grated but could be turned to white noise if you concentrated on the rasping gasps of your own breathing. What was truly disconcerting and gave credence to his counsel was when Captain Caveman ran past us towards the front of the pack, carrying his rifle in one hand while he held the bullhorn to his grinning mouth with the other. All the way to the front he sprinted with his siren's call of riding in the truck. Then he fell back, spending a little time with each man, urging them to end it all, to just get in the truck, before reaching the last man in the pack again. Twice more did he sprint to the front and fall back to the last man, toying with us.

"How is he so fast?" someone gasped again.

With mounting fear, we suddenly realized the hard truth. We were not the gods' gift to the unit. We were not physical specimens. We were the disgusting, dawdling playthings of the cadre who were literally doing laps around us. They did not need to play games or punish us unnecessarily. Some of us simply were not going to meet the standard.

At that moment, when that knowledge sliced deep into our self-inflated egos and cut us down to the bone, the first man gave in and got in the truck. He would not be the last.

CHAPTER 14

Rain, Rain, Go Away

So cold.

I cried. I cried so hard I could scarcely breathe. I wanted it to end. Had Satan appeared next to me and offered me a pen of bone, with blood dripping from the nib, I would have signed whatever parchment of skin he offered without even asking what the contract was for, so long as it took me from that pitch-black night. There was no hint of the moon or stars, only darkness forever and the ceaseless rain, so cold that each individual drop stung my face and neck like a bee sting.

So cold.

I cried but no one could hear me or see the salty tears of frustration as I stood "guard" in the frigid rain. Days without sleep had left me shaky and the dull throb behind my eyes was only made worse whenever I clamped them shut to let out a sob.

So cold.

Hell Week was living up to its name. I had been left behind to guard the radio at the forward operating base, as the rest of the team punched out to the observation post for whatever scenario the cadre had thought up for the night. Corporal Duncan was warm and half-sleeping under a poncho to keep the radio dry. Sleeping was against the rules and would have failed him immediately if he was caught. I cried, more frustrated than ever, not because he was doing wrong, but because it was not me warm and sleeping under the poncho.

So cold.

I cried and cursed the gods for their cruel indifference. I was one question away from throwing it all in. Finally, I made myself a promise in the dead of the darkest, coldest night I had ever known. If I made it through the night, I promised myself I would never be cold again. I promised myself I would never go camping or rough it on my free time. If I could just last a couple more hours standing still in the frigid rain, not able to see my own hand in front of my face, I would never willingly be that cold again.

So cold.

The rain ended, but that promise lives on.

CHAPTER 15

Gas, Gas, Gas

CS gas, or tear gas for civilians, is the equivalent of vigorously massaging wasabi up into the nasal cavity and packing it underneath your eyelids. It clings to your clothes and hair, ready for an encore at the first sign of sweat or when you foolishly wipe your eyes with your sleeve. It can linger for days on your clothes, just waiting to ambush you during a sleepy eye rub or an itched bug bite. Most units only experienced it once a year, an annual check to ensure you remember how to ugly cry after clearing a gasmask.

For a week of our lives, it was an alarm clock.

It was hard to sleep soundly, knowing the chances we were going to wake up in less than three hours to gas was exactly 100%. Hell Week had many defining features, but the CS-gas alarm clock was the most disconcerting of them all. What little sleep we were afforded was tainted by the knowledge that, when we were at our most vulnerable, there would be an attack.

We were not allowed to keep our gas masks out in the open, instead they were required to be kept nestled deep and inaccessible in their issued carrier, until the call "Gas, gas, gas" rang out. That did not stop most of us from sleeping with one hand slipped inside the carrier, with the rubber head straps pulled around to the front, to allow for the quickest seal to the face. At the slightest sound I would startle awake and rip my mask from the carrier, slamming it to my face hard enough to make my head ring, as I cleared the air trapped within with a hard exhale.

The hard sleepers and the slow to realize were punished mercilessly. We were in a mock forward operating base and were told we had to be ready for an attack at any moment of the day, especially when we slept. Actually, it seemed the enemy only attacked us when it was our dedicated rest period. Clever bastards.

I hated gas. I had gone so far as to buy an after-market carrier, that allowed the mask to be pulled out quicker, without the time consuming snags and tugging of the issued pouch, World War Two-era or Korean War at best. I was proud that not once was I gassed successfully during our mandatory sleeping hours, much to the disappointment of the cadre. I hated gas more than anything and gave up any amount of sleep just to avoid the horrible effects.

There were only a few rules during the day, when we were not "on mission," huddled around our sand map in our sparse firm base for the week:

No sleeping outside of the designated time. To be found asleep was to be packed onto the bus and sent home without another word.

No fraternizing with any other team. We were "alone" to test our team skills with the random warriors assigned.

Don't be more than an arm's distance away from your rifle. Be prepared for immediate-action drills at any moment.

Change your socks, constantly. Trench-foot sent an otherwise ideal candidate to the bus after days of watching the bottom of his feet slough off.

I tried to follow the rules. I really did.

I was digging through my ruck looking for a dry pair of socks when I heard the strange silence of a predator nearing. I looked up too late and saw my rifle being pulled back over my ruck; I lunged, my bare feet digging into the wet soil as I launched myself after it. Despite gripping the stock like I was dangling from a cliff; it was too late. The Spaniard had my rifle.

The Spaniard was a physical anomaly and a legend. We had watched, horrified, as he had ridden the front of our zodiac boat like a rodeo bronco during amphib week, holding on to a thin rope as he stood, feet straddling the gunnels, in bad chop on a moonless night. He laughed hysterically the entire time, daring the ocean to try to throw him as the rest of us held on for dear life. When that got boring for him, he started doing sit-ups off the front as we sped along, dunking his forehead back into the dark chop between growls.

"Let it go," he grinned, holding the barrel of my rifle.

This is my rifle. There are many like it, but this one is unfortunately mine.

"No," I whimpered, tugging weakly against his iron grip.

"Let. It. Go." I refused. In one swift motion I could not follow, he spun me around and pulled my back against his chest, the smooth handguard pressed against my neck. Slowly, he applied pressure until the tickle in my throat, a trapped cough, had me shaking. I would have let go if I could think straight, but the world was starting to end like an old *Looney Tunes* episode, the tiny circle of light growing ever smaller until …

That's all, folks.

I sat up, coughing, confused. The Spaniard grinned down at me from a few feet away.

"Come, Doe. Earn your rifle back."

I followed the Spaniard as he walked, efficiently snapping open my rifle and removing my bolt carrier with a quick flick of his wrist as he moved. Like a bad magic trick, he suddenly held up my firing pin.

"Bring this back to me and you can have your rifle. You have ten minutes to find it before your team joins you. Now, turn around."

I turned, facing away from him, and he threw the firing pin into a wide, shallow puddle the color of coffee with too much creamer. It was *Where's Waldo*, the military edition, and I got down on my hands and knees, crawling around the five-meter-wide puddle very carefully, sifting with my fingertips.

"And Doe?" The Spaniard chuckled. "I noticed you don't have your gas mask on you for once." I froze. I had taken off my leg carrier to change my underwear before my socks.

The Spaniard laid the CS-gas canister on the edge of the water, the top aimed out across the surface of the puddle, and pulled the pin. The terrible fog rolled over the surface and my lower lip quivered as I continued searching.

My only consolation was that I did not need my eyes for those nine minutes until my fingertips brushed the firing pin. It took hours before snot stopped coming out of my nose and what felt like blood from my eyes.

The house always wins.

CHAPTER 16

Trail of Tears

The lack of sleep began to tell. Tempers flared. Critical-thinking skills dulled until we were left with only the most primitive, artless thoughts.

By Day Two, we snapped at each other and tried our best not to close our eyes for fear of the cadre seeing.

By Day Three, the headaches made everyone wince, and most talk had been economized into single words and stowed until we needed to pass vital information for our mission.

By Day Four, we were rendered almost useless in our angry delirium.

But, by Day Five, we were so high on lack of sleep, all the pain and suffering slipped away and we were left grinning, idiotic husks of men tripping like we had been fed psychedelic mushrooms with our daily MRE.

Sleep-deprivation psychosis is subtle as it creeps into your thoughts a little bit more every moment you remain awake. It is like paint drying, hardly noticeable over its long evolution until even the most menial task becomes impossible.

There were seven men in my team, but as I took a head count on our patrol, suddenly there were 13 of us. I saw them, standing there, dark, shadow men nodding at me as I counted. I shook my head and counted again. Fifteen, then 16.

"Touch each man with your hand when you count," the grading instructor grinned. Six men let me touch their shoulder, and 13 shadow men all wandered away or disappeared as I tried to.

"Uh … seven? We're up?"

"Is that a question, Doe?" the grading instructor asked, his pen hovering over the grading sheet.

"No?"

An hour later, the patrol came to a complete halt when the pointman returned and informed the team leader we could not keep following the original route because a large, southern-style mansion stood in our path. We were hundreds of kilometers from the nearest human habitat in the mountains, but the team leader nodded and called a halt to see it for himself.

We detoured a full three hours out of the way, while our grading instructor chuckled, because the team leader believed he had seen the mansion as well, complete with wrought iron gates and manicured hedges. Contact hysteria made anything we said real to those around us.

One warrior spent 15 minutes banging on a tree with his fist. He believed the vending machine had stolen his money without spitting out his candy.

One warrior kept looking over his shoulder and talking to the imaginary film crew that was following him as he whispered a running commentary.

We were all lost in our own little dreamworlds as we tried to hold it together enough to seem competent and pass, all 13 of us in the team. No, 15. Nineteen?

On the very last night, I was slackman. My only grading criteria was that I did not lose the serial gear or radio batteries I was carrying in my ruck, which were dummy corded at least three times. All I had to do was not wander off or fall asleep and I would pass our patrolling tests for Hell Week.

Chewy and I were left behind at the patrol base to guard gear for the night. He was being tested on the radio, maintaining communication between the rest of our team, who had moved further forward to get eyes on the prize a kilometer deeper in the bush, and the instructors back in our mock firm base.

There was no illume. The moon had waxed in embarrassment and even the cruel stars hid their light behind the rain that raked us like enemy fire every 15 minutes. We were left one night-vision monocle to be used in emergencies; otherwise we had to use redlight and prove we could hide any trace of ourselves.

All I had to do was nothing, just not wander off and not fall asleep. For the record, I did not fall asleep.

Giggling.

"Doe?" Chewy called out into the pitch dark. "You okay?"

The giggling was joined by the sound of water being poured out onto canvas, but I did not respond. Chewy reached for the night-vision monocle and turned the dial, the viewing lens bursting to life with the intensity of a thousand green suns in the stygian darkness.

"Doe?" He put the monocle up to his eye and there I was, peeing all over our rucks, my own included, giggling like the mad hatter. "Doe, what the fuck?"

My head snapped up, my eyes two demonic glowing circles in my thin, leering face. I stopped peeing on the rucks and, to Chewy's horror, I charged. Before he knew what I was doing, I snatched the monocle from his hand and ran off into the dense underbrush of the forest, still giggling.

Still, I had not fallen asleep.

But, by the gods, I could polygraph that there were werewolves.

I wake up in a green forest that was constantly swaying and pulsing in the grainy viewing lens of the monocle, a living organism expanding and contracting as it drew breath. I am without my boonie hat, without my blouse, without my patrol harness with all of my pens, redlight, and small necessities.

I am without my rifle.

All of this is a dull ache behind my eyes, but tomorrow's problem. Right here, right now, I have to escape. I can hear them, out in the underbrush around me, sniffing, searching for my scent.

Werewolves are after me.

I look around the flat, dimensionless forest through the monocle and know without doubt that I am lost, but that I cannot sit still to wait for help to come. If I do not move, they will surely find me.

I begin walking in the bottom of a deep ravine, next to a small stream, my head snapping left and right at every small sound. It is the path of least resistance and seems as good a route as any.

I am terrified and very cold.

After walking 20 meters, I come to a damp, discarded jacket. I thank the gods for little miracles and slip it on, wondering if the owner had been eaten. I continue walking and after another minute I come to an unwanted vest brimming with pockets. It seems a handy thing to have so I slip it on. A little further on, a woman's floppy sunhat.

I giggle, realizing how silly I must look wearing a sunhat in the rainy dark.

This is all well and good, but the werewolves are still a problem, and sound as if they are getting closer. I hurry my pace, following the stream down towards whatever civilized dwellings might give me shelter until morning.

A few more minutes and I hit the absolute jackpot.

A gun. I pick up the rifle, smile, and continue downstream.

I am ready. I have what I need to survive.

"Oh, you fucking asshole," Chewy laughed as I stumbled back into our secret base. I keep saying how relieved I am and stare impassively at him as he ties me to the rucks with five-fifty cord, dummy cording me so I cannot wander off again. Ten minutes later, the radio hissed to life. The forward observers with the grading instructor are returning. We are returning to the forward operating base.

Chewy never said a word to any of the instructors about my harrowing adventure. A year later, at yet another quick funeral in-country, he and I would sob, hugging each other so hard I did not know if I would ever catch my breath again.

We did not return to our base, however. When we got close, we saw the big yellow bus, our beacon for the entire week, was idling just off the main road, and the cadre's entire camp had been broken down and stored.

We were done. We had passed.

We handed in our gas masks and our serialized gear to the smiling cadre who patted us on the shoulders as we tried to keep our knees from buckling.

In the first few rays of the sunrise, we shambled together into something resembling a formation and Captain Caveman stepped in front of the ragged group to say a few words.

"I'm proud for those of you who made it. Not everyone did and you all know how many you lost along the way. At the end of Hell Week, I like to play a song that should mean a lot to you by now and celebrate. Please bow your heads and close your eyes as we remember the fallen."

From some unseen speaker system, "The Star-Spangled Banner" blared, drowning out the sound of our own ragged breathing. A few of the cadre began throwing artillery simulations, giant firework canisters that exploded with the sound of a half stick of dynamite. Red, white, and blue smoke canisters were thrown, filling up the entire area in patriotic swirls as the morning breeze picked up.

It was one of the most beautiful things I've ever seen.

More arty sims began to go off. More colored smoke.

And then the first cough.

"Gas, gas, gas," someone cried, choking as the colored smoke began to sting our uncovered faces and unprotected lungs. From everywhere and nowhere Captain Caveman's booming laugh rang above the deafening explosions.

"Looks like your enemy doesn't think you're done. Emergency escape and evasion. Get to the POW camp."

The POW camp had been one of our targets in the rotation of nightly graded patrols, the furthest of them all unsurprisingly.

The bus pulled away in the opposite direction and we scrambled to try to find our team in the swirling chaos. We could not leave the area until our team was fully accounted for. Finally herded, we began what was going to be a 10-hour journey across every mountain and valley we had already patrolled, with mini-tests of every kind along the way.

We were supposed to build a boat out of ponchos and various materials that we carried, as we had been taught, but we could barely make our fingers work. We decided to just swim and risk the imaginary bullets as gas crawled across the surface of the river, making each stroke a terrible crucible.

We carried "dead" teammates and their equipment whenever we were moving to the next test. Chewy, all six-foot-five of him, died every time. Every. Single. Time. It was as uncomfortable for him as it was for us. His arms and feet were always dragging on the ground no matter how we tried.

When we got to the POW camp, we were given back our gasmasks and "The Star-Spangled Banner" began to play again, complete with a new, proud speech.

The speech was interrupted by yet another enemy gas attack, and we wondered how it was to run in a gas mask. We were saved the trouble. The filters had been changed out with fake, empty ones. We did not realize the switch until we had been standing too long in the gas, smug behind the foggy lenses.

The bus was still miles away.

The cadre, through all of it, were standing in the gas right beside us. They suffered as we suffered, except they always seemed to be grinning.

CHAPTER 17

Tall Tales and Taller Hills

There was something surreal about PowerPoint presentations in sniper school, the tiny Microsoft paperclip popping up in a ghillie suit, asking if we needed help calculating for windage and our target's relative height difference.

"And a shot right here, center mass, has the best chance of putting your target down, blowing out the heart or lungs. Next slide please. Next slide."

Even in one of the most challenging military schools, both academically and physically, we were still middle-schoolers. Our class flag, that I proudly carried most everywhere we went as a class, was bright pink with garish, sparkling tassels as long as my forearm. Our class motto "Athletes Not Mathletes" was scrawled in big, bold sharpie marker across the length. Whenever we ran (we never marched) as a class in our ghillies, it fluttered in the breeze for every warrior we passed to gawk at and shake their heads.

This was serious business.

Whenever left waiting for whatever individual test or instruction we were to receive on the thousand-yard berm, we would invent games that always devolved into sheer, lovely chaos. Bets and dares were commonplace, as were ludicrous personal stories that no one believed, but no one cared if they were true, not really. They helped pass the slow time of waiting.

Except Jeoffrey's stories. No one liked Jeoffrey. He was a shrill, entitled weasel of a boy, and a compulsive liar. Everyone groaned loudly whenever he opened his mouth to one-up whoever just finished telling their story.

We all know a "Jeoffrey." He could always be counted on to say the dumbest things to try to impress everyone but, worse, he always lied about abilities that could clearly be tested.

"I could jump that fence in a single bound," he would gloat.

"Then go do it."

"Oh, I pulled a hammie jumping my motorcycle over a car yesterday, so I'll have to do it later when, like, no one is around."

One fine day, he backed himself into a corner or, rather, an anthill. We had found the Empire State Building of the fire ant civilization and, like the clever, mature men we were, we began poking at it with sticks. As their name implies, a fire ant's bite is excruciating, a venomous burning that leaves a large, white "pimple" for days. They are the bane of every infantryman who trains where fire ants call home.

"I've been bitten by, like, a hundred at once," Jeoffrey scoffed, as we oohed and awed, our stick points jabbing into the huge mound satisfactorily.

"I bet you wouldn't stick your hand into that mound for ten seconds," someone snapped back, sick of his ridiculous mouth.

"Of course I would," he said defensively, and then put the nail in his own coffin. "But I would need, like, a hundred dollars to do it."

Jeoffrey had fumbled. I have personally watched an infantryman blow eight hundred dollars on a dancer who did little more than brush up against him for two hours. Money meant little to men who might not be alive to spend it in a few months, and during schools and training we had so little to spend it on, despite the paychecks being deposited like clockwork.

"I got ten bucks."

"I got twenty."

"Forty."

In short order we had raised a hundred dollars in pocket change and Jeoffrey was cornered. To his credit, or his complete lack of common sense, he took off his blouse and asked one of us to count out 10 seconds. That was Jeoffrey's second mistake.

He kneeled beside the enormous anthill, his pale hand hovering over the unaware denizens peacefully going about their business, and took one last look around, finding no face that held any pity or mercy. Realizing he had erred, he plunged his hand deep into the anthill.

It was the longest 10 seconds of Jeoffrey's life. Literally. The intentional gap between each spoken number was impossibly long. Like a horror movie, the pale skin of his arm was quickly covered by a moving fabric of fire ants bravely defending their home. Jeoffrey tried to keep a straight, stoic face for the first few moments, or one second by the verbal count, but when they reached his elbow, he cried out as if he was being burned alive.

It took almost a full three minutes of running around shirtless to scrape off all the kamikaze ants that had made it up to his shoulder, as Jeoffrey cried and danced like he was auditioning for *Footloose*.

It was the best hundred dollars ever spent.

CHAPTER 18

The Longest Flight

It was time. We were finally being shipped over to the Sandbox to fight.

The flight from the United States to Germany for a refuel and then on to the desert was about thirteen hours, depending on if the prevailing winds were with us. Our entire battalion was being flown over on one commercial airliner, complete with civilian stewardesses and pilot mumbling over the PA throughout the flight. The staff officers took first class while the rest of us filed into coach.

Derek, our platoon medic, had given out sleeping pills so we could sleep the entire flight, saying nerves might keep us too jazzed up to get the rest we would need when wheels hit the deck. He handed a few of the older, trusted warriors the sleeping pills to disseminate them around the platoon.

I was one of those older, trusted warriors.

I was also waiting in ambush to finally get revenge.

On one occasion, Kole almost blew a hole through the back of another warrior's skull during a live-fire training exercise in the kill house, where we practiced our raids and room clearing. If it had not been for Sergeant Bronx's utterly unbelievable reflexes, yanking Kole back by the carry handle on his kit, throwing the shot wide, a good man would be dead because of Kole's stupidity.

Kole was not allowed to train with a real weapon inside the house any longer and ran around with a stick having to yell, "pew, pew, pew" when he saw a target. On another occasion, in a battalion-wide competition with "paintball guns" on steroids, and a highly entrenched unit as our opposing force, Kole had gotten lost, taking the only possible wrong turn inside the complex we were storming, even after endless days of practice and dry runs. Instead of winning the day with what should have been a perfect run, our platoon was forced to go on a "rescue mission" to find him and his partner—the same rock he had almost shot in the back of the head—in idiocy. The embarrassment was almost unbearable.

Kole was not punished for any of this. It was kept from higher.

Kole was not on my team, but I sought him out personally to hand him his sleeping pill, the nice guy I am. His cherub face turned up in a halfwit smile as I dropped the pill in his hand, trying not to let my own feral smile show. He did not wait for water but palmed the pill into his mouth and swallowed, before returning to staring at pretty colors, or someone's jingling keys, or whatever the hell he had been doing before I had found him. I stood there for a moment, smiling genuinely down at him, before I moved on to hand out more pills.

We had known for weeks we would be getting sleeping pills on the plane. Derek had told us in advance to make sure none of us had any allergies or medical problems to the ingredients. No one did.

The entire platoon was staring at Kole as he sat looking around with a big, dumb grin slapped across his face. We smirked and got comfortable, propping neck pillows and tiny blankets up against the bulkhead to support our heads as we readied ourselves for our comas. The pills worked quickly and soon every single warrior on the plane was passed out cold for the long, boring flight.

All save one.

When we awoke 10 hours later, Kole looked flush with embarrassment and his pillow and blanket were stacked on his lap as he looked around, no smile on his face any longer. We grinned.

"You okay, Kole?" Derek asked, smiling.

"Yeah, fine, fine. Why?"

"You just look like you didn't sleep," Derek smiled.

"I couldn't. Those pills didn't work at all," Kole said, clutching his pillow tight in his lap.

"I think they worked just fine," I said across the aisle, smirking with the rest of the platoon.

Kole never got a sleeping pill. Kole, for being so young and already full of pep, received a rather large dosage of erectile dysfunction medication. The normally blue diamond pill had been painstakingly scraped down by my own hand to a pure white to match the other pills.

Kole had spent 10 solid hours on a flight full of sleeping men questioning his sexuality and trying to hide his unrelenting erection. The more he pushed his pillow down on it to hide his embarrassment, the bigger and harder his embarrassment would get.

We did not tell him until well after we landed and he had spent an awkward hour throwing bags with the rest of the lower ranks.

We would never hurt or tell on a brother, but we would embarrass the hell out of him.

CHAPTER 19

One-Sandal Country

Dawn broke on our first day in-country, on mission.

Suddenly, with the sun rising, we were confronted with what would be our first and most lasting impression of the terrible, forsaken land we found ourselves in. It was a paradox of pastoral antiquity smothered by a layer of modern refuse.

There was no breeze during the night, so the four "fire watches" manning the heavily sandbagged posts were spared, having only to deal with the barnyard smells that perfumed our own firm base, a three-story house we had silently occupied during the early hours of darkness when the moon had not yet risen and one could only guess if his eyes were open or closed if he foolishly removed his night-vision monocle.

There was a surprising amount of vegetation. Tall, sharp grasses hugged the banks of the numerous canals and tight clusters of palm trees dotted the landscape in between the dark, loamy fields that broke up the countryside into an enormous checkerboard of low vegetables and grains. The pungent smell of the rich, fertile earth permeated everything. If I closed my eyes I was reminded of Vermont in the spring.

It was not the barren, desert wasteland we had envisioned during our countless cultural-awareness PowerPoint presentations back in the States. There were no sculptured dunes rolling across an endless sea of bleached sand. There were no lone figures perched with a flintlock rifle riding a camel silhouetted on the horizon, like a scene out of *Lawrence of Arabia*.

There was no endless Sandbox. It was a lush, verdant land near the great rivers, a gorgeous cradle of civilization frozen in time.

No amount of greenery, however, could make up for the sheer destitution.

As the breeze picked up, the true smell of Iraq was overpowering. It knotted the stomach and caused us all to swallow constantly. The metallic taste of bile pushed up the back of our throats as the morning breeze moved toward the sun, carrying with it the stench of burning refuse and the human waste that festered in stagnant puddles and the frothing eddies that lined the canals. Black irrigation trenches, filled with dead animal carcasses and alien soda bottles, dissected the land like a giant spider web as far as we could see in every direction.

Our firm base, a three-story "mansion" of flaky cement, with its vast, vaulted dome in the foyer and stained-glass windows, did not have one stick of furniture inside it. In the kitchen, there was only a miniature, electric range-top stove, a decrepit easy-bake oven that was rusted and looked as brittle as the month-old flatbread stacked in a corner to rot and mold. Onions, so old they had begun to collapse and melt to dark syrup, lined one of the pans stacked in another corner under a thick blanket of flies. The bathroom, a narrow, windowless room directly off the kitchen, smelled of ammonia and defecations that did not quite make it into the four-inch-wide tube that ran out of the house and ended 10 feet before a greasy, rainbow-colored canal.

The only comforts of any kind were 30 floral-pattern sleeping mats stacked in an empty room of the mansion for when the owner's relatives spent the night, a common occurrence in an area where indigenous farming families were constantly being displaced by men with guns from both sides.

Occupied houses made for the safest firm bases. Empty houses had the nasty habit of being rigged with low-grade, homemade explosives. The brightly colored sleeping mats smelled of piss and the dead-skin smell of bed sheets in desperate need of washing. We laid our poncho liners down on the mats to catch a few hours of sleep before the next watch rotation and our first patrol.

The "house" next door was far worse. It was scarcely a house, clinging voraciously to stay within the definition of the word as the dictionary explains it. The cement walls leaned and crumbled with enormous cavities. One-third of the cement roof was missing, giving us a perfect view of the one-room hovel from our elevated, third-story positions. There was no kitchen. There was no room set aside for defecation. The roof watch we relieved told us an elderly man, tending an oil lamp all night, had defecated in two of the four corners during his vigil. We laughed in disbelief until the gradual sunrise slowed our laughs into a silent, wide-eyed disgust. There had been no exaggeration.

Colorful glass shards and rusted tin cans were spread about the yard like antipersonnel landmines, just waiting to sink deep into the dark, bare feet that darted about in morning ritual. Empty sacks and cloth scraps blew about in the morning breeze, accumulating in the windless corners of the walls and in the razor wire strung across any possible point of entry to our firm base during the night. Tethered cattle roamed the yard to the very ends of their frayed rope, nibbling on what little grass they had not stomped dead into the dark earth. It was hard to imagine these cows produced either milk or meat. Their skin was two sizes too tight for their bones, as if it had been made of cellophane and wrapped across their bones to simply keep them from falling apart. Every twitch and movement of their sinewy muscles was exaggerated by their malnourishment, as they spent their idle time in between meager feedings chewing at the dead roots and mud in a futile effort for just a few more calories.

Everything—the house, the land, the animals, the people—was broken and starving, casualties of a smoldering war of cat and mouse.

The sun was still touching the horizon, turning the sky a stunning tangerine color. The world was quiet. Even the cattle stood silently in respect for the calm before the storm. Only the breeze made the slightest bit of sound as it whispered through our Kevlar helmets. At the moment, the world was peaceful and still.

It was hard to imagine there was a war on, that men and women on both sides were being killed daily. It still seemed like a bad dream. It was not tangible for us yet. It was still something far removed from us.

A beautiful young girl of four years danced out of the house into the yard from the hovel next door. She was dark and delicate. Her thick elbows and knees stood out awkwardly against her brittle arms and legs. Her enormous dark eyes and frail body gave her the look of a doll as she danced about in childish delight. It was a moment or two before she noticed the garbage-strewn razor wire strung across the gap in the wall between our abutting yards, good fences making good neighbors and all. She stared at it cautiously for a moment before skipping closer.

We peeked out over our sandbag posts, smiling. We were fortunate. Our first encounter with a local did not involve flicking our thumbs down across the safety catch of our rifles as we tightened our hands around the pistol grip, just as we had been taught.

The girl was a beautiful, bright-eyed child. Perhaps, we thought secretly as we watched her smile and dance about, perhaps this country is not as bad as we have been taught. Perhaps there is beauty here after all. We said nothing aloud, though. We kept our heads low and continued to scan the horizon for possible threats while we snuck long looks at the little girl dancing at the hem of our razor wire.

She saw our Humvees, parked around the house in a fan shape to avoid a single mortar destroying more than one at a time, and her eyes became huge black pools. She clapped and rubbed her fingers along the bottom of her pink, sun-bleached dress that looked as if it had been crimson when it had originally been bought or sewn together by one of her relatives. The young girl finally looked up far enough to see our sandbag posts and the eyes peeking out from under our helmets. She waved as best as she had been taught, her elbow moving twice as much as her hand. A sense of relief fell over us.

Children, we had been told, were a good indication of how the people in an area felt about Coalition forces. If the children were scared and fled, the village was against us. If the children smiled and waved, the village was still against us but at least they were going to be civil before they tried to kill us.

We waved back and the girl was delighted. She continued waving. We waved back. She waved harder. We waved back. She waved so hard that her whole body was shaking back and forth. We realized she would not stop so long as we continued to wave. We stopped waving and sunk down into our sandbag positions. The girl continued waving for five more minutes, switching hands three times before tiring of our seeming indifference to her genuine amusement. Our smiles grew larger as she danced across the yard.

What a beautiful child, we thought. Perhaps they were all as beautiful.

The young girl stopped in the middle of the yard and clutched at the edge of her dress with both hands. Her back and shoulders tightened. She stooped slightly as if she had been slapped across her stomach. She looked down at her bare feet and suddenly pulled her dress up into pink bunches under her armpits. Naked, she looked like the cattle, sinewy and malnourished. She stooped lower, her ankles touching and her emaciated legs bending at a 90-degree angle. We stared, confounded by what kind of odd cultural habit we were witnessing.

Without a noise, the young girl defecated. It was wet and dark as it splattered across her tightened calves and ran down over her ankles, finally pooling around her tiny, bare feet. The girl looked down at her feet and then awkwardly over her shoulder at the backs of her legs. She was frightfully stoic. She examined her predicament for a moment longer and then let go of her dress, which fell lightly back down to her knees. The young girl stood, gave each leg an ineffective shake, and then danced off to another corner of the yard to play.

"Fuck ... this ... place," someone said behind me, expressing the sudden and violent reaction that had gripped us all.

We were definitely not in Kansas anymore.

CHAPTER 20

Beggars Can Be Choosers

He held the crippled boy like a towel.

The boy's arms and legs dangled uselessly over his father's arm, one of each on either side, while his father balanced the diaper-clad child on his forearm. If it were not for the crook at his father's elbow acting as a resting place, the boy's head would have dangled as aimlessly as the rest of his body. The boy's one eye, not wrapped up in bandages like the rest of his head, stared out from under his enormous, gauzed forehead and looked from post to post. His father, dressed in a long white robe, lifted the boy a few inches higher and tilted his head upright to give a better view of the fantastic fortress that had sprung up next to their one-room hovel overnight.

The father pointed at our Humvees and rooftop posts, whispering to his son in hushed wonderment. The boy's eye rolled up toward our rooftop posts and a shudder rushed through his body, almost unbalancing him but for his father's vigilance to such attempts. The father leaned his black, matted hair down to the boy's face and listened as if to hear the ants walking across the loamy ground. The father nodded his head in understanding and, with his free hand, lifted one of the boy's arms up. After a moment, the boy moved his hand to and fro unsteadily, using all the concentration his frail body could muster. We watched, disheartened, and preoccupied by the gunfire we had heard in the distance an hour before.

The father released the boy's arm, which fell limp, and pushed his own arm out sideways behind the boy's view. He waved, gently at first but with increasing vigor as we did not respond in kind. Finally, one of the rooftop posts waved back in a tiny, quick burst that caused the man to smile and nod lightly. He held the boy up higher and once again lifted the boy's sinewy arm. The boy attempted another wave and received waves from every post that could see the two figures standing at our razor wire. The boy wriggled in seeming delight as his wave continued to be returned by the watches.

Suddenly, the father dropped the boy's arm and pointed to the boy's head. The game of Iraqi charades was afoot.

First gesture: the boy? Bandages? Gun? The boy? You already said the boy. His head? The boy's head? The boy's head, we say and tap at our helmets. The man nods and then points to the yard.

Second gesture: yard? House? Dirt? Filth? Yard? Idiot, we already said the yard. Stop saying things that have already been guessed. Field? Does anyone else realize that he cannot speak English? Ground? Yard? Stop saying yard! Cow? Moo, as in cow? Moo-cow?

The other post put his fingers up to his helmet in the shape of crude horns and mooed. The man nodded furiously and wagged his finger back toward his enormous, chaotic yard where three tethered cows were grazing on the rubbish scattered about. The man then feigned slamming his palm against the boy's bandaged head.

Third gesture: hit? Slap? Slam? How could a cow slap a boy? Kick? The cow kicked the boy in the head? The cow kicked the boy in the head! He has no idea what we're saying, does he? Shit.

The other post put on his "horns" again, mooed, and then hit his head with his palm. The man nodded his head, pointed at the boy again, and then pointed at his own mouth. The boy had yet to take his gaze off the rooftop positions as his father implored us with his hands. There was no need to guess his last gesture. It was universal. We would see it for the rest of the deployment everywhere we went. Some would go so far as to pat their stomachs before they put their hand to their mouth like they were eating.

They wanted food.

We made a hasty search of the rooftop and a candy bar was produced, a treasure of our first wave of care packages from home. After a moment of deliberation, it was decided it should be thrown over into the abutting yard by the closest post. Getting up from behind the post for only a moment, the nearest post heaved the candy bar like a baseball. The chocolate bar, melted given the heat and its long ride in a sweaty pocket, sailed over the razor wire and landed with a quiet puff of dirt 10 feet from the man and his son. For how awkwardly his son was balanced, the man moved effortlessly to the candy bar, his son's limbs waving back and forth like a pendulum, and scooped it up. The father held up the candy bar for us to see. There was a certain triumph in his movements and, after tearing at the plastic with his teeth to remove the top half of the wrapper, he placed the gooey end of the chocolate bar near his son's mouth. The boy's mouth fell open loosely like a ventriloquist's doll. His father wrestled the melted chocolate past his son's cracked lips and paused for a moment. The boy's mouth shut slowly, trapping a small gob of the chocolate in his mouth.

There must have been a change in the boy's demeanor too subtle for us to recognize at a great distance, for the father suddenly threw his free hand up, candy bar and all, into the air. A slow, contained dance followed in which the man moved his feet back and forth while he sung to his child in a language that we had studied in classes but, hearing it for the first time, sounded like a smoker making baby-talk, a quiet gibberish with hacking tones and inflections.

It was oddly beautiful.

There were nine of them suddenly, standing just outside the wire and putting their dark, dirty hands to their mouths and rubbing their stomachs, as if we had blinked and nine starving children suddenly came into existence opposite our rooftop posts. The man holding his son swatted at the new children as they noticed the colorful wrapper and pawed at him for a hunk of the dark, sweet chocolate. He laughed and held the candy aloft, where even in their highest attempts they could not reach. After a handful of failed attempts, those who had been pawing at their father joined those who stood at the fence calling out hunger pangs in low, miserable tones.

"Mistah! Food, Mistah," said one of the tallest, though we could not accurately guess his age. They seemed ageless in their poverty, neither young nor old, simply haggard beyond anything we had ever seen. Those who were able took up his call and increased their gestures with a newfound fervor of shared language. The mangled English chorus increased in pitch with every passing moment. The father did nothing to quiet them but continued to feed his enfeebled son, beaming with masculine pride and gratitude as he pushed bite after bite into his son's nutcracker jowls.

"Think they'll stop anytime soon?" asked the only post not able to witness the spectacle from the far side of the roof. The end of his question was punctuated with a further increase in the children's audible violence against us. "Do we have any food to give them? Maybe that'll shut 'em up."

MREs were produced and examined. There was a science behind choosing an MRE for consumption (for certainly they were not chosen for any type of enjoyment). Important decisions had to be made at the very first. Did one want a decent main entrée and little else, or did one want an inedible entrée but a handful of mildly enjoyable sides? The chief meal designers must have called a meeting and unanimously decided that, while trying to please all the people all of the time is impossible, pleasing half of the people half of the time is a far better goal to set for themselves.

After our "Rooftop Committee to Decide Upon the Worst MRE" voted and unanimously came to our conclusion, we took a minute for a thorough inspection of our surroundings and then launched a Country Captain Chicken MRE over wall and wire.

Sharks do not attack so ferociously.

The children were fighting before they even knew what the prize was. The MRE disappeared into a maelstrom of swinging fists, sharp nails, and gnashing teeth. The children were suddenly gladiators pummeling each other by all means available as if in a terrible battle for their very lives. As it was, they were battling over an MRE that had neither entrée nor side palatable enough to save it from every rat-fuck box we made, but still they tore recklessly at the smooth, tan plastic wrapper and each other.

A little girl with shit adorning her calves was tossed aside and took to sobbing. The tallest boy, the one who had started the chant, swung his arms wildly like two great windmills in an attempt to force his way to the eye of the storm. A smaller boy was clobbered brutishly and lay quietly on the ground.

Finally, after 30 seconds of anarchy, the violence stopped. A victor had emerged.

Through size alone, the tallest boy stood over the MRE victoriously. The other children leered and kept circling just outside of striking distance, ready to assault en masse at the slightest sign of weakness. The boy stooped and retrieved the MRE. The circle ground to a halt and it was suddenly very quiet. He tore at the corners of the MRE with his teeth and managed to come away with a ragged triangle of plastic. He looked up at us defiantly and poured out the contents of the MRE at his feet. The other children turned away from the pile and joined him in staring defiantly at us. Even the father, seeing what we had thrown to his other children, stared up at the rooftop post, the wrapper of the candy bar already forgotten and blowing across the yard.

By ones and twos, they disappeared into the house until there was only a pile of MRE guts left in the yard and the wrapper blowing across the fields. It was once again silent except for the morning breeze.

"I see they've had MREs before," one of the posts commented, as we hunkered down in our positions to finish out our watch.

CHAPTER 21

Know Your Frenemy

"Two is one, one is none," we told ourselves as we began to pack and put our gear on for our first patrol.

Extra batteries and water were squirreled away in every pocket we could find. Suddenly, on the cusp of our first patrol, the three of us who had never been to combat could not seem to pack enough extra gear in case the worst should arise. Our team leader, Ballas, smiled and sauntered about the firm base preparing his patrol brief with an ease that slowed our buzzing minds, but only slightly. Our assistant team leader, Boom, checked our gear multiple times, ensuring we had not forgotten anything or taken too much, if there was even such a thing.

Both Ballas and Boom had the calm look of experience, having been deployed to the exact same spot only one cycle earlier. The three "boots," warriors not yet forged in the crucible of combat, wore the look of complete horror that uncertainty brings. We were both excited and anxious by the prospect of making contact on our maiden voyage out into the dust and tumble. We had trained every day for what seemed like years, practicing our reactions and drills until we dreamed them, bounding back in elements and assaulting through while we slept fitfully. We had no idea what to expect.

We were told it was a cache sweep as we gathered around Ballas and the laptop he had prepared his route brief on. We were taking one engineer in support and making a seven-kilometer movement to the northwest of our firm base. The local populace was suspected of housing insurgents and weapons caches. We needed to pay attention to how people were acting toward us. It could change from one group of houses to the next, depending on how the immediate family in that specific area felt toward us. Insurgents could be housed next to Coalition supporters, though it was unlikely; we were briefed insurgents tended to brutally murder and make examples out of Coalition supporters. Still, not everyone in the country was our enemy.

Or so we hoped.

It was a mild day as we stepped out into the open air. Spring persisted, clinging to the horizon in clusters of gray clouds that spelled rain in our distant future, but right then it was bright and warm. We squinted in the sunlight as Boom got accountability and gave the thumbs-up. We weaved in between the Humvees like a heavily armed snake.

We all had our jobs. I took point. Ballas followed in trace looking for possible caches while Spears worked the radio. Clark assisted Spears with the radio when we stopped and helped spread the weight of the heavy radio batteries and accessories between the two of them, while Boom took up rear security. Ringo, our platoon's attached engineer, stayed toward the middle of the formation working his metal detector. As we filed out into one of the many fields, we pushed out into a wedge formation and began our first sweep of the area.

As we moved into hostile territory, I was thoroughly convinced we were about to be attacked. If not that second, then the next.

Or the next.

Or the next.

Looking back at the other boots—Spears and Clark—I could see the feeling was understood as mutual. Our eyes darted back and forth across the field, narrowing on every bush or possible crux of our destruction. Our hands caressed the safety of our rifles like children terrified to stop touching their mother's hem, as if our rifles would betray us unless under the constant reassurance of our sweaty fingers.

We were filled with both ecstasy and gut-clenching terror. Nervous virgins on the cusp of the first touch of a trembling naked body, we moved across the fields not knowing what to do with our shaking and clammy hands.

Ballas was no longer smiling, but his eyes were still soft and friendly as he looked about the fields leisurely. There was a method to his madness, we were later told. "You cannot see the forest if you are only staring at the trees." Ballas would go on to be known as "cache boy" for his uncanny ability to find the buried arms and ammo of the Insurgency. It would be as much of a curse as an homage, sending our team out on sweep after sweep due to our near-constant success but, right then, on our first sweep, we only knew of the soft fertile soil filling up the tread of our boots and the tall grasses leaning east toward the rising sun.

The body could not sustain the constant state of vigil we demanded of it. The hair on our necks could only stand straight for so long. The adrenaline could flood the muscles and produce the comforting shiver of preparedness for only a short duration. After an hour, it felt as if we had humped our full kit over the Rockies. Our steps shortened and we became clumsy in our sudden exhaustion. Ballas and Boom had not missed a step, moving as fresh as when we first left the firm base. They smiled. They looked around leisurely but carefully. It was only when there was a sudden explosion that their true colors shone through. In a flash, Ballas and Boom were on a knee, Ballas facing the unknown threat and Boom facing our six o'clock, in case of a complex ambush. We boots were slower to react but only by a fraction.

Time stood still. The world was a photograph.

In the middle of a dark field, six figures kneel, rifles pulled tight into their shoulders, fingers lingering just outside of the trigger guard, straight but ready to apply the even pressure that would send our rounds accurately down range. No slapping the trigger. Slapping the trigger pulled the round. Slow, steady pressure until the break of the round, releasing the trigger only until the hammer resets, no more, and then the slow steady pressure again until the first round is the second and the second is the third. Their hands tremble but it is not unwelcome. Their hands are vices, twisting the rifle into itself until it feels as if it might break in half. Their bodies are steel, each beat of their heart resounding in their chest like an enormous bell tolling their coming calamity. Their dilated eyes see everything and nothing, focused on a plane a thousand yards away but seeing every detail in between. Each man plays the soldier's version of "Duck Duck Goose" with every visible object (non-hostile, non-hostile, non-hostile, hostile!) just waiting for the inevitable moment when the goose will present itself and the great chase will begin.

We waited like marble statues for what felt like an hour, though only seconds passed.

Ballas laughed and dropped the barrel of his rifle an inch.

An ancient belt-driven tractor had backfired in an adjacent field. Ballas laughed harder and signaled for us to continue our movement. We all began laughing to ourselves, a nervous, rapid chuckle that instantly relieved the tension tugging at our stomachs and burning in our muscles. It felt unusually good for something that did not seem all that funny.

But we laughed anyway, heartily and to ourselves. It was just a glint of the gallows humor to come.

We grinned as we moved, as the comedy of defying death, if but for a little while longer, still tugged at the corners of our mouths. We finally relaxed, our movements becoming more natural with each continued step we took. The exhaustion was a fading memory, replaced by a far more visceral feeling of awareness. Everything was clearer, crisper. Each sense was distinct and precise. It was a feeling we would begin to crave as time passed and would try to recapture through recreation but inevitably fail. We would come close, but there was nothing that reached such a high back in the other world, the civilian world a million miles and a million lives away. It was the feeling of being intensely alive in our own skin.

It was the feeling of flirting with death with each step.

We moved in silence, save the occasional scuffle of our boots as we dug in for traction on the constantly varying soil. Slight inclines that should have been a simple matter of leaning into them, had the soil not been damp from the persistent rains, had become miniature "Slip-N-Slides" we had to awkwardly maneuver up, while remaining ever vigilant. Declines were no better, more skating or surfing than hiking. Eventually, after an hour, we gained our legs and began to move efficiently across the fields, canals, and vegetation that lined both.

As we passed each cluster of houses 200 meters off to our right, closer if Ballas warranted the necessity to check any suspicious hills or fresh digs, we watched with great interest as to how our presence was received. Our area of operation was notorious for its localism, their fierce desire to have the area be run by the heads of the families and religious leaders that resided within its boundaries, rather than by any outside force or influence.

The people who resided within the area were anti-Coalition forces. They were also venomously and violently opposed to the Insurgency. They were simply for themselves; all outsiders were considered hostile regardless of what flag they lived and died under. There was only their law within the region. If it were not for the palm trees, one might mistake the area for the Old West.

As it was, we were not received at all by the adults. The locals we passed took almost no notice of our presence. The parents of the children swarming about the dirt yards did not usher their children inside with heavy hands and harsh whispers. But they did not wave either. They watched our movement with little interest, the demands of the hungry mouths and blocked canals far outweighing any little pleasure or slight they may have derived from our skirting their fields. We were not the first soldiers they had seen. Ballas and Boom had patrolled the same area on their previous deployment with only a handful of incidents across the entire battalion. Be it the battalion's historically small footprint in the area, the lack of a well-organized insurgency, or just a general apathy—whatever the reason—our presence in the area seemed to be of little concern to those living there.

The children, fresh to the delights and fears of outsiders moving about them, scurried and jumped about, pointing their tiny fingers at the tan figures moving on the horizon. The bold children moved to the dirt mounds lining the canals to command a better view of so foreign a sight, while the meek majority of children peeked out from behind the trees and outlying buildings to catch a glimpse. We must have looked like turtles, our kit and giant rucks giving the impression of enormous round torsos and backs with thin limbs sticking out of our "shells." The children made eyes at each other and put their hands over their tiny mouths when they giggled.

We moved extraordinarily close to a cluster of houses to inspect a knot of scrub vegetation sprouting up directly next to a mound of soil. We caught the attention of a young boy on his way to school, his books gripped tightly to his chest. School supplies were very limited; paper was a luxury for most of the families in the area. The patrol halted at the mound and the ground surrounding the possible cache was searched for possible booby traps. With no visible signs of a trap, the patrol spread out from the mound to provide 360-degree security for Ringo and Spears, who had volunteered to work the shovel for the first shift should the need arise.

The schoolboy forgot his destination in the face of so extraordinary a sight as six men guarding a bush. He waved. Those of us who could see him gave a quick, halfhearted wave back, hesitant to remove either hand from our rifle for any extended amount of time. We were vulnerable out in the open. Well-placed rounds from any one of the buildings could prove particularly fatal for such a small patrol without any reliable cover. We were exposed; appeasing the young boy was not the top priority.

Still, the boy persisted.

To his wave, the boy added a small hop whenever his hand was straight above his head. This achieved a collective smile from those who could see it. The boy was doing a one-armed jumping jack with a load of schoolbooks tucked under his other arm. Eliciting a smaller response than his first attempt, the boy moved to more desperate means. Dropping his books, the boy started in with full-blown jumping jacks complete with screaming. Clark began counting cadence out loud for the boy. "One-two-three, ONE, one-two-three, TWO, one-two-three …" The boy was in perfect time.

Another set of eyes had noticed the spectacle and moved closer to the boy to inspect. A cow, as high in the shoulders as any we had ever seen in the other world but carrying only a quarter of the weight, moved up behind the boy. Its slow, constant movement brought to mind the *Jaws* theme music as it ambled closer. The boy himself was in a fury of movement, trying to gain recognition from the soldiers suddenly guarding the bush out in his father's field, if proximity implied ownership as it usually did in the area. He might never have seen Coalition soldiers so close before, and he would be damned if he was going to walk to school without the story of the "fat" soldiers having waved back at him.

The cow had broken into a trot. It was easily as tall in the shoulders as the boy standing fully. The boy was about to be rammed; those of us watching took a sharp breath in anticipation of the event. It was almost more then we could bear watching, as the distance between the boy doing clumsy jumping jacks and the cow dwindled. The terrible laugh was already growing inside us all. Impact was imminent.

A mere foot from the boy the cow stopped dead, only its ratty tail still moving back and forth, slapping each flank. We exhaled, slightly disappointed by the outcome.

"Stupid cow," someone grumbled.

The cow, still unnoticed by the boy, lowered its head to the ground.

"No. Oh, no," I begged to no one in particular. The cow lashed out with its enormous pink tongue, and the boy's notebook and a handful of loose papers were pulled into its mouth. The boy, now breaking a sweat, took no notice as the cow ground his homework between its square teeth, a ticker-tape parade of confetti falling from its mouth as it ingested basic grammar and adding fractions. The laugh that was growing inside of us was now escaping in small chuckles and silent shakes. Finally, Clark yelled to the boy and pointed behind him, more out of curiosity for how the boy would react than any real desire to see him cease his strenuous exercise. It was worth the effort.

The boy turned slowly, as if not quite understanding the hand gesture of "behind," or wary he was being misled by a group of foreign turtles silly enough to guard a bush that grew out of every piece of soil not sown for harvest. The cow looked at the boy unapologetically as it masticated his homework in long, cartoonish movements of its thick lower jaw. The boy flew into a rage, screaming at the cow and making wild gestures to scare it off. The cow stared back blankly as it finished off the boy's notebook. It was not until the cow got its tongue around one of the boy's textbooks that the boy finally tried to recover his work. He tugged the textbook free of the cow's mouth and cracked the cow on the crown of its head with the damp book. The cow lowered its head in seeming defeat and the boy lowered his voice, until he realized the cow had simply stooped to retrieve another stack of papers from the ground. The boy cracked the cow on the head again. The cow raised its head, more out of ignorance than defiance, and the boy wrestled the papers from its mouth. The papers did not come away unscathed.

The boy quickly bent and retrieved what was left of his schoolwork from the ground before the cow had time to lower its head again. Satisfied his remaining schoolwork was safe, the boy turned back to our security positions and began his one-armed jumping jacks again.

Dry hole.

There was no cache under the bush or in the mound. It was time to move the patrol on. We waved at the boy. Satisfied, he sprinted off to school to tell the tale of the soldiers who guarded bushes and how a cow really did eat his homework.

In high spirits, we continued on with the patrol. The firm base was once again in view, our enormous loop being almost complete; only a few fields remained to be crossed. A sudden surge of energy filled us as the end of the patrol neared. The area seemed friendly enough and there had been no sign of any caches. There was none of the hostility that was expected during our briefs. The country seemed to be turning the corner. If this continued, we were not going to be needed in the area much longer.

Ballas halted the patrol and moved up beside me.

"What's up?" I asked.

Ballas surveyed the scene carefully, his dark, Greek eyes sharp and unusually somber. He pulled his rifle into his shoulder and stared through his optic at a cluster of houses 300 meters perpendicular to the direction of the firm base. He lowered the rifle for a moment, squinting at the same spot with his naked eye, and then pulled the rifle back up again.

"That mound has been bothering me," he said without pulling his eye from his optic. I pulled my own rifle up and scanned the direction of interest. There was the normal cluster of one-story houses, bars in the windows, and a dirt yard bleeding seamlessly into the dirt driveway. A few sparse grasses speckled the yard, and a tiny mud oven still sighed a few wisps of white smoke from the early morning cooking as it had been at every other house on our route. I dropped the rifle from my shoulder and tried to squint as Ballas had. Whatever was drawing his eye, my virgin eyes could not discern anything out of the ordinary. Ballas guessed as much by the look on my face and led me on target.

"See the palm grove," he said, waiting for me to draw up and acquire. "All right, now go ten meters to the right. There is a low, long plateau butting up against the yard between that palm grove and the field to the right of it."

It was like trying to see the unicorn or sailboat in one of those magic-eye posters where the eyes must be crossed and unfocused just so to make the image pop out of the wavy blur. I did not know what I was looking for. I suddenly felt very stupid and inexperienced. I wanted so badly to see what Ballas saw. I was letting down my hero. I stared harder until my eyes shook in their sockets and it felt as if they were about to pop out altogether.

Nothing.

I sighed and closed my eyes.

There!

As I opened my eyes to admit my failure, they caught a glimpse of something impossible to put into words but equally impossible to deny. Something was just not right.

"It's too uniform," Ballas said matter-of-factly. "It's too neat."

I could see it now—the almost-perfectly-level plateau with its equal lengths, widths, and heights. It sat lower than the palm grove to the left of it but only inches higher than the bed of the field to the right from where we stood. Ninety-nine out of a hundred people would have missed it, would have rationalized the perfection as some little illusion, some trick of earth and light. Ballas had seen it as if there had been billboard signs all the way leading up to it.

We formed back up into our wedge and moved toward the area, cutting our route back to the firm base by a 45-degree angle. The excitement that had filled us at the sight of our firm base had become a hard knot in our stomachs. The presence of the uniform mound muddied the clean feeling of the area being as friendly as we had begun to hope. Our movements were slow and deliberate. Our skin tingled with the sensation of being watched.

The mound was bigger than it had first appeared. Its flat top sat two-and-a-half feet above the level of the dirt yard and surrounding fields. We must have been on a slight incline looking down at the position, blending the mound's silhouette, for as we moved around it checking for any snares, it was obvious someone had taken an enormous amount of time preparing it. Without any evidence of snares or traps, we formed a perimeter and sought the best cover we could find, which was not much. We were no more than seventy meters from the nearest house. They would not even have to aim; just put the stock into their hip, squeeze off a burst in our direction, and chance alone would give them a fair probability of hitting someone in the patrol.

Ringo, our engineer, began moving the metal detector over the far side of the mound in precise, overlapping rows. If there was something here, it would be found, we were assured. Ringo smiled constantly, and his John Lennon glasses gave his face a friendly, passive look. He told stories of his beautiful wife and their future plans when not on patrol. He was kind and courteous. He had no chip on his shoulder and he turned the other cheek when slighted. He was a pacifist.

Most of us wondered what the hell he was doing there.

Three-quarters down the mound and still nothing. Ringo continued sweeping with steady conviction, smiling while he listened to the tones whining out of his metal detector. On past occasions when there had been a hit, Ringo had stated confidently what the object was that the metal detector had picked up before Spears even had time to work his shovel into the hard-packed mound. To our amusement, Ringo had been spot-on each time. An old can sounds different than a large nut and bolt, sounds different than a 155 mm round, he said humbly, but it all sounded like a baby screaming in his ear to the rest of us.

We were losing steam. What looked certain to contain the entire stock of weapons of mass destruction so heatedly debated over back in the other world had produced only two cans, a shapeless fist-sized piece of metal, and an assortment of what looked like tractor pieces. This fact did not lessen the tug in our stomachs; in fact, quite the contrary. Our gut told us that here, in this spot, danger was rife. If there was no danger, our guts had led us astray. For men who were required to live by their intuition, that was a far worse feeling than being shot at.

A sudden screech cut through our thoughts and fear. The metal detector groaned loudly, enough to startle even Ringo.

"That doesn't sound like a can," Ballas quipped coolly, a thin smile pulling at the corner of his lips. Ringo nodded absently and moved the metal detector, still whining, forward. The whine remained steady as he moved. Ringo stepped forward another half foot, another foot, another three feet, and still the whine warbled loudly.

"Tin can? Gods, it's a tank," Boom said over his shoulder, watching Ringo's movements out of the corner of his eye. Ringo moved the wand back and forth over an area roughly five-feet square without the whine changing volume or pitch. He ran the wand outside of the square, leaned his head closer to the metal detector, and then moved the wand back over the area, listening to something with great interest. After a moment, he removed the wand again and then placed it over the area, off the area, and then back on the area, his face never changing from scientific meditation. Off the area. On the area. Finally, Ringo placed the wand gently on the ground in silence. Everyone in the perimeter turned an ear in his direction to hear his prediction. Ringo remained silent for a few moments biting his lip, his eyes focused somewhere beneath the dirt.

"Well?" Ballas asked, breaking the silence. "What is it?"

Ringo bit his lip two more times thoughtfully before finally giving his speculation. "I have absolutely no idea. I've never heard anything like that."

"But is it a tank?" Boom asked smiling.

Without a word, Spears moved in with his shovel and began working the dirt with swift, powerful blows. A world-class athlete, Spears made quick work of the hard-packed soil. In less than a minute, he was a foot deep. Looking at the scene, one might conjure up images of *Treasure Island*, of pirates digging for gold while their shipmates looked on eagerly. We were suddenly heavily invested in the endeavor. We hoped for treasure of some kind.

TUMPT!

Spears pulled back his shovel. Both he and Ballas peered into the hole to see what the shovel had hit. Spears scraped the shovel against the bottom of the hole awkwardly, leaning it against the side of the hole after a moment to use his hands. He stood up, his dirty hands holding a box a foot-and-a-half long and half the width. It resembled something like a large gray sardine can. Ballas worked the lid and, after a momentary fumble, removed it from the can. He grinned and held up what looked like an eight-inch anti-aircraft round slightly larger than the American .50-caliber rounds. It was one of a hundred in the box. Ringo ran the wand back over the enormous area; individually, we did the math in our heads.

There must have been sixty or seventy such cans in the mound.

Ballas reached for the radio.

"Well, boys. The area is definitely not friendly."

CHAPTER 22

Close Encounters of the Fourth Kind

Sleep came hard.

It was not that we weren't dog tired, laying there on our damp poncho liners, sweating through our green T-shirts and the tan flight suits tied off around our waists, hoping for sleep to eventually overtake us. We were exhausted. It was only spring, but after a long winter workup of sleeping bags and wool watch caps back in the States, the desert sun beat down on our firm base with an intensity that drained all our energy almost as soon as it peeked over the horizon. The sweltering, sticky heat made us wiggle and slap at the "bugs" crawling all over our body, though it was always just beads of sweat.

We had been out all night on a cache sweep, moving in the cooler times, when we were also at the greatest advantage under the cover of darkness. It had been 80 degrees at midnight and our eight-kilometer movement—over berms and through the dark, muddy fields that would suck a loosely tied boot clean off—had taken its toll. Our eyes were heavy, and we pined for sleep, but the sweat running off our foreheads and into our eyes kept us squinting and tossing on our mats in a vain attempt to find a comfortable position. Every position was an uncomfortable one in the sweltering heat and every piece of material buffering our skin from the mat was soaked completely through. Whenever we moved positions, and the material had a chance to dry in the arid breeze, a large white sweat ring was left. Position after position we shifted, ring after ring formed until our flight suits looked like topographical maps of the Rocky Mountains.

Clark was on watch on the roof manning the 240 Golf, a 7.62 mm machine gun, while the rest of the team "slept." Every hour another teammate replaced the last as we shuffled through our endless loop of rooftop watch of the four posts we had set up during the initial raid on the house, after filling sandbags and moving hundreds of pounds of bulletproof glass to the roof. We had worked until each position afforded as much protection as could be had, without moving an entire Abrams or Bradley up onto the roof, an idea Sergeant Bronx would have staunchly supported and enforced if it had been even remotely tenable.

We slept until it was our watch; we did our watch until it was time to do another patrol; we patrolled until we were exhausted. It was a vicious circle of military life, one that every warrior knew all too well.

Boom was stripped down to his green T-shirt and black shorts, reading on his mat as the sweat puddled in the cavity of his chest between his tight pectoral muscles. Without a breeze, the syrupy sweat stuck to the skin at the base of the little chest hairs for what seemed liked forever. We blew down the length of our chests in an attempt to speed up the evaporation process and possibly cool our bodies for a second or two, but in the end it did nothing other than make us lightheaded.

Ballas and Spears were halfway through a deck of cards, taking turns doing the amount of push-ups shown on the card they flipped over until they finished the deck. They often went through the deck twice before moving onto their abdominal routine, a searing eight minutes that left the muscles almost completely exhausted. I was attempting to scribble an impossible letter on a sheet of notebook paper. Each time I tried to begin the letter, the edge of my hand and wrist touched the paper, depositing half a cup of sweat, which soaked into the paper in dark, widening circles. I could get the first few words down before the pen moved over one of the dark splotches and began tearing the paper rather than depositing ink.

A single gunshot pierced the rural silence, and the team looked up at the ceiling in unison—like dogs trying to locate the origin of an unfamiliar sound. The shot had not been a 5.56 mm, the round used by U.S. military forces, which had a distinct high-pitched crack when fired. The shot had been a lower pitch with a bit more oomph behind it; 7.62 mm, the official round of the Insurgency. Sergeant Boom was suddenly sitting up, his book tossed aside, and his ear cocked to the ceiling. He was opening his mouth to say something to the team, something important by the look on his face, but a burst of gunfire drowned out his words. We heard what he was saying, but it was distant background noise compared to the sound of the incoming gunfire peppering the side of the firm base, like fat raindrops on a tin roof. After a moment, the words finally registered.

"To the roof," Boom yelled, hopping to his feet. There was no fear in his voice, no panic causing the slightest quiver. There was only excitement. The last deployment offered no gunfights for Ballas and Boom, only the occasional improvised explosive device (IED), one of which gave him his unlucky nickname when he was almost killed. The opportunity for Boom and everyone else to have a proper stand-up fight had finally arrived. There was no need for any further commands or guidance for preparation. This was the moment everyone had been waiting for.

The team was on its feet only a beat behind Boom. Our turtle-shell plate carriers were thrown directly over our T-shirts, no one wanting to take the time to shimmy their top half fully into their flight suit. Boom did not even reach for his flight suit, tossing his flak jacket and helmet right on top of his shorts and T-shirt. Half-dressed in clothing but fully dressed for battle, the team scrambled to the rooftop, bounding up the stairs while skipping two or three with every long, powerful stride. Everyone wanted to be the first to the roof, the first to burst out into the fray.

The sudden sunlight was blinding.

During the deployment workup, we shot tens of thousands of rounds. We had shot from sun up to sun down, and then we turned on our night-vision equipment and shot through the rest of the night. We had done endless dry practices, going through our exact movements with the empty gun as if we had a loaded magazine in and were intending to shoot. We had done up-down drills in the rain, a hellish drill in which Sergeant Bronx would call out one of three firing positions—standing, kneeling, and prone—and those taking part in the drill would move into the next position as fast as possible. Palms and knees had been shredded by the sharp rocks. Five minutes and the quads burned with lactic acid. But we had pushed on, hoping that one day we would find ourselves in a gunfight and that we would be the quick, rather than the dead. We had loaded and snapped our rifles up on green silhouette targets proportionally sized to an average human male, though one with a disproportionately thick neck. We had shot at these green bodybuilders almost every day for the seven-month workup, trying with every round to hit the six-inch circle drawn on the upper chest and the two-inch-by-four-inch rectangle drawn on the head where the eyes would be, the brain box.

We had shot in the pouring rain. We had shot with bitter mountain winds biting at our cheeks and numb fingers. We had shot with flashlights. We had shot with night vision. We had shot from our backs just to see what it would take to make a hit if we found ourselves injured or thrown to the ground. We had shot until the skin on our hands peeled and blistered.

And then Sergeant Bronx had us shoot more, adhering to the belief we needed to learn how to shoot and keep the cycle of the weapon when we were exhausted, as we would be in combat.

"Only us snipers get to fire a calm, rested shot," Sergeant Bronx would say with a smile, fingering his fabled "Hog's Tooth," a necklace given at sniper school graduation, through his shirt.

We had pretended with each shot that suddenly we were there, face to face with an insurgent, the muzzle of his AK-47 already ascending toward the moment when the barrel would be pointing directly at our heart, our lungs, our anything, and our enemy was beginning his gentle squeeze of the trigger.

Seven months of practice and the movements had become muscle memory. The rifle seemed to move almost without thought as it was brought up from the low-ready, muzzle toward the dirt, into the pocket of the shoulder. Spread the legs, take a step with the lead foot toward the target. Lean forward, the body weight shifting to the lead leg. Bend at the waist. Place the entire body behind the rifle to reduce the muzzle movement on the recoil. Twist the rifle in the hands in opposite directions to steady it. Apply even pressure to the trigger. Squeeze. Reacquire sight picture. Squeeze. Reacquire. Squeeze. Squeeze until the drill is done. Squeeze until the threat is lying in a pool of his own blood, two shots to his heart and lungs and one shot to his brain box.

Training for exhaustion required willpower to move the slow hand with hardly any strength left behind it. But there was no training for the adrenaline.

As we bounded to the roof, we realized that energy was the last thing we would have to worry about. There was no precedent for the amount of adrenaline and endorphins our bodies were pushing through our swollen veins. We were shaking so much it was almost unnoticeable, the way a hummingbird seems to be floating in air with its wings hardly moving.

The light was blinding as we burst out onto the roof in a four-man train, huddled closely to the man in front of us just to be sure we were not late, that we would not miss it. It took our eyes just a moment to adjust to the afternoon. There was not a cloud in the sky and, for three o'clock in the afternoon, the sun was still quite high. It would not set for close to another five hours. There were hardly any shadows, the sun touching everything and everywhere.

Without hesitation, Spears ran to the roof wall closest to the origin of the gunfire. As he moved, his rifle came up and was aimed as if he had been born doing it. His face was calm, vacant of any wild emotion, fear, or excitement. Everywhere, as other teams followed us onto the roof, people were ducking behind the wall encircling the roof to take cover, where they would not be shot but would not be able to engage, either. Spears stood in stark contrast. He began engaging the two gunmen who were firing blindly from the corner of a store in the market our firm base overlooked. The wall gave Spears cover from the stomach down, but he made no attempt to sink lower, as the increased cover would have required him to move into a less-stable shooting position.

Spears had not conquered fear; there was simply no fear inside of him to conquer. Sergeant Bronx had drilled it out of him. Though rounds continued to impact the firm base, Spears took no notice. He was focused on his targets, taking well-aimed shots at the small amount of flesh they exposed as they stuck their AKs around the corner and squeezed off short bursts.

Ballas took control of the roof, yelling out for different people to move to different areas of the roof in case it was a diversion, in case the real attack was about to be sprung from the opposite direction with rocket-propelled grenades, crew-served weapons, and the most dangerous course of action, a vehicle-born IED, or VBIED, slamming into what might be an unguarded side of the building if everyone rushed to the gunfight. The Insurgency had done it before, we knew, catching units off guard and feigning an attack, setting the bait of an honest gunfight. Like moths to a flame, the units had focused solely on the sporadic gunfire, hoping for a few easy kills to post in their daily intelligence summaries.

They never saw the sniper a few hundred meters away looking for the key leaders, or the Bongo truck loaded with a few hundred pounds of homemade explosive bearing down on their exposed flanks. Too late the units had realized their mistakes, usually with an officer or platoon sergeant spraying blood from the ragged exit wound in his neck, or the flash of orange light that precedes the deafening detonation and shockwave of a few hundred pounds of low-grade PE4 disintegrating the side of a firm base, a Humvee, or the seven-ton truck loaded with confused troops.

Our platoon poured out onto the rooftop like a hundred-dollar red ant hill, eager to defend our tiny mound of dirt. Like a steel porcupine, there were suddenly guns facing every direction from our firm base. Those facing the direction of the gunfire rained down hell into the market. All the civilians had just happened to leave two minutes before the gunfire, a sure sign of an impending attack in the usually crowded streets. Boom fired 40 mm grenades on the far side of the building the gunmen were hiding behind. Clark on the 240 machine gun laid down suppressive fire, ensuring the gunmen could not risk accurate fire at the firm base without moving into a cone of bullets that was slowly eroding the corner they had just been firing from. They needed to retreat or wait for Boom to bracket their position with grenades.

It was not as we had imagined. From the moment we had picked up a rifle for the first time with the intent of killing in our most basic training, there had begun a question in the dark recesses of our heads that begged for an answer that few would ever get the opportunity to find.

How will I act when the first bullets begin cracking next to our heads?

Will I cower? Will I be a hero? Will I shit myself and shiver in uncontrollable panic? Will I remember to fire my weapon? Will I freeze up? Will I kill? Will I do what needs to be done when the time comes?

Some never have an opportunity to find out an answer and spend the rest of their lives wondering.

Those who do find an answer are not always happy with what they find. Some, and usually those who boasted the most, find themselves freezing up or too panicked to come out of cover. They are swallowed whole by terror, by the Great Fear of dying in a pool of their own warm, crimson blood thousands of miles from their home. They are consumed by their own thoughts of failure.

And then there were men like Spears, Clark, Boom, and Ballas, men who functioned like clockwork when the time came. Men who stood on the wall hardly thinking at all, only acting on their instincts, their training, and the required arrogance that whispered over and over they would not die that day, that it was not yet their time. These were the quiet men, the men who never claimed a thing about their bravery. These were the men who would be at a bar years down the road and, when pressed to answer the questions "What was going through your head? What were you thinking?", would sip at their beers for a moment and then shake their heads. "Nothing. I wasn't thinking," and they would mean it. They just did. There was no thought behind their actions.

No Medal of Honor recipient ever ran through a hail of gunfire to save a friend thinking, "I should not be doing this. I'm going to fail. I'm going to die. I should go back." No one ever jumps on a grenade thinking, "This is really going to hurt." The bravest acts in the world were done without a conscious thought, only the instinct of what is right. The brave act, without waiting for the rational side to weigh out the pros and cons. If everyone in war weighed out the pros and cons of their actions, there would hardly be a hero among the ranks, if there were any ranks left at all.

Suddenly, everything was silent.

The machine guns and the M4s going off around me recoiled without a sound, the expended shells dancing around the rooftop in a noiseless ballet. My own rifle was firing round after round down range, but I could not hear it. I could not even feel the pressure of the recoil in my shoulder. The rifle felt weightless in my gently shaking hands. I did not notice the weight of my kit or the way it was digging into my left shoulder because one of the Velcro tabs had peeled away and folded back on itself. I did not notice the high-pitched ringing in my ears as tone after tone was destroyed by the sheer volume of all of the weapons firing at once in such close proximity, despite the issued hearing protection.

I would notice these things later: when I was exhausted from carrying the extra 90 pounds of weight; when my shoulder was bleeding from a deep ravine where the Velcro tab sawed into the flesh; and when my hearing tests would come back as partially deaf.

For every sound I could no longer hear, the scene was still extraordinarily vivid. Directly in front of our firm base, a canal ran on the far side of the driveway, forming a moat between us and the marketplace that lay only 50 meters on the other side.

The word "market" is deceiving. It brings about images of fat butchers with white aprons and colorful fruit stands full of beautiful, exotic fruits from *Aladdin*. The scene sprawled out in front of me could not have been further from this.

The canal was dark brown and frothy in the backwater. Human waste and garbage floated on the slow current until it got caught up among the reeds or in one of the many eddies. There were streaks of rainbow glinting off the surface from the gasoline and oils dumped upstream by the "car garage," two clay ramps that allowed someone to get underneath an automobile with relative ease so they could drain the fluids into a channel that led right to the canal. On the far side of the canal, the back half of a yellow bus sat rusting. Every window, bar, and bolt that could be stripped had been. Next to the bus was a long, narrow building made of cinderblocks but without any mortar or bonding agent holding them together. It would not have taken much to push an entire side over, and the building was sagging inward on the two longer walls. There was a three-foot pile of garbage stacked up next to one of the far windows where the tenants threw out their waste.

Bordering the road on all sides of the intersection were structures that resembled something like a child's fort. The materials used for the constructions ranged from concrete to sticks and straw, and hardly any of them used less than three types in conjunction. The most common construction was cinderblock walls, scrap-metal roofs with straw filling in the cracks and rusted holes, and large branches and sticks for support. There was some colorful writing on the doors and cockeyed signs, but gray was the primary color. It muted everything down to the feeling of a dying Midwestern town 40 years after the factory or the mine had shut down. If it were not for the normally bustling streets, it would have looked like a ghost town that had been dead for a century.

I saw everything so clearly, as I fired round after silent round into the corner of the building the two gunmen slipped behind. Everything was so bright and detailed. Time had slowed to a crawl, and I could see each shell eject from the side of my rifle, tumble in the air like a thin brass acrobat, and then fall to the ground beside me to join its brothers. I was yelling in something of an excited laugh, but even I couldn't make out my words, if I was even trying to make any. My eyes were glued to the intersection where the gunmen fired from and to the impacts my rounds were making.

This was tunnel vision.

We had been told about tunnel vision, that when rounds started coming toward us, we would most likely revert to our training and the rest of the world would melt away. This is not a good thing. I was becoming so engrossed in a 10-degree field of view that I lost sight of the other 350.

If it were not for Ballas, 20 men would all have been standing on one side of the rooftop all staring with superhuman concentration at the same 10-degree field of view. If it were not for Ballas, the other 350 degrees would have struck us down with complete immunity from our senses. As a team leader, Ballas had gotten beyond the tunnel vision.

It was only another half-minute before Sergeant Bronx was up on the roof redirecting the platoon. He moved quickly but with great care. This was not his first gunfight. A highly respected operator, a close-quarters-combat shooting instructor, and winner of the team-leader-of-the-year award, Sergeant Bronx had spent his career training for conflict. The small exchange of gunfire we were experiencing was very little in comparison to what his dark eyes had seen.

But it was our first rodeo and he treated the situation accordingly. We were all adrenaline and jittery excitement. We needed to be harnessed and commanded or it would only be another minute before we expended every single bullet we could get our hands on.

Gain fire superiority; that is the first rule we had been taught. We made absolutely no attempt at economy.

"Cease fire," Bronx yelled, waving his non-firing hand in front of his face. On his second yell, the command began to be passed around. Slowly, as the command was screamed around the roof, the guns began to shut off their fires. "Cease fire," Bronx continued to yell until he was satisfied the silence was not just everyone reloading at the same time.

"Is anyone hurt?" Bronx yelled, looking around the rooftop to ensure every post and possible attack point was manned. The assistant team leaders got positive confirmation from the rest of their team that everyone was unscathed and sounded off.

"YEAH!" someone suddenly yelled out, his grin enormous and suddenly infectious. "That. Was. Awesome." The whole rooftop laughed, the high of the battle taking hold. We were alive. We had survived the attack.

Bronx did not laugh, not even smile, but found Clark, who was the first to see the gunmen. How many? What kind of weapons? What did they look like? What were they wearing? Did anyone see which way they went?

"Prepare for a follow-on attack," Bronx said.

The laughter subsided. Suddenly, every vehicle within sight was suspect and scrutinized through the three-power scopes mounted on the M4s. Suddenly, everyone was an insurgent carrying out phase two of the attack.

The shaking got worse. Our limbs were trying to shake free of our bodies. The overwhelming urge to piss became all-consuming. Everywhere on the small cement roof, men were beginning to silently evacuate their reactions into plastic bottles, poorly. For most, it was their first brush with death. Some were second guessing their particular choice in occupations while others were grinning at the obscene feeling shooting up from their every nerve. It was written on each person's face.

Spears would be addicted to adrenaline, motorcycles, and base jumping from heights barely inside the safe limits just to push the limits.

Clark was an operator for life.

Boom went on to become a mercenary for hire.

Ballas was just pleased that we, his "boots," were unscathed and that we did so well.

I was thankful I could not see my own face. I was not sure I wanted to know what it said by the awful feeling in my guts.

Sergeant Bronx paced the roof three more times, like a prizefighter in the locker room before the big fight. He was stern but obviously pleased with both his men and the state of readiness his firm base hummed with.

Let them come.

Finally, after a full five minutes of silence that hung on the air like a year of hard labor under the blistering sun, Sergeant Bronx gave an order.

Waiting to step off on patrol with a broken down .50-caliber SASR and sniper-hide kit.

Stepping off on a weapons-cache patrol with a combat engineer manning a metal detector.

One of many weapons caches dug up on patrol. Waterproofing was sometimes poor.

View from a rooftop post of a firm base overlooking a small cluster of shops.

A primary school watching a patrol shuffle by, hoping for candy.

A beautiful blue lake where high government officials had their vacation homes.

One of the abandoned vacation homes turned into a company firm base.

Practicing long-range marksmanship with a .50-caliber SASR at the range.

A proud father and his two sons posing after a rare successful knock-and-talk.

The "Recon Bodyworks" gym brought out to a company firm base.

A Recon Marine holds rooftop security during a monsoon.

Waiting out of the sun in a tightly packed Humvee for follow-on orders.

Further away from the rivers, camels roamed the desert sands.

A fording goes awry and a team of Recon Marines wait for a wrecker.

Celebrating Thanksgiving with a lavish meal of noodles and peanut butter.

Captain Rusher surveys his platoon's dispersion after taking over an abandoned house.

The abandoned royal mansion in the middle of the blue lake.

Some of the beautiful architecture that still remained standing.

Ballas and Spears catch some rest while I brush my teeth waiting for our next mission.

The Humvee after the IED that injured Ballas and Spears.

Where Ballas had been sitting, directly over the IED.

On line at the range practicing our up-down drills.

A casual sniper hide providing overwatch, with antipersonnel and antivehicle options.

Catching a quick nap during a long-range "observation and interdiction" mission.

My second team waiting to step off on mission, carrying team hide kit.

Waiting to step off on patrol with my second team.

From left to right in Oakleys—Boom, Spears, Ballas, Clark.

"Snoop and Smokey," he said pointing at Ballas and another team leader. "Take your two teams and get ready for a BDA.* We step in five."

To Sergeant Bronx, everyone was either "Snoop," "Smokey," or "Stupid" and everything was a "Who-yah." It was as entertaining as it was confusing, but he always patiently waited until we figured out what he wanted.

Boom herded us back down into the team room while Ballas coordinated with Sergeant Bronx on the route and the order of movement. We were all nerve endings and sweat. Boom put his flight suit on fully and the rest of us did the same. We checked our kit, our grenades, and reloaded our magazines. Boom double-checked our load calmly, as if this was just another cache sweep and we had not just been engaging insurgents in a known sanctuary for hostiles. Extra magazines were loaded and stored wherever we could fit them in our kit.

"Do we need to bring our back plates or NVGs?"† Clark joked. *Black Hawk Down* was watched and rewatched endlessly by most of the warriors.

"Nah, but we do need to write our blood type on our boots," Spears replied. Spirits were high.

It was eerily quiet as we slipped out of the firm base and began weaving our way down through the barrier plan toward the market square. Only 10 minutes before we stepped off, the market had been bustling with commerce and throngs of locals catching up on the rumors and news of the day. Men had barked out their wares and children had been laughing as they chased each other around the refuse piles and broken cinderblocks, left where they had fallen years before. The noise had been constant and calming.

Rarely was the local populace kept in the dark about an upcoming insurgent attack. It was bad business for the Insurgency to anger their camouflage and human shields, without whom they would be easy to spot and far easier to engage without the worry of collateral damage.

The insurgent group that had attacked us, we were debriefed later, was comprised of mostly the local citizenry being led by a few more experienced men from "out of town." The majority of the insurgents lived within twenty kilometers of where our firm base sat and, for all their hatred, they were careful in warning their neighbors about their intentions.

The citizens were battened down in their cement houses, covering their heads with their arms and holding their malnourished children tightly to their breasts. They did not peek out from the windows or cracked doorways like in the movies. They were curious, but not curious enough to risk a look.

Even the stray dogs had scattered, though the meat carts and food stores had been abandoned and lay unguarded, ripe for scavenging and gorging until the dogs were

---

* BDA stands for "battle-damage assessment."
† NVG stands for "night-vision goggles."

shooed away after the panic had passed. Only the chickens remained—arrogant, noisy animals that seemed to fear nothing and pecked at the ground casually as the patrol snaked by them. They seemed to be the only animal that could not sense the danger or, if they did, they understood the danger of a rifle was insignificant compared to the cleaver that every single one of them would find their necks under when they could no longer fornicate or produce eggs.

Not an indigenous creature moved but for the chickens.

Approaching the crossroads, the market's center, we began posting and taking up security positions on every danger area we came across. Sergeant Bronx moved toward the corner of the building we had been engaged from and looked for signs of the insurgents' whereabouts and condition. He ducked behind the corner and then peeked out at our firm base slowly, trying to see what the insurgents had seen, to see what weakness they had seen that had made them decide it was a good idea for two men armed with AK-47s to attack a hardened structure containing 25 armed and well-trained men. The other 10 of us held our sectors of fire and eyeballed everything. Sergeant Bronx squatted at the corner and looked at the ground around him.

"At least one of 'em is hit," he said, fingering a splash of blood with his tan Nomex glove. It was hard to discern what caused the wound, the gunfire or Boom's 40 mm grenades, given the size and shape of the blood. But there was blood, a good amount of it, and that was all that mattered at that point. The insurgents did not come away from attacking us unscathed. We had. On the scoreboard in our minds, we had won a small victory.

"They must have pushed back into the village using the side of this building for cover," Sergeant Bronx said, standing and tracing their escape route with his dark eyes. "Stupid or Smokey, is there blood over there leading between those buildings?"

The two warriors slowly walked in a large arc, pieing off the corner, and then moved a few meters down the alleyway. They called for Sergeant Bronx after a minute; he moved to their position. There was another spattering of blood in the alleyway, though nowhere near the amount there had been at the corner of the building. The three emerged from the alleyway and Bronx briefed the rest of the group on their findings.

"Can everyone hear me? All right. Snoop found some blood in the alleyway, so we know they ducked into the alleyway after one of 'em got hit. Looking at the map, the firm base can see the whole western side of this row of buildings, so they must have crossed back over the road to the east, further down where we can't see 'em. We're going to move south down this road in two stacks. Snoop, you'll take that side. Smokey, you and your team take that side. We'll move south until we hit the eastern road or anything that looks suspicious. Any questions? Good, great."

The sun was merciless, baking us inside our sweat-drenched flight suits and flash frying any exposed skin. We moved deliberately, cautiously placing our boots as we shuffled down both sides of the road in two stacks. Each stack ran like a game of leapfrog, the operator in the front holding on the first danger area he came to. The next warrior in the stack moved past him and took up the next danger area as the third warrior passed him to take up the next. When the last warrior in the stack passed the first, he tapped him on the back and said "Last man," letting the warrior know the stack was moving past him and he had become the last man. After a few seconds, he pivoted, checked his rear security, and then moved up, tapping the next man on the back and saying "Last man." Each stack protected the other and each man protected the next moving past him by covering the danger area being crossed.

The adrenaline was still high after half an hour, and the stack had moved 200 meters down the road, which was dense with multistoried buildings broken only by tracts of thick vegetation perfect for an ambush. It was slow moving with so many danger areas to cover as the stacks pushed on. Sergeant Bronx laughed.

"You're all moving average now, but let's see how we're doing in another hour. How we doing on water?"

The water situation was under control at the moment. Everyone had grabbed at least one bottle before stepping off, if not more. Water had been the last thing anyone was thinking about. Somewhere, hidden in the crumbling cement structures or thick, shadowy vegetation, two armed men were hiding. They would fight to the death if they were trapped and already wounded. The adrenaline and endorphin spike that occurred with each new danger area kept the feelings of thirst and hunger at bay. There was only the hunt, and we were tracking the most dangerous quarry.

The market was long, and each space large enough to hide a man had to be cleared before moving on. We were short on men for such an enormous task. The 11 men on the BDA were clearing the equivalent of two or three city blocks, checking every nook and cranny for gunmen. An unseen gunman could ambush us from behind if we passed them by.

After another hour of bounding and dirty clears, the stacks were beginning to tire. The feelings of thirst and hunger were no longer being kept at bay. Water was being consumed in large mouthfuls and the snack foods that had been squirreled away in the different pouches were being produced and eaten in single bites when time and security permitted. The sun did not seem to have changed positions from directly over our heads. There were no clouds or trees to shade us from its heat, and the sweat ran into our eyes and mouths. The 90 pounds of kit digging into our shoulders began to feel heavier with each step. The slightest kink or fold in the gear began to saw into the shoulders and hips slowly and painfully. Skin was scraped away layer by pink layer until it was raw and seeping water.

This was what Sergeant Bronx had us train for. It had not been the initial gunfight that worried him, knowing the adrenaline would push us beyond any feelings of worry or fatigue we may have felt. It was this newfound feeling of pain and exhaustion he had tried to train us for, drilling us well beyond the point where we believed we needed any further instruction. Whenever someone finally bitched during a long drill, Sergeant Bronx would grin and reply that we were near the point where the real training would begin. When the whole platoon seemed ready to quit, sometimes vocally, Sergeant Bronx said that was the point when the knowledge would be needed the most.

There, in the 110-degree heat baking off the pavement in hazy waves that we moved slowly across, we were beginning to understand his method. The kit, the Kevlar helmet, the rifle—they all seemed to be getting heavier by the second as we shuffled down toward the east road. An hour-and-a-half after the attack and still not a soul moved outside of their houses as the 11 warriors bounded slowly down the main road waiting impatiently for the imminent attack.

Propane tanks lined the road outside each house, stacked in a pyramid shape like the bottles of the ball-toss game at the county fair. Each tank could hold up to twenty or thirty pounds of homemade explosives and the thick metal cylinder would fragment just like our own grenades, throwing fist-size pieces of metal going Mach Jesus in every direction. We studied every tank as best we could as we bounded past them, but there were too many and time was not on our side. Each minute we spent out in the open was a chance for a well-aimed shot from the shadows of a window or the dense underbrush. Each minute we spent bounding was more water seeped out and a little more weight dug into the shoulders.

There had not been any sign of the gunmen for an hour; we were moving further from the protection of the heavy guns of the firm base that scanned for any movement, ready to suppress and destroy anything that threatened us. Soon we would be beyond their sight range and their help should the worst happen. It was comforting knowing we never just brought a gun to a knife fight; we brought a nuclear weapon. Fire superiority, while looking excessive in the form of the military's budget, was essential for the protection of the troops on the ground.

Nothing says "Don't shoot at me" like the reprisal of better training, better weapons, and superior manpower. No bully on the playground punches a kid twice his size, especially when that kid is surrounded by all his friends and they all have baseball bats. The gunmen had not stayed and fought it out. They had taken off running as soon as they were met by our wall of bullets and grenades.

Two hours into the battle-damage assessment and we found ourselves passing outside of visual contact of the firm base and the protection of the heavy guns on the roof. The 11 operators on the deck were alone in the maze of crooked streets and poorly built houses. The rest of the platoon could not rescue and reinforce us without first breaking down the firm base, a very timely process, and mounting up on the Humvees. There were too few left to send a rescue squad without the firm base becoming open to attack. Forces would be spread too thin.

We bounded down the street out of range, without a safety net, and with exhaustion pulling at our limbs. Our flight suits, made of a fire-resistant material that was not designed for prolonged use in the searing heat, were soaked completely through. The sweat was simply pouring out too fast for the material to dry despite the lack of humidity. Our eyes were angry red with the salt and dust that had beaded up on our brow and washed into the corners of our eyes like the constant drip of a leaky faucet.

We passed by an open gate, the barren driveway cutting across the threshold leading up to a ramshackle house that had bars on every window but no glass. Faded curtains hung motionless in the windless bake of the day. The darkness between the gaps and tears in the cloth seemed impenetrable. We shuddered as the stack began to bound past.

From a blind spot behind the wall hugging the gate, a man walked out into the opening.

"Don't move," one of the stack yelled, leveling his rifle at the man's chest. He stopped moving, less from the verbal command but from the universal language of the gun. When a gun is pointed at you, stop moving. Do not make any sudden movements. Do not talk back.

The man, dressed in a black man-dress and wearing only one leather sandal that looked as if it had seen its last spring, stopped in the middle of the open gate with his hands down at his sides. He was smiling.

The stack had also stopped moving. Confusion rippled out to its ends, who had heard the yelling but otherwise had no idea what was happening. Bronx, who had placed himself near the front, began moving back toward the middle. Safeties were flipped off and holographic red-dot sights were dancing across the man's thin, bony chest as he stared dumbly at the rifles. He had no weapon and there was no blood anywhere on him. Our minds raced.

Suicide vest? Grenade in his pocket? Why is he just standing there? Distraction for a complex ambush? Why the hell is he just standing there smiling? Trigger man for an IED placed on the side of the road? WHY THE FUCK IS HE JUST STANDING THERE?

"He's slow," Bronx yelled, giving the man a wide berth as he circled the gate. "He's mentally challenged!" Still, none of the guns moved.

"Hi," Bronx said and waved at the man. The smile widened and the man waved back sheepishly. "Go back inside," Bronx said, pointing to the crumbling, dark house. "Just go back inside." The man looked back over his shoulder to the house and then back to Bronx. We did not have time to be dealing with a mentally challenged man tagging along with the stack. Every minute we sat in the open street, our survival rate dropped closer to zero. Bronx took a quick step toward the man, as one would do to try to scare off a curious dog. The man, startled, took an involuntary step back.

"Get inside," Sergeant Bronx growled, his normally smooth, calm voice given over to a harsh threat. The man responded finally, shuffling off back toward the house. Without another word, Bronx signaled for the stack to continue moving and began walking back to his place near the front of the stack.

"Gods, I almost shot a slow guy," one of the stack said laughing, more out of a sense of relief than any real comedy. The others around him grinned back with the same sense of relief.

We continued pushing down the roads and side streets, trying to be as thorough as such a small group could. With such a small footprint, it was very possible the insurgents had simply skirted our group and already been secretly transported to a nearby relative's home to receive medical care. It was impossible to know, so we did the best we could and kicked in every single door that could hide someone behind it.

Our lack of water was becoming an issue. What little we had brought had run out, and the heat only seemed to be getting more intense. It had taken us two-and-a-half hours to penetrate so far into the village so thoroughly. Even if it took us half the time to get back, we were in trouble.

Sergeant Bronx called a halt to try to coordinate a resupply from a motorized platoon running missions north of our position. They were scheduled to travel back through the village we were currently searching; it was only down to luck that the insurgents had not been a bit more patient. The streets were horrifically narrow and there were too many windows for too few turret gunners to stop a determined sharpshooter from getting at least one well-placed shot off.

"Get some cover, we're being resupplied in ten," Sergeant Bronx passed. We had stopped on the eastern side of the village that hugged the river like debris left after floodwaters had receded. Every man sought cover, but we were still vulnerable and did not hold the home-court advantage. There were propane-tank stacks everywhere as well as dark windows that peered out onto every possible piece of cover.

I took a knee behind a stone wall that overlooked the river, the narrow cement one-lane bridge that cut across it, and the dirt road that ran parallel to the river on the far side. Just beyond the river was another cement-block village, their family and their allegiance possibly completely different though only separated by a few hundred meters.

"Call anything out that you see," Sergeant Bronx said, checking everyone's positions and ensuring our defense had no gaping holes in it.

For the first time, I did not feel we were the invincible American military. I did not feel as if we could take on any enemy and come out victorious. I suddenly felt very alone and very exposed. For the first time, I realized death was not just a possibility but a very distinct chance. Despite the heat, I felt my blood begin to freeze.

What the hell had I gotten myself into?

Before I had any further time to dwell on my decisions, a man dressed in a gray *dishdasha*, a long man-dress, walked up onto the far side of the river and stopped at the intersection between the bridge and the dirt road running parallel to the water. I placed the crosshairs of my three-times-magnification scope on his frail chest and watched. He was not surprised to see us. Most indigenous would suddenly start, give a look of utter confusion and dread, and then quickly retreat from whatever direction they came from. Instead, the man seemed to be expecting us and mildly amused, smiling to himself.

"Got a guy on the bridge watching us," I shouted. Sergeant Bronx slipped up behind my position and eyeballed the man.

"Keep watching him. If he breaks rules of engagement, take him down," he said over his shoulder as he turned to walk the length of our defenses again.

Our rules of engagements were clear. To engage the man, he must either be actively engaging us with a weapon or be an active forward observer, helping an ambush or IED team, usually spotting and relaying information via radio or phone.

Right then he was just a man amused to see us, which was disconcerting in its own way. No one was ever amused to see us. I took turns looking at the man through the scope and then looking around at the bigger picture with both eyes, to ensure I did not miss something terribly important just because I was too focused on one odd man.

In the distance there was a rumble of diesel engines. Our resupply had entered the northern fringes of the village. I smiled. I could almost taste the bottled water we all so desperately needed.

The man on the bridge heard the engines too and, to my utter horror, he removed a cellphone from his pocket.

"No, don't do it," I whispered to myself and closed my non-shooting eye. "Don't do it, don't do it."

The man placed the phone against his head and said a few words before throwing his head back in a fit of laughter.

And just like that I was suddenly within the legal limits of war to kill a man. I found myself thrust in the very position I had sought out when I signed my life on the dotted line and swore my oath. I did not smile at the thought.

He had given every indication he was a forward observer and I flicked off the safety on my rifle. A human life was suddenly up in the air, awaiting my decision.

But I couldn't do it. I froze and my brain was overwhelmed with conflicting emotions and thoughts.

What if he is just a guy who happened to get a random phone call?

What if his wife has just called him to remind him to pick up some goat milk?

What if he has just called in to the IED team that their target is en route and to arm the device?

What if he is telling the insurgents that all of those propane tanks that were rigged up with homemade explosives were in perfect position to take out my entire group?

What if he cannot see us and has no idea he will find us on the other side of the bridge while on his way to visit his sick father?

What if he has just called for reinforcements?

There had not been a single offensive shot fired by any member of my unit yet. None of the sniper teams had taken a shot. No platoon had ambushed and engaged the insurgents yet. We had just fired back defensively two hours prior, a reaction. That round, that single round sitting in my chamber would be the first one fired aggressively and would be put under the most scrutiny. A misjudgment on my part could lead to a full-blown investigation and my being severely reprimanded.

What if he is just a civilian?

What if my indecision kills every single one of my friends?

What if I am wrong?

What if I am right but fail to act?

And in a split second the decision was stolen from me. The man took two steps behind a cement pillar, the crumbling remains of who-knows-what, and disappeared from sight, not to be seen again.

I braced my body for the explosion of propane tanks, or the alien sensation of my soft pink flesh being torn apart by gunfire.

But none came.

Not that second.

Not that minute.

Not even when the resupply trucks rendezvoused with Sergeant Bronx and dropped off more water and food than could last us a week.

Nothing happened. We finished our BDA and bounded slowly back to our firm base without further incident, the whole time my brain trying to grapple with my choice.

Despite my not killing a seemingly innocent man, I was unsettled with my indecision and would remain so for the rest of my life.

Less than a month later, if I had been put in that exact same situation again, I would have shot the man with the cellphone without faltering.

I do not say this out of anger or hate, or any other petty emotion. I say this because I know what it is to watch friends die terrible, screaming deaths and to believe those deaths were my fault. I know what it is to bear the burden of their terrible shrieks each day, but especially every night for years when the reoccurring nightmares kept me from sleep like the harpies of myth.

It is an easy thing to judge and Monday morning quarterback the actions of adolescent young warriors a thousand miles away. But they had watched as the ones they loved were blown apart, burned, and riddled with bullets. They had to shower off the dried viscera from their skin and the skull fragments from their hair, but it never ever washes out, not fully.

Each time they left the wire, they knew there was a good chance some were not coming back.

CHAPTER 23

It's the "Little" Things in Life

There were bottles of piss everywhere.

The entire rooftop of our firm base smelled of ammonia. Clear plastic water bottles drank during the night—and then refilled one-third, one-half, three-quarters—lined the gray cement wall around all the four rooftop posts. One of the most natural effects of adrenaline withdrawal was the overwhelming urge to urinate. After the exhilaration of clearing the house, the need to piss was paramount. Some of the bottles were less than halfway full and dark brown, indicating whoever had filled them was becoming dehydrated from filling sandbags or hauling them to the rooftop. Most of the bottles were light yellow and still translucent, indicating an adequate level of hydration and the motivation for filling the bottles throughout the night. A handful of bottles were neon yellow, the color a yellow highlighter would make if it was dropped into a bottle of water and left to bleed out. These were the supplement junkies' bottles; horse-pill vitamins taken twice daily, to enhance workout recovery, left the piss inside the bottles syrupy with excess B vitamins.

The piss inside of the bottles did not smell. The bottles had been capped with squat, white plastic tops and were quite secure. It was the piss on the outside of the bottles and on the roof that smelled something awful. The roof was speckled with tiny piss stains no bigger in diameter than a dime. The bottles themselves sported discolored streaks of mineral deposits on the outside of the plastic where the piss had dried in the morning sun. To every watch, it looked as though the watch before them had no bowel control or accuracy whatsoever. We snickered and made jokes at their expense. How could someone miss? The hole of the bottle was not that small, we quipped, as we scanned the horizon and took large swigs of water, our own morning piss percolating inside of us.

We found out one by one that the hole was that small. Rather, it was not the hole that was exceptionally small but our inability to see the tip of our own barrel to aim that plagued our first awkward attempts. The flak jackets we wore were loaded down with eight to ten magazines filled with twenty-eight 5.56 mm rounds each, fragmentation grenades, flash-bangs, night-vision monocles, water bottles, a variety of global-positioning systems, maps, compasses, pens, medical kits, 40 mm 203 grenade rounds, Beretta 9 mm pistols, 9 mm magazines, batteries, radios, protractors, suppressors, throat guards, and a groin protector that hung well past mid-thigh. The urge to urinate overtook us suddenly and, one by one, we crowded ourselves into our sandbag posts with a plastic water bottle we had emptied and little sense of embarrassment. While still watching our sectors of fire, we tried to unbutton our trousers and pull ourselves out. The groin guard, firmly attached to the bottom of the flak jacket, flapped against our hands and impaired any hope of seeing our own manhood past our other gear. With one hand we felt for the opening of the bottle while the other held the Kevlar flap enough out of the way. It was like trying to refuel a plane mid-air, blind.

There it is.

Good.

Now, the tip.

There we go.

Excellent.

Push the tip against the opening of the bottle.

Cockeyed.

Pull back, try again.

Still cockeyed, only in the other direction this time.

Pull back, try again.

All right, that feels lined up.

We craned our heads to try to catch a glimpse of the situation, but the groin protector blocked any chance and we dared not move our alignment. "Good enough" should not be a phrase allowed in a sentence involving piss and a small-mouthed water bottle, but we allowed our warrior arrogance to cloud the issue. It should be aligned; that was good enough to let loose the deluge.

Fuck.

There was piss all over my boots and trousers. The horizontal alignment was spot-on. The vertical alignment, however, was lacking. Never having to piss in a point target before had left us with a gap in our knowledge of our own bodies. The lip of the water bottle split the stream into two camps, one half finding its way into the bottle with the other half ricocheting off the water bottle, staining my trousers, boots, and the roof like a lawn sprinkler. By the time I had realized what was actually happening, since I could not see past my groin guard, it was far too late. I pinched off what was left and realigned, though still poorly. After I finished, I capped the bottle and placed it on the wall by the others.

"I pissed myself," I announced, wiping my hands on my trousers.

"So did I. I think we all did," the other post replied smiling, but there was little consolation in that. We all secretly promised ourselves that the next time we would take more care, that next time we would take the time to properly align. We shook the feeling of failure off and went on with our shift, hoping no one would notice the piss on our boots already drying in the morning sun.

We were relieved by the next watch shift and, as we descended the staircase, we heard them snicker about the piss stains all over the roof. We grinned. They were drinking water by the gallon in anticipation of the noon sun. It was only a matter of time before they found out the truth.

The hole was just that small.

CHAPTER 24

Milataree Jeanyus

After what seemed like a very unsuccessful first month of counter-insurgency operations, it was deemed by whatever higher authority that we needed to get more active in our pursuit. Our clandestine observation posts rarely saw anything out of the ordinary, and our "knock and talks" yielded even less, as we literally asked the townspeople point blank, "Hey, seen any bad guys?" Or, if we were trying to be more subtle, "So, I like your squalor. It's quite, ummm, dirty. Say, if you were a bad guy, what shack on this street might you live in?"

Talking to Coalition forces was frowned upon by the Insurgency and, after we left a house, the insurgents would sometimes visit whoever had spoken to us to voice their objections. The conversations were rather one-sided. Needless to say, few people ever wanted to talk to us knowing their next-door neighbor was watching and ready to call the insurgents—or worse, the neighbors simply were the insurgents.

"No bad guys in this village," everyone would say with a smile.

Great, mission accomplished. Well, that was certainly easy.

Can we go home now?

Our platoon was pulled into a company firm base, a rather large concrete mansion that dominated a vast, open tract of unplanted fields that stretched out in every direction for half a kilometer. We had been called in for the brass to do a face-to-face to plan a follow-on mission given our current one had fizzled out and devolved into us hoping the insurgents had labeled their safehouse "Secret Hideout" like in the old cartoons. A new course of action had been decided and was being disseminated.

As we pulled our convoy of armored vehicles into the yard, Sergeant Bronx growled. The roof bristled with antennas and equipment, an enormous beacon to any insurgent that there dwelled someone of importance in the chain of command. There was little overwatch and virtually no barricades protecting the house from a suicide vehicle laden with explosives. When boots hit the ground, Sergeant Bronx ordered a complete overhaul of the firm base security; we set to work. We were glad for the distraction, as too many officers in tight quarters never brought anything good for the enlisted men.

In addition to rolls and rolls of razor wire being unfurled across every possible entry point, the roof was stocked with an inordinate amount of heavy weapons, each pointing in a different direction with as many overlapping fields of fire possible; .308 sniper rifles and a .50-caliber SASR (special-application scoped rifle) were loaded and placed in the middle of the roof under a waterproof tarp, ready to be shouldered by their highly trained owners in a heartbeat. Even the platoon's M32 grenade launcher (imagine an old Western revolver; now imagine it was built for a giant and shot grenades instead of bullets) was loaded and left waiting.

In the matter of an hour, the firm base had been transformed from a soft, fluffy target into a fortress that even the most suicidal insurgent would think twice about before trying to assault. They would get a simple warning of a red flare being tossed skyward. If they did not heed that warning, the fields of razor wire, the mobile dragon's teeth, and the shouts of the rooftop security, they probably did not have good intentions and would be stopped short of their intended target.

With no rest for the weary, we were sent out on foot patrols to secure the perimeter of the firm base and check for any nasty little surprises that might be lurking just out of line of sight from the rooftop. Without warning, the gray sky opened up and released a deluge like the wrath of an angry god. We groaned and shook our heads, wondering who had just said, "At least it cannot get any worse."

The soil of the lush green fields absorbed the morning rains like a black sponge, turning it from a cracked, dry surface, hard as cement, into slate soup that would suck a boot off and dry as hard as glue on everything it touched. Foot patrols became slow, messy affairs that felt like some kind of nightmare in which no matter how hard we tried to move forward, our cumbersome weapons and equipment weighed us down to a slogging crawl. Patrol times doubled as dry irrigation ditches turned into impassable mires of unknown depths.

I stumbled and fell constantly while running point, trying to remain alert while picking out solid footing for the team on quickly degrading terrain. I swore each time I fell on my ass, much to the amusement of the rest of the guys. We were hours behind our projected return time and, when we made our final turn back toward the firm base, we all breathed a sigh of relief. It would be good to finally get out of the rain.

Right on cue, the rain stopped as we made our way the final 300 meters into the protected perimeter of our razor wire and small-arms range.

Just our luck.

We tromped into the firm base and began removing our cumbersome armor turtle shells when the crack of a rifle resounded off the walls. It was a single shot.

A sniper.

"Roof," Sergeant Bronx bellowed and with that the anthill was disturbed. Men in every state of dress, but fully armored, poured out onto the roof, ducking below the high cement walls surrounding the roof.

"Which direction?" someone yelled, and the roof watch pointed to the east, a tiny cluster of houses on the fringes of the enormous soggy fields.

Without hesitation the platoon medic grabbed up the M32 grenade launcher and aimed it in the general direction that had been pointed out, lobbing all six of the 40 mm high-explosive grenades into the sky in rapid succession.

For a moment, everyone stopped to watch. The cluster of target buildings was somewhere around eight hundred meters away, twice the range of the M32 in ideal conditions. After a moment of dead calm, six massive explosions blew mud a hundred feet into the air as the shells detonated in the middle of soggy fields, just shy of three hundred meters from the firm base. The explosions were deafening but still not as loud as the cheer that went up from all those on the roof in witness.

"That was fucking awesome," someone cheered.

"Why would you even do that?" one of the team leaders ribbed the medic. The medic grinned.

"We might never get another chance to fire that thing and I wanted to see what it could do," he said, chuckling.

Sergeant Bronx positioned the rooftop defenders swiftly. Most of us were simply ordered to duck behind the cement wall out of sight while those shielded behind two-inch-thick bulletproof glass scanned every inch of the horizon for signs of a follow-on. If someone was foolish enough to take a second shot, our three snipers, five heavy weapons, and fifteen rifles would rain down destruction in a matter of seconds.

We squatted, eager and grinning. A minute passed and no one moved.

Two minutes.

Three minutes.

Four minutes and our legs began to burn with lactic acid in our awkward squatting positions.

Five minutes and our combat readiness devolved into witty bitching and uncontrollable squirming.

"They are sending out a second platoon in Humvees to check it out. We're overwatch," Sergeant Bronx relayed, his head tilted as he listened to the orders being passed. We stood and watched as a four-truck convoy of Humvees raced out of the hard-packed driveway and into the fields, making a straight line for the cluster of houses the shot was presumed to be taken from.

"Well, that's a terrible idea," a quiet voice said behind me. I turned and found one of the company level officers watching the overly armored vehicles fan out into a wedge formation. "No one read your team's report about the mud, I guess."

"Sir?" I said, unable to repress a grin from my face. The good captain returned the grin and sighed.

"They might make it halfway," he said, shaking his head. "Those Humvees weren't even designed to carry a quarter of the armor they have bolted onto them. It's like putting a tank turret over a Volkswagen Beetle."

The good captain was wrong. They did not make it a quarter of the way. The lead Humvee suddenly nosedived deep into a patch of mud and sunk up to its hood with a loud whine of its overworked engine. The rest of the convoy stopped short and surveyed the lead vehicle, passing communications on their platoon's net that we could not hear. After a minute, a foolproof plan must have been agreed upon.

The second vehicle revved its engine, spun its tires for a moment before gaining traction, and then sped forward at full tilt in a line that would take it 10 feet to the left of the lead vehicle. It roared, churning up mud and speeding forward for a moment, only to come to a lurching halt exactly in line with the lead vehicle. Both vehicles revved their engines for a moment as if the situation might have changed and then fell silent.

"Well, that was something," the good captain beside me chuckled and turned to survey the rooftop defenses. "Your platoon looks good. I have ..."

The good captain was cut off by a loud roar of a diesel engine, and he quickly turned back to the half-stuck convoy. His face took on a look of horror as a third vehicle raced forward, this time at a 45-degree angle away from the others.

"No, no, no, no, no," the good captain moaned. "Who is leading that convoy? Benny Hill?"

Before anyone could answer his question, the third truck came to a sudden and completely expected halt as it sunk into the black bog of foreign soil. Everyone on the roof tried to stifle the amusement that was bubbling up, but all it took was one snicker and everyone exploded in laughter. Even the good captain could not help but hold his stomach as he wiped a tear from his eye. He struggled to regain his composure, shaking his head as he looked out on the three stranded vehicles. He keyed his radio and smiled.

"Gods, someone call a wrecker here before they send that last vehicle to free the other three."

It took the wrecker, an enormous tracked vehicle, three hours to arrive at the firm base and free the stuck vehicles.

Presumably, the sniper escaped.

Or laughed himself to death.

CHAPTER 25

The Night Written a Hundred Times

My therapist at the VA hospital said it was not my fault. My therapist said these things happen, and that I cannot blame myself. He told me to write out what happened, again, and again, and again.

My therapist said each time I wrote down the events it would help me see how illogical I was being, how I was trapped in a vicious cycle of guilt and blame. He said each time I wrote about that night, the reoccurring nightmare may lose a little of its stranglehold on me.

For six months, I slept only one out of four nights without waking up crying and sweating through the sheets, unable to fall back asleep for fear of slipping back into the nightmare.

So I wrote it, again, and again, and again.

I killed four of our own men.

It was a good idea on paper. Everything always is.

It is said a military plan is perfect until the first boots hit the ground; then it goes straight to hell. Good intentions and keen intellect can produce a finely crafted battle plan, but it can never account for everything. It never factors in chaos, how absolutely strange and counter-intuitive human beings will react in a life-threatening situation.

No plan is ever drawn up with malice, or with posthumous medals in mind. Succeeding earns medals. Succeeding saves lives. Every battle plan is crafted to succeed.

Our battalion commander was a man who wanted to succeed and bring every one of his boys home safe. He stuck his neck out on several occasions for his warriors and planned our every move to ensure we minimized our exposure to the dangers of war. He was an admirable man and he cared for each soldier under his command.

But there is no accounting for everything in a plan.

Our battle plan was for the whole battalion, about one hundred and twenty shooters, split into small teams of six or seven men, to cordon off an enormous area of land, sealing it off from the rest of the world while assault elements swept through the houses looking for any insurgents, or signs of insurgent activities. No one would be allowed to leave or enter and our unexpected blitz into the area would snare some top-level insurgents with minimal risk. Either they would stand their ground for our assault units to deal with or they would be driven like frightened deer into the waiting guns of those manning the corners of the cordon.

That was the plan anyway. Problems arose the moment we hit the ground.

We were too few shooters with too much land to cover effectively due to the unexpected amount of lush vegetation that reduced our visibility considerably. For a land referred to as "the Sandbox," it was still something of a jungle near the river.

Worse, it was not our land and the two-dimensional aerial maps were no match for generations of firsthand knowledge. We did not know the goat paths through the islands of vegetation that could hide men and supplies. We did not know which cluster of houses "supported" us and who was watching us with malice behind their smiles, or who would point a finger in the right direction or use that finger for a slow, steady squeeze in our direction.

We could only hold the line in our designated area and do our duty.

Our platoon's particular spot was on the southwest corner of the cordon where the only single-lane road staggered on east after a 90-degree elbow. We were tasked to occupy that elbow and try our best to keep eyes on both axis points.

The major problem was that the road was elevated about ten feet above the fields it sliced through; the furthest we could see in either direction was 200 meters before the road snaked around another cluster of palms and dense vegetation, as if the engineer who had originally designed the road had been blind drunk the day he had staked it out on the ground. By the map's reckoning, we were supposed to have almost a thousand meters sightline both north and east, far past the next team. We did not. No platoons or teams anywhere had the sightlines that were planned for.

The cordon had become one giant sieve without any means to cover every escape route, or even a fifth of them. Our giant spider web of overlapping fields of fire and protection had devolved into tiny islands of armored Humvees, all fending for themselves, while our assault units did their best to cover the treacherous farmlands at half the speed that had been planned for.

"This isn't good," Sergeant Bronx muttered as he strode up and down our lines, five armored trucks spread out in an "L" shape, all parked within sight of one another for covering fire. Our platoon commander, Lieutenant Rusher, nodded his head and continued to monitor the battalion chatter on the net with a grim look. "Sir, this really isn't good," Sergeant Bronx repeated. "We have been sitting here too long."

We had been static for almost twelve hours, sitting in our trucks eating MREs while we tried to pass the time playing the "Would you rather" game. The game never lost steam as we rotated out our watchman every half an hour to keep fresh eyes on the situation.

"Would you rather clog the toilet on a first date or first day at a new job?"

We had not seen anything suspicious all day.

"Would you rather lose a foot or a hand?"

The owners of the few houses nearest to our position had brought out flat bread and tried to beg for food.

"Would you rather be homeless or go to jail for the rest of your life?"

They played soccer in their yard and invited us to play.

"Would you rather fight Bruce Lee or Mike Tyson?"

We politely declined and continued to watch our tiny corner of the bigger picture, which looked more like a Sunday afternoon in any suburb back home, not the big, bad "Sandbox" we had been warned about.

"Would you rather be buried or cremated?"

Still, we kept a watchful eye on every inch we could see. It was not much, but it was ours.

"Would you rather die now gloriously, in a great ball of fire, or later in obscurity?"

"This really isn't good, Sir," Sergeant Bronx said, marching up and down the full length of our position, yet again. He looked like a starved panther behind bars at a zoo, tensely pacing as he awaited the opportunity to spring on anyone foolish enough to draw near. Based on his brief stories, he had been in combat zones the rest of us could only have imagined, a warrior without peer in the entire battalion and a warrior used to the ebb and flow of battle. "If we aren't out of here by nightfall, things could get much harder for us, Sir."

"Noted, Sergeant, but we hold until ordered otherwise," Lieutenant Rusher replied. He would never openly agree with the sergeant in front of the men, but his tone suggested deep reservations of his own.

Night fell, despite our prayers that the assault elements hurried the hell up before the entire battalion was caught out in the open and in the dark.

Sunset was not a long, drawn-out affair. Only minutes after the sun touched the horizon, the world fell into complete obscurity. Illumination was almost zero, the moon refusing to show its face in the night sky. Our visibility plummeted to however far we could focus with our night-vision monocles, which was surprisingly far given such a small battery device, but not nearly as far as we hoped given the entire countryside was out to get us.

From the moment we were inducted into the community, we were drilled that darkness was our greatest asset. We were silent, nocturnal killers who wore the darkness like a cloak, and the darkness protected us like a mother when we were deep in her bosom. We moved in darkness and we ambushed in darkness.

But darkness is a two-way street.

Suddenly, we were the known quantity, an enemy easily studied in the bright desert sunshine and tracked by the deep rumble of our diesel engines when we were to leave our position, despite the darkness. Our mother had abandoned us.

Finally, the order was given for our planned withdrawal. But the original plan had called for slow daylight driving. We would creep along carefully knowing brother platoons were only a klick away if contact was made. It was no longer daylight and, no matter how vigilant we were, any edge we had possessed had been lost to the absolute darkness. We could only react now, "prevention" slipping away with the last of the sun's rays an hour before.

"Get out of the driver's seat. I'm driving," Boom said, opening the driver-side door to our Humvee.

"Are you serious?" I said, unable to believe what I had just heard.

For the entire deployment workup, I drove the team's Humvee. Every training exercise and every road trip we went on, it was me behind the driver's wheel, practicing for when we would have to do it for real, for when we hit the Sandbox. Everyone needed to know their jobs and be able to do them in their sleep. For hundreds of hours, I had sat behind the wheel of our Humvee, and only a handful of times had I been "killed" or "wounded" in training exercises, forcing me to relinquish my position.

There is a certain feeling of control that goes with driving a vehicle rather than being a passenger. A passenger is a puppet of fate and must suffer events he cannot direct. Everyone has gotten into the "I want to drive" fight with a friend or loved one. It is not that you do not trust them; it is simply that you trust yourself a whole lot more. It is not a new fight. It is as old as the first animal-drawn vehicle. He who holds the reins has control.

That control, that feeling of absolute power to manage and manipulate events as they occur, was suddenly being taken away.

"You kidding, Boom? You told me I was driving the entire mission."

"Not kidding."

Worse still, I was put up in the turret to man the heavy machine gun. It would be my job as lead turret gunner to ensure no vehicle approached our convoy from the front or sides, to watch the entire 180 degrees for possible rocket-propelled grenades or snipers, check the road for improvised explosive devices, guide the driver through situations where the height advantage was useful, and also keep track of how dispersed the rest of the convoy was becoming.

I did not argue further with Boom. He was above me in the pecking order and it was my obligation to do as he said.

It is widely hypothesized special operations' lack of disciplined rank structure, as we called each other by first, last, or nicknames without rank, was a travesty and led to myriad problems with command. I could not agree less. Boom was not only my assistant team leader, the micromanaging sledgehammer of the team as opposed to the remote father figure of the team leader, but he was my great friend. I respected him and respected our friendship, and it was because of this friendship and respect I would follow his commands despite any personal beliefs that opposed them. I find I can say no to a stranger when told to do something dangerous; it's much harder to say no to a friend.

I did not agree, but I followed orders.

I slid up into the turret and checked my heavy gun, stashing my rifle in an easily accessible position in case the worst should happen and the heavy gun suddenly stopped working in a time of need. Everything seemed in working order, and I prepped my road flare in case of unexpected oncoming traffic.

I shook my head dejectedly in the darkness before flipping my "nod" down over my eye. As I looked around with my night-vision monocle, my stomach sank as I realized how very small a window into the big, bad world it made.

"Convoy is moving," Ballas announced with the radio hook hanging down from inside his helmet. "We're moving. You good up there?"

I lied. I was nowhere near good, but no amount of stalling would make it any better.

"Yep."

We began to creep along and I felt my knuckles burning as I death-gripped the cocking-handle assembly of the big weapon, ready to rack it back at the first sign of danger and charge it with black-tipped, armor-piercing 7.62 mm rounds. My other hand was draped across the top of the feed tray to steady the weapon, while holding onto a red-star cluster flare that would be the first step in my escalation of force with unknown situations.

Flare. Warning shot. Engine block. Kill shot.

The little green world looked surreal as I swung my head back and forth, checking the windows and doorways of the village down the steep embankment to our left. Everything swam in unnatural shades of green that terrified me and at the same time made my eyes tired. My world had been reduced to 20 fuzzy degrees of dream-vision.

As the lead vehicle, we were given a head start before the rest of the convoy began to rumble behind us, a kind of scout element helpful in identifying ambushes before the rest of the convoy got too close. I could hear the rest of our vehicles, but I had not turned my head to check on their dispersion yet. We had traveled only 200 meters past the first bend in the road, which we could not see around during our cordon.

"Are we up?" Ballas yelled. I began to turn to see if the entire convoy was within sight.

Thunder and daylight.

My brain reeled at the sudden idea the sun had inexplicably risen and illuminated the world around me, while a great summer storm had broken at the exact same moment.

It was not until I was turned completely around that I realized it was not daylight reflecting across every surface. It was fire, the biggest bonfire I had ever seen. A 60-foot-high, writhing column of bright orange and yellow almost twenty-five feet across had sprung up from the ground just behind us. I gasped involuntarily, bewildered fear grabbing my insides and twisting them until I thought I would not be able to take another breath again.

The enormous column of flame spouting from the road did not terrify me. It was what was inside the column of flame that would forever haunt my dreams.

The next Humvee in our convoy was floating 20 feet off the ground inside the flames, doing a glacially slow front flip in place, as if suspended in liquid fire.

"Stop," I screamed. But I did not say it aloud, only silently mouthed the word that was lost to the unadulterated horror gripping my mind.

"Stop," I hollered again, but it only came out as a whisper.

"Stop," I finally managed to say just loud enough for Boom to slam on the brakes.

Time stopped. Metal and flesh hung in the air like a terrible nightmare, frozen in the brilliant flames like it was trapped in amber. After the initial terrible rumble and whoosh, there seemed to be no sound accompanying the chaos as my mind began to narrow the horror into fewer senses to stave off complete collapse. The sight alone threatened my boundaries. The Humvee danced impossibly amid the flames, defying gravity as it tumbled.

Had I the ability to simply disconnect from my brain forever at that moment I would have, just to escape the unrelenting horror of bearing witness to the madness. But I could not. I watched, frozen, as the world began to move again in slow motion, as if I was being forced to sear each individual frame of the dreadfulness into my memory before being allowed to move onto the next.

Ernie, the turret gunner of the vehicle, was awkwardly swimming 10 feet in the air out in front of the column of fire, his arms and legs flailing instinctually to try to find equilibrium. He had been tossed like a stone out of a catapult but was saved from the fire. Some of the doors had blown open from the overpressure, vomiting out two parodies of the human form, living, breathing torches covered in burning diesel fuel. Their limbs flailed wildly, fanning the flames as their mouths opened and closed in inaudible screams that died in their blackened throats.

After a full, gradual rotation, the Humvee crashed back onto its melting tires in a brilliant shower of flames and black, choking smoke. It came to a rest immediately, an enormous inferno of cooking gear and meat.

One of the figures thrown from the vehicle had been tossed over the embankment and was running around in the field wildly, his body ablaze, and the 80 pounds of gear wrapped around him fusing together as it burned and melted. The more he ran from the pain, the greater the flames grew. His lungs were seared black, so he ran silently among the vegetables and irrigation ditches, a living, dancing effigy.

The other burning figure thrown from the side of the vehicle slapped the crumbling road and made no attempt to flee the pain, only to lay there shaking and twitching as he opened and closed his mouth in a silent plea.

He was not dead, but he silently begged to be. Death would have been the greatest mercy. He would last three weeks in an endless pain that no medical intervention would touch, over eighty percent of his body charred beyond recognition.

The turret gunner landed heavily, but miraculously still able to move. He bounced twice and stood up as soon as he stopped moving. Without a second thought, Ernie ran back to the blazing inferno without the slightest bit of hesitation. Despite the hundreds of rounds of ammunition cooking off, Ernie dove into the raging fire and attempted to pull his other team members from the burning wreck. The flame-retardant material of his gloves and his sleeves melted under a heat they were never built to withstand.

Ernie burned. He burned the skin on his hands and arms willfully and knowingly. He pushed his own flesh into the flames to save his friends. Ernie burned himself out of love for men who were not his own blood, men he had only met six months before. That is the greatest, most selfless form of love possible.

But he could not save anyone and was pulled away from the flames by Sergeant Bronx, kicking and demanding to be let go despite the skin on his hands melting. Bronx held tight. There was no one left in the vehicle alive to save. We could see their blackened husks in between the sheets of fire.

Our medic took over the immediate scene. He never raised his voice, only gave orders in the calm manner of a man who was in complete control of himself.

I, on the other hand, was not in control of myself.

I twirled around, racked back the charging handle of my heavy machine gun, and spun the turret in the direction of the village we had stopped directly in front of. I narrowed my vision down the front-sight assembly, visible only because of the pyre, and aimed that beautiful, perfect implement of death at the first doorway to catch my eye. I pulled the dense plastic stock close into my shoulder and began my slow, steady squeeze of the trigger, bracing myself for the kick since I had removed the T&E* for quicker target acquisition at close range.

I prayed for movement. I prayed to all the gods I could think of for some poor bastard to stick his head out of the doorway, or peek around a window cover to check on the devastation, so I could watch his face disappear in a fine pink mist. I promised my soul and other priceless things to the darker gods, if they would only grant me the chance to enact my revenge, to slaughter mercilessly those who had perpetrated such a horrific, cowardly act. I did not want justice, no trial and jury. I wanted blood, pain, and suffering.

Kill them all. Every single last person I could reach out and touch with my black tips.

Some were innocent, I knew. Some might have no idea what had just occurred. Some would have known but would have been too scared to warn us for fear of their entire family being executed. I would pity them and cry for them later perhaps, but not at the moment. Right then, they were all one, a villainous them.

---

* Traverse and elevation mechanism.

Some were innocent, but not most. Most had smiled through their teeth at us and quietly kept watch as an improvised explosive device was buried in the road only 100 meters from their front doors. They had come up to our static position and engaged us in happy conversation, acting as diversion, while their brothers and fathers were busy planning our death. They had smiled and offered us bread while they kept our guard low and our attention fixed.

And their plan was ruthless. On top of the already deadly improvised explosive device, they had buried an unknown amount of five-gallon diesel containers to burn those who may have survived the blast. It was the fire that killed at least two of the four warriors. They were untouched by the explosion itself, being thrown from the vehicle by the overpressure inside the vehicle. They may have had concussions and little else had it just been an explosion, but it was fire that kissed them for the last time. The villagers had planned for our deaths to be painful and terrible beyond comprehension.

Kill them all.

They all knew, even if they did not help.

Every single one of them knew.

Kill. Them. All.

A thousand lives for each one of my brothers.

A thousand, hateful lives for each of the beautiful lives of my friends.

I did not fire. It was not a moment of clarity, or a sudden realization such actions would be morally and legally wrong that stayed my hand. There were simply no targets to fire on. I could only tremble and gnash my teeth, fingering the trigger while I willed my enemies to show their faces.

The insurgents would never be so foolish. Though they had destroyed an entire Humvee and killed four men, our remaining convoy was still bristling with enough heavy weapons to completely level a small village if given the justification. A single shot fired in our direction, and the whole of our barely controllable wrath would reign down until all weapons ran dry. They stayed in the shadows and watched us rage without vent.

They sat in the shadows and watched us burn.

Kill them all.

Kill them all.

And then, kill me.

Twelve hours later, we sat in our team room in silence as the chaplain did his best to console our losses. Two warriors had died at the site of the explosion. Two more warriors were burned beyond recognition but holding on, more than eighty percent of their bodies charred black wherever the flame kissed their beautiful, delicate skin. No one had any delusions about their survival. It was not a matter of if; it was only a matter of how many weeks and days.

Lieutenant Rusher entered the room and waited for the chaplain to finish. The chaplain nodded to him and slipped out of the room quietly.

"EOD[†] just came back with their summary," Lieutenant Rusher said, his eyes bright red and puffy with irritation. I winced and felt bile fill the back of my throat as I slumped forward. I already knew what he was about to say. I felt the judgement deep in my bones as soon as I saw the column of flame. I stared at the floor, unable to look any of my brothers in the eye.

"It was not a command-detonated IED," Lieutenant Rusher said. There had been no triggerman, no buried wire that ran from the explosives off into the vegetation that simply needed a small battery to initiate the device. I felt my body tighten as I prepared for the next sentence.

"It was a vehicle-initiated device," he announced. "Christmas light configuration. They ran it over."

The guilt was overwhelming. I could not breathe and wanted to run from the room, but I found my whole body had locked up tight.

It was my responsibility as the lead turret gunner to watch for such devices on the road in front of our vehicle, to yell out when I saw a strange lump of dirt piled up over an initiation device that looked like the bell hose at a gas station or a wide, flat square of dirt-covered metal that resembled a bathroom scale. It was my responsibility to ensure the safety of the convoy from IEDs.

And I failed.

I failed and good men died because of my failure.

I was not careful enough and did not see the initiation device. I had let it pass right under my gaze and under the tires of beautiful human beings who were doing their jobs, watching the flanks to protect me, confident the point vehicle would not let an IED slip through. Men were relying on me to have their backs, to protect them from quarters they could not watch, and I had failed.

Their deaths were my failure.

Their last gasping breaths of burning flesh and diesel fumes were on my head.

I wanted to die. I wanted the pain in my heart to end.

I begged the gods to return those men to the earth and take me instead. I silently begged and pleaded they should take me instead.

Take me, I screamed into the void.

Take me, it was my fault. Give my brothers their lives back. Give them back to their mothers and their fathers, to their wives and siblings. Please, take me. Take me instead. Give me all their suffering and their death.

Punish me, not them. It was not their fault.

Please, please kill me.

---

† Explosive ordinance disposal, the crazy bomb-disposal warriors who swept and disarmed IEDs in-country.

But I did not die. I sat shaking, wishing for death and knowing it would not come to me then. Their deaths were mine to suffer. There would be no escape from the guilt and the shame that crept into my every thought and emotion.

Death would be a liberation; I knew there was no freedom for me.

A week later, we were ushered into the team room only to be greeted by the chaplain clutching a Bible. One of the two warriors had succumbed to his extensive burns and died.

We bowed our heads in a moment of silence and I daydreamed of slipping my mouth around the wide barrel of my breeching shotgun as the chaplain spoke words of peace and serenity I would never know again.

But one idea stayed my hand.

Revenge.

The chaplain met us again two weeks later as we piled into our team room to unload our heavy weapons after a mission. We slipped off our plate carriers and stood fingering the loose threads of our beige flight suits until the entire platoon was assembled, a fifth of the original shooters no longer with us as we stood shoulder to shoulder. The second warrior had finally succumbed after three weeks of pain that even the strongest painkiller could not fully mask.

I prayed to the gods for death, but again it did not come. I had lost hope for so simple a solution to the overwhelming guilt I felt each time I looked around at the faces of the men beside me. I had been put back into the driver's seat of our vehicle. The two minutes I had been given the responsibility for the safety of our platoon had been enough.

And so I write it again, and again, and again.

No Rest for the Wicked

Less than a full day after the explosion, we left the wire on another mission. Stiff upper lip and all that. This was war.

Dinner and a Show

The predeployment briefings were quite clear: do not eat any of the local cuisine or imbibe any liquids not from a sealed bottle of known origin.

No exceptions.

It was an easy rule to follow at first. Everything about our surroundings assaulted our senses in such a way that made the stomach clench; any idea of hunger dissolved into a mild sense of nausea. The smell of burning rubber and rotting vegetables did little to whet our appetites for the first month.

I can remember the first time we were given an MRE in Basic. The future warriors oohed and ahhed as we ripped open the vault-like plastic casing and dumped our treasures in front of us. It was like Christmas morning. We were shown how to make pudding from the cocoa powder mix, a creamer packet, and a little water. We nearly lost our minds when we were shown how to use the heating pouch to warm our meal to a few degrees above room temperature. MREs seemed like manna from heaven and we looked forward to the day when we were allowed to take as many as we could hump out on mission.

After a month in the desert, the mere sight of the tan package made my stomach knot. I loathed everything about them, and dreaded whenever we had to pick out eight or ten from the cardboard box of assorted meals to pack for our next mission. It was always a choice of the lesser of 12 flavored evils.

There was no right choice. There were only choices that seemed less horrible than the next. The major decision was always a palatable main-meal pouch and no worth-while sides, or a completely inedible main meal with some decent accoutrements.

When the first perfect stranger offered us candy—in the form of fresh vegetables, hummus, and fresh baked flat bread—I took it without question.

Our platoon had taken over a house to hold out in for a day before moving out again after dark. Our host, if one was to call a pseudo-hostage such a thing, was most gracious. He told stories of how the insurgents had come into his village and threatened the heads of the families with great violence if they did not hide some of the insurgents by pretending they were visiting family. Some of the families had refused and the insurgents were swift and cruel in their punishment. The families retaliated, and suddenly the 75-square-mile area of farmland became a checkerboard of families who were either in bed with the insurgents or fought them tooth and nail.

To celebrate such an unexpected pleasure of helping the forces aligned against the insurgents, our host prepared a feast. The women of the house brought out trays the size of truck tires piled high with steaming bread, freshly picked vegetables, and thick spreads that resembled hummus but came in myriad different flavors and textures.

"Eat," he said beaming, putting his hand to mouth in the universal sign.

"You first," Sergeant Bronx replied, smiling. Poison was not outside the realm of possibility and Sergeant Bronx took no chances with the warriors in his charge. The interpreter translated and the host nodded his understanding. He sampled a bit of everything to show that none of it was tainted and then beamed again.

"Eat!"

"If you eat this, you all know there is a good chance of Montezuma's revenge. So, eat at your own risk," Sergeant Bronx said.

I did not hesitate. I grabbed a handful of warm, earthy bread and shoved it in my gaping maw without a second thought. I followed it with some vegetables slathered in various dips, quickly followed by more bread. There was a white, milky substance that tasted like sour cream, but in drink form, and I sloshed down even more bread with the liquid. Clark sat down beside me smiling and the rest of the platoon looked on as we made a significant dent in one of the enormous platters of food. We ate and ate, laughing quietly at the knowledge that in a day, perhaps less, our digestive tracts would in all probability be overwhelmed by bacteria foreign to our bodies, leading to an indiscriminate purge. The baby would be thrown out with the bathwater and there would be nothing to do but ride it out.

"Crazy idiots," someone mumbled as he shook his head at our satiated faces and round, full bellies.

We thought we had been spared but, two days later, our bodies went into full revolt. Nothing could have prepared me for the utter lack of control.

A single gurgle and I had, at most, twenty seconds to find a "safe" place to squat down before my body simply let go. I spent an entire day within arm's reach of a toilet on base. I would drop down with my flight suit at my ankles and sweat profusely, as all the water I had tried to replace in the previous three hours sprayed out of me like a showerhead in terrible spasms. Nothing stayed in my body for more than a few hours and, no matter what color it started out as, it all came out a stygian black that only had a chance of being considered "normal" in hospice facilities.

"You, Spears, and I are going on a mission tonight," Ballas said with a grin. My stomach gurgled in reply and I bent forward. "Told you not to eat that shit."

"I'll be fine. It's much better now," I lied.

"Let's hope so. I need you tonight. Sniper OP looking for a shithead that is suspected to be digging in an IED on a stretch of road we use occasionally."

There was no better mission than a long-range ambush on an unsuspecting fiend. The risk was wonderfully low while the payoff was disproportionately high. The only problem was gambling on exactly which patch of road the insurgent might decide to take the shovel to rarely paid off. Still, the chance to watch Ballas put a round center-mass into an insurgent who never even saw us was worth whatever gastrointestinal hell awaited me. Whatever microbe was swimming around in my guts would run its course either way.

We snuck into a cement house under the cover of darkness and rounded up the family. We handed the father a clearly printed index card that read in Arabic: "We are U.S. military forces conducting an important mission. We need you to hand over all cell phones and weapons in the house. Please stay in the room we show you and do not come out until we tell you it is safe. Thank you for your cooperation."

While Spears kept security from the rooftop, Ballas held security on the family while I looked for a room without windows in the house. Once found, I searched every possible hiding place, of which there were few. Once we were confident there were no weapons or means of communication hidden away, we corralled the family inside the sterile room. We put our fingers to our lips; they nodded in understanding. I stacked some empty tin cans against the door as an early warning device should the family open the door before we came to get them. We slipped up onto the roof and Ballas deployed his scoped rifle while we set up our security.

Two hours later, our unsuspecting digger had not arrived.

My stomach gurgled and I inhaled sharply. "Going down," I whispered into my headset.

Ten seconds.

I scrambled across the roof and stumbled down into the stairwell.

Seven seconds.

I tore at my zipper as my stomach groaned loudly.

Five seconds.

I ripped down my flight suit and held open a wag-bag underneath my squatting body, one hand in front and one behind, on the landing of the stairwell.

One second.

There was a contraction in my torso that left me breathless and gnashing my teeth as I tried to keep from shaking so hard that I might tumble down the next flight of stairs to the ground floor. I heard someone stir in the family's room.

Time's up.

I could not breathe in between contractions; I gave up on holding the bag. I dropped it and gripped the handrail with one hand, while keeping my rifle clutched tightly into my shoulder, and trained on the door the family was hopefully sound asleep behind, with the other. Aiming for the wag bag had ceased to be a priority.

"Oh my God," I moaned as the contractions brought thick beads of hot sweat to my red, strained face. "Fuck," I whimpered as I felt my body kick repeatedly, my abs pulling so tight between breaths I thought my spine would snap.

Things could not get any worse, I thought.

The cans in front of the door toppled over with a shrill metal clatter. I threw the barrel of my rifle across my arm, straining to keep my body upright, and with a flick of my thumb a red holographic crosshair suddenly appeared, floating between my eye and the doorway. I steadied myself for the firefight that was about to ensue, as my body spasmed and evacuated black water into what I hoped was a plastic bag and not my flight suit.

We had placed a lamp beside the door and erected a small, hasty barricade in the stairwell to block the view of anyone standing in the doorway to the windowless room. It would take but a moment for their eyes to adjust and make out my silhouette, but a moment was all I would need.

The door swung open a foot and I pulled the rifle tight into my shoulder. Despite the well-built automatic rifle gripped in my hand, I had never felt so vulnerable in all of my life. I had always hoped I would not shit my pants after being shot, but I had never figured on being shot while in the middle of shitting my pants.

A little four-year-old boy with enormous brown eyes slipped through the doorway and toddled up to our hasty barricade.

I moved the crosshair back to the doorway as the boy stood silently at the foot of the stairs. My body, suddenly aware the boy was not a threat, released a terrible wave of contractions that made me shake violently.

"Ohgoddddddd," I whimpered, my voice drowned out by the outrageous sounds coming from my shaking hips. "Ohmyfuckkkkkk."

The boy continued to stare up at the barricade and suddenly opened his hands up to the sky and shrugged.

"Mistah," he called out. "Okay, mistah?"

"Fuuuuckkkk," I moaned as I shook and drooled from my clenched mouth.

"Mistah, okay?"

"Go away," I moaned.

"Mistah," the boy said, turning his head to the sound of my voice. "Okay, mistah?" He extended his hands forward, fingers splayed, in supplication.

"Go back to sleep," I whispered and then grunted.

"Mistah?"

"Pleeeeeeease go back to bed," I begged, tears running down from the sides of my cheeks. The boy stared at the dark shadow moaning from behind the crude, childish fort constructed out of sheet metal and blankets.

"Okay, mistah?"

"Yes," I mewled. I tried to think of the Arabic word for yes and tossed out the two possibilities that popped in my mind. One of the words must have been right, because the boy cocked his head sideways in skepticism and then dropped his arms to his sides after a moment. He stepped back away from the stairs and moved silently to the crack in the door. Before slipping through, he turned once more.

"Okay, mistah?"

"Yes, yes," I whimpered and threw out the magic words again. He shrugged, slipped back inside the room, and pulled the door closed behind him.

I lowered my rifle and grasped the banister with both hands, laying my sweating forehead down across my forearms as I sobbed quietly.

And then as fast as it had come on, it was gone. My stomach was mercifully quiet and my chest slowed its heaving until my breath was steady and even again. I took a deep breath, wiped my brow, and then cleaned myself up with a wet nap. It was like cleaning up the Exxon oil spill with a bathroom handcloth.

More than anything in the world, I suddenly wanted a drink of water. I crawled back into my position on the roof underneath the beautiful stars and drank deep from my Nalgene.

"You okay?" Ballas said over our three-man net. I could hear his grin in the question.

"Think I just scared the shit outta some kid. I think he thought I was dying on his staircase. I kinda felt like it there for a minute."

"Everything good?" He was not asking about my stomach.

"All asleep and contained."

CHAPTER 28

One Square Kilometer

There was to be a major raid, the type of mission that got the platoon all hot and bothered when the order was given in our small briefing room. Raids entailed everything we loved about our jobs: breaching, close-quarters combat, and the absolute rush of entering a building, when we would flow like water through the structure, every room a complete mystery as to what waited for us on the other side of the door. It was a dreadful, adrenaline-fueled gameshow.

The mission itself was a hasty raid on a time-sensitive target that had just popped up on the radar in our area of operation. The compound he was supposedly holed up in was small—three two-room cement buildings—and, with the element of surprise, it would be done in less than a minute if everything went as planned. Sergeant Bronx gave out truck assignments and went over where they would be parked during the raid itself to allow no escape for runners, while we grinned and shook with excitement.

"Given that this is hasty and we don't have time to coordinate exactly when, there will be no IED sweeps in the hours prior to our going in."

Our team—Ballas, Boom, Spears, and Clark, with me driving—was still the suicide vehicle, the first vehicle in our platoon convoy and the one most likely to trigger a pressure-plate improvised explosive device (IED). That made every detail about the route to our target and the route out our grave concern. EOD, the crazy bomb-fondlers, usually performed IED sweeps regularly on the routes most traveled. It was regular enough the enemy was used to it and would not correlate an IED sweep with a raid or any other action. Without a sweep within the past few hours, chances were high something would be waiting for us. Worse, the route to the target was a name that made us cringe and our hearts tighten each time we heard it.

River Road was a death trap, a natural ambush site that could not have been better suited to putting our convoys in a neat little row, like the hard-to-miss targets of the boardwalk shooting galleries. The road was narrow, only wide enough for two very slender cars to pass with an extraordinary amount of care and concentration; otherwise, it was a one-lane road for a Humvee. There was no break-down lane.

The entire road was six to ten feet higher than the dark, loamy fields on either side, to protect it from constant irrigation and the threat of the Euphrates during the rains. The banks were sheer, a straight drop from the side of the road down to the fields, a rolled Humvee just waiting to happen if a driver took his eyes off the road for even a moment.

River Road was also the only road to get where we needed to go. There was no other game in town. The options were to drive a convoy down River Road, rolling the dice and puckering our asses until we could make diamonds, or try to drive across the muddy fields that would swallow a Humvee just as easily as a boot, which was no option at all.

River Road was the gravesite of four warriors of our platoon, almost twenty percent casualties in one horrific IED attack during our first month in-country. Every time the name was mentioned during briefing, my stomach would clench, my face becoming tight as I fought back anger, guilt, and sorrow in equal measure. It was Russian roulette and there seemed to be fewer and fewer empty chambers each day.

"We did have time to go see EOD and they are sending one Buffalo with us to hold security on site and sweep for IEDs on the way in and out."

A Buffalo was a ponderous, stretch limo of a semi-truck. Unlike a Humvee, it was built with the idea that it would be blown up. Where a Humvee was a flat-bottom vehicle and would channel an IED blast up into the crew compartment, a Buffalo was built on a giant metal V-frame, like the prow of a ship to cut through water, only angled toward the ground so when the blast did come, it would simply be pushed out and around the crew compartment. They were not indestructible—enough high-grade explosives will destroy anything—but they were damn close.

The element of surprise is a lifesaver. What the enemy does not know, they cannot defend against. If you hit a target fast enough and with enough violence of action, only the most battle-hardened enemy will not be shocked and quickly overwhelmed. With surprise, casualties can be reduced and the rate of survival skyrockets. Hit hard and fast, hesitate for nothing, not even if a brother goes down. Finish the fight.

Speed is key. Speed is life.

Speed is not driving down the most dangerous road at five miles an hour behind an enormous Buffalo as its crew looks for IEDs. Not that we were not grateful to have our chances reduced of being blown up, but we were trading one evil for another. We were telegraphing our intentions and destination. Our Humvees were outfitted like no other unit in the area, a rag-tag gypsy caravan bristling with heavy guns and gear, and intelligence had come in that whenever we rolled out of the base, the enemy was quick to alert each other our unit was on the move.

At our current speed, if there was a high-value target in the area, they would know we were on our way to snatch them up, albeit painfully slowly. They would barely have time to make lunch, pray, take a nap, pray, irrigate a field or three, pray, and then escape with their lives by leisurely walking down the road in the opposite direction.

I hit my head against the steering wheel as we rolled along in broad daylight. Ballas, Clark, and Boom were trading stories and jokes while Spears rocked back and forth in the turret, shaking and trying to channel his excess energy. It was like taking a train when we knew we should have flown. Sure, we were going to get there eventually, but it was a strange way to conduct a lightning-fast raid.

We made a slow turn onto a straight stretch of the road, muddy fields on either side for almost a mile. With such a long line of sight, I let the Buffalo crawl further and further away in front of us, spacing out the vehicles to maximize our fields of fire and just for something different to do to keep my mind occupied. At our rate of travel, we were still 20 minutes out from our target; we needed to stay focused while we waited.

"Convoy halt," the Buffalo commander passed across the radio. "Possible IED."

All vehicles stopped, and the gunners began traversing their fields of fire looking for anything out of the ordinary. It was just dark, fertile fields for hundreds of meters in every direction, bordered by the ancient river on our right and dense patches of forest out on our left. The Buffalo crawled up further and parked. A long robotic arm that ended in a giant claw suddenly jerked to life from its roof like a lame transformer.

"Yep, we got an IED," the Buffalo passed. Was that glee? Were they actually happy? "Going to try and disarm now."

The claw moved in shaky fits until it slammed down into the dark patch of gravel where the pavement had either been removed or had simply crumbled away with time. The claw dug in and, within a moment, a loud explosion rocked the Buffalo on its giant frame. Every warrior in our truck braced and our heart rates soared—the body's natural reaction to the dangerous and unknown.

Suddenly, loud crackling screams came over the radio. They were hit, I thought, horrified. The IED had done more damage than it seemed.

The screams suddenly quieted and cleaned up, and I could focus on what they really were: laughter. Those crazy EOD bastards were laughing that the IED had gone off and rocked their truck. The dark humor of their job was unbelievable. The EOD teams had lost and replaced more good warriors than any unit in-country. Their mortality rate was sickening to hear. It was a macabre job and their laughter sent shivers down my spine.

"IED neutralized and …," The Buffalo's message was cut short by a loud explosion in the field between the river and the road. Enormous chunks of black earth were thrown skyward from the giant crater that suddenly appeared 50 feet past the Buffalo.

"Incoming mortars," Ballas growled into the radio headset. The second mortar was already in the air and landed on the opposite side of the road, 40 feet short the Buffalo. The mortar team was bracketing the Buffalo, dialing in the distance by overshooting and then adjusting quickly, knowing the Buffalo was somewhere close to the middle of their first two shots. The third mortar smacked into the side of the steep bank the road was perched upon, gouging out a deep cave and kicking up dirt onto the Buffalo itself.

One more click on the dial of the mortar sight and the next shell would be walked directly onto the flat roof of the Buffalo, which would be as effective as tin foil at protecting the EOD boys inside. The IED had done its job, luring us into a clever ambush. The Buffalo was not fast enough in reacting to what was happening.

The sound of the explosion was deafening, and our bodies instinctively tightened. We clenched our eyes shut as every object not bolted down in the truck rattled and danced around amid the chaos. The explosion reverberated in our ribcage even after the sound had ceased.

The second explosion was baffling and we opened our eyes to see the Buffalo sitting only a little ways down the road, still intact, no sign of a mortar impact anywhere.

"Left," Spears yelled down from the turret, where he had an unobstructed view of the entire landscape. Like some surreal tour of hell, everyone in the cab turned their heads and looked out the driver-side windows, our mouths agape.

An infantryman is issued a rifle and grenades, and perhaps a slightly bigger .50-caliber machine gun or a Mk-19 "tennis ball launcher of death," but the effect is generally a single small hole that has to be carefully aimed to do anything more than sound impressive. We had come to believe that we, with our bullets and collective war cry, are the most terrifying enemies on the battlefield and that our little barrels are the biggest things anyone has ever seen. The arrogance of the infantryman knows no bounds as he holds aloft his rifle as if it is the thunderbolt of Zeus himself.

But our arrogance crumbles, turning to envy and awe, at the sight of a full-fledged artillery barrage.

Out of our driver-side windows, an entire forest was being leveled. Miles away, counter-battery had detected the mortar fire, reverse engineered the trajectory, and "pinpointed" the position of the enemy mortar team, all in the time it had taken the first mortar to land. By the second mortar, the eight enormous artillery barrels, which made out rifles look like toothpicks in comparison, had turned and began their reply.

For two straight minutes, the artillery boys let loose on a square-kilometer patch of forest and fields. The deep bass of the explosions were riddled with the squealing of palm trees being torn apart and thrown a quarter mile in every direction. Dirt was thrown skyward and rained back down in heavy clods with each detonation, mixing with the smoke and creating a gritty haze as the last few shells screamed down from the heavens.

When the explosions had stopped and the dust began to settle, we stared incredulously at the destruction wrought. An entire swath of earth a kilometer across had been deforested and churned up as if ready for fall sowing. Somewhere among the dark chunks of earth were the two mortar operators, now broken down into tiny bits of fertilizer, their perfect hiding place for their ambush in the forest suddenly nothing more than a smoldering pock-marked wasteland.

Somewhere far away, the artillery boys were lighting cigarettes they had been loath to dash out when the counter-battery klaxon had begun to wail. They were joking and smiling, beginning the cleaning process of their giant pieces unaware they had just saved the lives of five EOD warriors and killed two enemy insurgents. To them, the blip on the computer screen that had suddenly showed up finally stopped blinking after forty or fifty shells, and their job was complete.

Death from afar.

After a minute of staring at the bedlam the shelling had produced, we were on the move again, carefully avoiding the bathtub-sized hole in the road where the IED had detonated. We moved even slower than before, EOD poring over every inch of road, looking for the secondary IED that the common enemy tactics suggested would be there. After countless explosions, a forest being leveled, and our nerves being fired and frayed countless times, we finally arrived at our target, somewhat lacking the element of surprise.

Dry hole.

Our target had fled. Or grown old and died. Either way, the house was completely empty upon our arrival and our raid took less than two minutes. We conducted a thorough intelligence sweep but, had there been anything of importance, our target was not in enough hurry to leave it. Forty-five minutes later, we mounted back up and turned the convoy around, shaking our heads in resignation.

It was time to drive back the exact way we came.

CHAPTER 29

Allah, Pelé, and Coca-Cola

Most of our actionable intelligence was spotty at best. We had fantastic, secret-squirrel assets, but the missions they produced were few and far between. Most of the time we would action on word from an informant who had heard something from a guy who had been told by his brother who had overheard a parrot repeating something his owner had said. We kicked in doors and launched night ops on a local's gossip, hunches, and trash-talk.

A vendor in the village we had been running our missions out of had come up on the radar as something of an informant for the insurgents. It was rumor, second-hand gossip from a third, fourth, even fifth, party, but we needed to shake him down regardless. Better to shake him down and find nothing than find out later we let someone slip through our fingers.

Plus, it gave us a chance to potentially draw out some men of ill intent when we rolled up in their main market and began putting the screws to some of their people. We secretly hoped someone, or multiple someones, would be ignorant enough to shoot at us and begin a firefight. Besides the heavy guns mounted on our vehicles and the snipers Sergeant Bronx had inserted ahead of time in overwatch positions, the sheer amount of air assets on station, just itching to go Winchester on some ramshackle, cement hovel full of insurgents, was staggering. Fire superiority was a term Sergeant Bronx lived by and woe to the poor fool who took a potshot with an old Russian-surplus bolt rifle or AK-47.

We hit the market fast and hard, rolling up like a sandstorm out of the blue skies. Within sixty seconds of the first Humvee passing into the market, the entire area was cordoned off and the warriors had made entry into the suspect shop and the two flanking it, hitting all three simultaneously.

One of my complaints about the indigenous people was they did not properly respect the M4 carbine we carried. Enormous warriors suddenly pointing the business end of a 5.56 mm high-velocity boom-stick of death in someone's face should have terrified them.

But it did not. Not even in the least.

They would stare at our rifles impassively, as if trying to stifle the yawn creeping up in their jaw, and sometimes, much to our prideful indignation, smile. It was not just our M4s. Any rifle was considered dreary to them and viewed with all the stark terror one would give someone pointing a rubber band at their chest.

It was the most deflating and anticlimactic thing about any raid. The least they could do was pretend to be scared.

It was not actually their fault. For decades, men had been pointing rifles at them and for decades they had survived. Every indigenous owned an AK-47 and found our carbines just as ordinary, if not a bit "tinier."

Our target looked up at the three men who had stormed his shop, pointing their weapons directly at him, and did not even bat an eyelash. He calmly nodded his head and waited for our interpreter to slip out of the Humvee and come inside when the area was completely secure.

"Search the shops. Top to bottom. Don't. Break. Anything," Sergeant Bronx barked, and the warriors went to work, searching every possible place a weapon, or information, might be hiding.

"Let's take him in the back for a talk," Lieutenant Rusher said quietly to the interpreter, motioning for the man to lead the way through the door to the storeroom. He made no motion to move and stared blankly at the lieutenant. There was a strange moment of hesitation in which the lieutenant visibly sighed, realizing the man would be a hard case and needed extra incentive.

Lieutenant Rusher drew his pistol from its holster and held it casually in front of him, the barrel pointing down a few inches in front of his feet.

As if jolted by a sudden electric shock, the man jumped at the sight of the pistol and began to sweat despite his lifetime in the searing heat. He bowed his head slightly and held up his hands in supplication.

While every indigenous owned an AK-47, only the brutal assassins of Saddam Hussein had historically owned pistols. For decades, Saddam's secret police with their shiny pistols had tortured and executed their own citizens with complete impunity. An Abrams tank with its 105 mm rifled barrel was just a worthless pile of scrap metal compared to the awesome, fear-inducing power of even the cheapest .22-caliber pistol.

Without hesitation, the shop owner led Lieutenant Rusher and the interpreter into the back room while we tossed the shop from top to bottom and then back up again.

The indigenous knew the Coalition warriors could not hurt them. The threat of torture or violence was something of a joke. They knew, unlike the insurgents, Coalition warriors' hands were tied no matter how big their talk. Coalition warriors would feed them, house them, clothe them, if need be, and then release them if nothing was found. Being held captive by the Coalition forces was the equivalent of being forced to stay at a cheap bed-and-breakfast for a day. They reveled in our soft, nonviolent ways.

But there were other threats that could be made. The insurgents had absolutely no compunction about torturing and killing anyone they deemed a threat. They knew nothing of the geography of Geneva and struck out against any Western conventions.

How does one become a threat to the insurgents?

Help the Coalition forces.

Even if the person had been an insurgent up until that moment, they would be hunted down and killed the second they were believed to have given up any information.

We did not need to threaten violence. We only needed to remind them we could leave them as if we were bosom companions, or we could leave them as if we did not get any information from them, gnashing our teeth and leaving the store in seeming disarray. The choice was theirs.

Help us or we leave smiling.

Help us or we leave patting you on the back and laughing jovially, best friends in a moment of merriment.

Help us or our seeming friendship will have your head stuck on a pike by dawn, courtesy of the insurgents and their supporters.

We left all the knickknacks and merchandise sprawled neatly across the floor waiting for a word from Sergeant Bronx. He stepped into the tiny back room with Lieutenant Rusher and came out after just a moment.

"Leave it," he said with a smirk. The shopkeeper had been cooperative and we had gotten what information we wanted. Lieutenant Rusher returned to his vehicle to radio up to Company, telling the shopkeeper to act as if we had trashed his store out of anger for his being uncooperative. The shopkeeper nodded, his eyes angry and resentful. He had been placed unceremoniously in the middle of a lethal Catch-22 and he knew it.

He began to wave us out of his shop angrily, his mouth drawn up into a sneer. I do not think he had trouble finding his motivation for the scene.

"Wait," Sergeant Bronx said, pulling a small wad of paper bills from one of his many pouches on his plate carrier. He held up a rainbow of various bills in front of the shopkeeper and smiled.

The shopkeeper squinted to make out the value of the myriad bills held in front of him. His eyes widened.

And just like that, the hard-pinched anger in his face softened into a genuine smirk of blissful greed.

"Soda," Sergeant Bronx said quietly. The shopkeeper practically jumped to the ceiling in his eagerness to fulfill the sergeant's simple desire. The bills offered were obviously far in excess of the value of everything in the ramshackle store combined.

The shopkeeper madly stuffed two mismatched plastic bags full of ice-cold soda cans until they seemed on the very edge of tearing. His movements were hurried and comical as he tried to deliver the goods as fast as possible to get his hands on the money. He sprang over to Sergeant Bronx with the straining bags and held them as high as his scrawny, shaking arms could.

"Give them out to the boys," Sergeant Bronx said, and one of the warriors took the bags from the shopkeeper, disseminating them among the platoon after we left the market. As soon as the bags were smuggled into the nearest Humvee, Sergeant Bronx held the bills out for the shopkeeper.

"Tell him he hates us," he told the interpreter. "Tell him to badmouth us loudly, as often as he can." The shopkeeper nodded as the interpreter talked and then held out his hands for the bills.

"And then tell him that we'll be back with more money if he tells us what the others say back."

The shopkeeper bowed his head when his fingers touched the bills and he shook his hands at us in a sign of thanks as he secured the bills in his palms. It was more money than had passed through his hands in five years; he had said so as he profusely thanked us.

"I think we made a friend for life," Sergeant Bronx whispered as we left the shop in a seeming rage. Our anger at the shopkeeper was seemingly implacable as Sergeant Bronx turned back to the shop and screamed obscenities, pointing his thick, gloved finger at the shopkeeper as if the simple act could cut the man in half.

"How much money was that?" I asked as we walked away.

"Probably about sixty dollars American," Sergeant Bronx said laughing. "Not a bad price to buy a friend who was just interrogated at gunpoint."

CHAPTER 30

Red, White, and Blue on Blue

Despite our highly advanced U.S. military shovel technology, the "sand" we had heard so much about before being deployed felt like trying to dig into cement. The yearly rains and the endless sun had baked it into a nearly impenetrable hardpan. What had taken a three-man team two hours to dig back in practice in the fertile, loose soils of the U.S., suddenly was a race to be done in six or seven hours before the sun rose.

We took turns, as two held security while one chipped away at the soil with a spade shovel, cut halfway up the wooden handle to make it more portable. Spears, one of the fittest human beings I had ever met, always took the first turn with the shovel and seemed to revel in pitting his body against the exhausting hardships. I would dig next, then Ballas would round off the rotation before Spears took his next turn.

Illumination from the moon was 100 percent, a big, fat full moon high overhead, spilling as much light as the sun did minutes before sunset. It was breathtaking in the vast, wide-open country. It made everything look like the old black-and-white cowboy movies that would be filmed during the day and simply given a darker tint in the developing process to simulate "night" on the prairie.

After an hour of digging, a pair of A-10 Warthogs roared overhead, low enough that we could feel them pass. Their blunt, stub-nosed profiles were awe-inspiring. The A-10 was not so much a plane as an enormous 30 mm Gatling cannon with some wings glued on, like some child's outlandish drawing of the ultimate war machine. In the first second it could put approximately fifty-five rounds of depleted uranium, armor-piercing slugs inside a 40-foot diameter from 4,000 feet in the air. From there the rate only increased once those barrels got howling.

We watched in silent veneration as they swept low looking for prey.

"So cool," I whispered. Spears smiled, pausing his digging for a moment to admire them, and nodding in agreement as we continued to watch.

Ballas did not take his eyes from his handheld FLIR* system as he scanned the lonely stretch of road for heat signatures between the main "highway," a water pump, and generator being run and guarded by a reservist unit. There had been chatter this particular stretch of road was of interest to the insurgents and we were tasked with overwatch for three days.

"Ballas," Spears whispered. After a moment he repeated himself. "Ballas."

"What?" Ballas replied.

"Those Warthogs just banked back hard a few klicks out."

"They see something?" Ballas asked, turning to Spears.

"Seems like. They hit the turn-around pretty fast."

"Keep an eye on 'em."

Spears and I watched as the Great White Sharks of the sky finished their tight turn and headed back over our heads, lower than before.

"Ummm," Spears whispered. "They just did it again."

Ballas put his FLIR down and looked out to the horizon where the Warthogs completed their second tight banking turn in less than a minute. They glowed majestically in the bright moonlight.

"Get the flag and firefly," Ballas said evenly. Neither I nor Spears moved. "Get the fucking reflector flag and the IR firefly," Ballas barked sharply.

The Warthogs had indeed found a target. Three in fact. Three unidentified men digging into the side of a berm at night only a short distance from a known insurgent target. They had found their prey.

They had found us.

"Here they come," Spears said. Ballas got on the hook and gave a blunt report of our situation. The Warthogs had fallen into formation for a gun run, one in front of the other ready to light up their target in turn before making a follow-on run until all 2,700 tank-killer rounds were gone.

"The fucking flag and firefly," Ballas growled. We had agreed the enormous orange rectangle was too much of a risk to keep out in the open given the sudden winds; if any indigenous spotted even the smallest orange speck, we would be made. I had kept it in my front pouch, easily accessible along with the infrared "firefly," a pulsing beacon that alerted anyone with night vision in a few klicks' radius to our exact location. Old-generation night-vision goggles had just been found in a local raid on known insurgents. We were briefed to only use the firefly when making ourselves known to Coalition forces.

Easily accessible is a relative term when two of the military's most fearsome war machines are bearing down on you at only a moment's notice.

The Warthogs were closing fast as I tore the flag from the pouch and ripped it open as wide as I could manage and flicked on the firefly. Ballas and Spears each

---

* FLIR stands for "forward-looking infra-red."

grabbed a corner and pulled it taut above our head, our frail bodies shaking like children hiding from sharp claws underneath a thin sheet.

The Warthogs dove in on us for the final two klicks. Perhaps it was my imagination, but I swear I could hear the barrels beginning to spin as they readied to rain down hell on our position. It was either that or the high-pitched squeal that had begun escaping my mouth.

And at the last possible moment, both Warthogs banked hard to the right, aborting their gun run as they spotted the orange "oh shit" flag and the enormous IR pulse that sprang to life as we sat holding our breaths.

As the Warthogs roared off into the distance, we all began laughing violently, the mirth of slipping through death's grasp making us dance with unspent adrenaline.

"Well, that was close," Ballas quipped, returning to his FLIR. "Of course, the first time we actually see air patrolling and it's when we're digging in." Spears and I lay on our backs panting and trying not to think just what would have happened if the pilots had seen the flag a second later. A single flick of the fire mechanism would have left very few pieces for anyone to identify us by. We laughed quietly for a few more moments but subsequent bouts of nervous laughter surfaced in waves, like aftershocks after an emotional earthquake.

For six hours we dug our hide as deep and camouflaged as humanly possible. It would not do to just throw the moist, darker dirt from underneath the baked surface all around the hide, forming an enormous arrow that screamed "come investigate," to every farmer who had tilled the lands for countless generations and knew the land like the faces of their own children. For the hide to work, it had to blend seamlessly into the background, to eyes that had seen the same land for tens of thousands of days.

By first light, we had completely buried ourselves in a low berm, moving enough earth in the dark to create a hole seven feet, by seven feet, by four feet deep. Tight-weaved mesh netting, mostly covered by a thin layer of dry dirt, made a one-way window through a deep notch we had cut out of the front of the berm. To a passerby, the irrigation berm seemed to look as uninterrupted as it had for decades. Only a bird could see the high-powered scoped rifle scanning the road or the three men laying on their stomachs waiting patiently for their prey, roasting in the intense summer sun.

An hour later, an enormous dump truck rumbled up the side road toward the highway. Three men sat in the cab looking out at the sides of the road as it crept along.

"Hello," Ballas whispered, and moved himself behind the scope of his rifle. Spears reached over and checked the ammo belt that fed into the enormous 7.62 mm machine gun he had humped out to the hide. All he had to do was rack the charging handle and 200 armor-piercing rounds would be at his disposal should the situation begin to go south. We had humped out an additional 800 rounds that were staged beside the stock should they be necessary.

We all prayed it was not. Three men in a hole, no matter how well armed, are still prey.

I took up the binos and we all watched as the truck rolled to a halt next to a large culvert at the side of the road. All three men got out and began looking around to see if they were being watched. Spears wondered out loud if the Warthogs were still on station as Ballas closed his non-dominant eye and relaxed his cheek into the adjustable stock.

"One's got a black box," Ballas whispered. I rolled over and got on the hook with Lieutenant Rusher, informing him of our situation. The quick-reaction force (QRF) would be on their rumbling vehicles within two minutes and ready to respond to our position within three more minutes. Five minutes until the cavalry arrived should the situation dictate.

"Shit," Ballas snarled. "They went on the other side of the truck. I no longer have visual." I relayed his words directly to higher.

"Lieutenant says take the shot if you get positive ID," I repeated back to Ballas.

"I got nothing," Ballas growled. "Come on, show me something."

We waited in silence for almost a minute before Ballas exhaled sharply.

"Fuck. They don't have the box and they're getting back in their truck. I can't take the shot. I did not see them emplace it. Say again, I did not see them emplace."

I passed the message up to higher and we waited for orders. The truck began to gain speed and barreled toward the obscurity of the highway. Higher was not responding.

"Fuck 'em," Ballas growled and fired three shots in rapid succession. He grinned as the vehicle slowed and rolled to a stop. "Down."

I held the hook to my ear and looked inquisitively at Ballas, awaiting his orders. His smirk only grew as he surveyed his marksmanship and then turned his head to look at me.

"Tell higher that they need to get a tow truck out here immediately. I immobilized the vehicle by shooting the tires, and we need to take these shitheads in for questioning."

It took a little less than five minutes for the QRF to roll up the drivers and drag the truck off to a secure location to be searched thoroughly.

"Lieutenant says to remain in place and watch the IED," Spears relayed as he began his turn on the radio. "All local units have been informed of its position and we're to babysit. If anyone comes to claim it or check on it, we take them down."

"Let's just hope they didn't have a chance to call anyone and warn them," Ballas said, stretching his back before lowering himself back into position behind the scope.

Traffic had been nonexistent on our stretch of road. The insurgents were notorious for threatening the locals about the placement of their IEDs, not out of some sense of Robin Hood-like chivalry, but because IEDs were expensive in both materials and their high cost in mortal danger during building and digging in. The last thing the insurgents wanted was to waste an IED on some local Bongo truck carrying empty water barrels stacked so high it was always on the verge of tipping over. They were quick to put the word out which roads were "under construction" that day and woe to anyone who did not heed their warning. Even if they did not trigger the IED, there was a good chance the insurgents would execute them as an example later.

Between the word being passed to all Coalition forces and the insurgents threatening the locals, everyone and their mother in the entire area had been informed there was an IED emplaced on the crumbling water-pump road.

Everyone except the reservist unit.

The four-truck convoy of mismatched Humvees rumbled up the road from the water pump, aimed directly for the IED ahead of them. The three of us all shared a look of horror; Ballas grabbed the hook.

"There is a reserve unit from the pump moving up onto the IED," he informed higher. Higher cut the conversation short, flipping over to whatever frequency the reserve unit was supposed to be monitoring. The vehicles continued moving forward to their obliteration.

"We got to stop them," Spears said, throwing on his helmet and standing up. Ballas nodded and Spears took off running across the field, his arms held out in an iron cross as he screamed to get the convoy's attention.

I threw myself behind the heavy machine gun and Ballas got down behind the scope. No words were spoken, but we both had the same exact thought. If any gunner in the convoy began to open fire at Spears, we would stop them and suffer the consequences later. Spears would live at any cost.

Even laden with 70 pounds of extra weight strapped around his chest, Spears hurtled toward the convoy at a pace that could have seen him on a podium in another setting. He drove himself onward, pumping his thin, muscular legs despite the burning in his lungs. The convoy was bearing down on the IED; Spears only had moments to get them to stop before the lead truck would roll its front tires directly over the spot where we had seen the men disappear with the black box.

"Stop!" Spears screamed, waving one hand in front of his face, palm out in the gesture for "cease-fire" while he held his rifle by the barrel at arm's length, showing he was not a threat. "Stop!"

Like the mighty Tyrannosaurus Rex, turret gunners hunt by movement alone. Mandatory ear protection coupled with the thunderous rumble of the diesel engines drown out any possibility of hearing warning sounds. Five senses are reduced to one, creating a dismal reliance on sight alone. Any sharp, distinct movement is translated into a probable target and acquired with great haste. The decision time to fire on and neutralize a threat, before being blown into a million tiny pieces, is staggeringly low, especially when taking into consideration that most of the trigger-pullers have barely just received the right to vote, buy pornography, and still cannot legally drink for some years.

It is a profound and terrible burden.

Shoot and possibly face court-martial for mistakenly killing an innocent.

Hesitate and possibly get you and every warrior around you killed.

No CEO making millions of dollars has ever had to make such weighty decisions. It is left to warriors who cannot legally drink yet, and whose take-home pay is pocket change.

Thirty feet from the convoy and Spears had still not been spotted. We watched in dread as he stopped and jumped up and down, waving his outstretched arms as he screamed.

And then he was noticed—as a suspicious person with a rifle who suddenly just appeared only 30 feet from the convoy like magic.

Insurgent.

Suicide bomber.

Target.

The turret gunner of the middle vehicle wracked the first round into the chamber as he wheeled his heavy machine gun around to take aim. He was already putting his shoulder behind the weapon and trying to line up the front sights on Spears's chest.

"Fuck," Ballas whispered to himself, aiming his scoped rifle at the heavy machine gun, hoping to knock off the gunner's aim or destroy any of the firing mechanisms inside.

"Stop!" Spears screamed, pushing his arms out in the iron cross and staring down the turret gunner. Ballas began a slow, steady squeeze on the trigger and the turret gunner began his.

Everything came to a dead stop. The convoy skidded to a halt and for a few seconds there was only the low rumble of the engines.

"How the fuck did you not see me?" Spears screamed, his adrenaline swelling his muscles and pushing his heart to flutter like a hummingbird's.

"Go take over and get him back here," Ballas said with a grin. Spears was tremendously slow to anger, but when it spilled over it was a sight to behold. He was one of the last people on earth I would want to fight when he had been pushed over the edge and saw red. He was all twitch and pent-up aggression.

I ran up behind Spears and clapped my hand on his shoulder.

"Ballas wants you back in the hole. You're a better shot than me should these assholes get us into trouble. I got this."

Spears turned and loped back to our hide with effortless grace. He looked like a big cat, sleek and always straining against the potential energy of his muscles as he moved. I smiled and forthanked the gods the turret gunner had the good sense not to talk back.

"Who is in charge here?" I yelled.

"That would be the major," the turret gunner yelled down.

"Tell him to back this convoy up two hundred meters. You're almost on top of an IED."

The orders were obeyed with the utmost haste and in less than a minute the convoy was a safe distance from the IED. I stood on the side of the road and waited to liaise with the platoon sergeant, or whatever lowly corporal had been placed in charge of such a rabble. The four trucks were a rash convoy, with only three having heavy weapons, two facing forward and back, with the third desperately traversing, trying to cover both sides. It would not take much of an ambush to see all these men dead or captured. It had been a poorly thought-out idea from the start.

I was not met by the acting platoon sergeant. Instead, the major himself tumbled out of the third vehicle and walked up to me. I swallowed hard.

I was a corporal, four rungs up the enlisted ladder. Not low enough to be treated like an indentured servant of the first few ranks but still not high enough to be given any real respect by the staff enlisted or higher. It was a gray rank, easily looked over for both menial labor and any position of real command in our community.

The major was 14 rungs above me on the ladder. There were 13 ranks between us that would obey his every order without question. If he was a junior vice-president of a company, I was still working in the mail room as a low-level head sorter.

"What's our situation, Sir?" the major asked, stepping up in front of me with two corporals in tow playing the role of his personal bodyguards.

Sir?

I looked down at my dusty bouncer laden with 10 magazines, grenades, and a small personal radio. My flight suit's Velcro nametape was hidden underneath—my identity, unit, and rank right along with it. I grinned to myself. The major had bought in to the belief I was some sort of ranking, high-speed operator. We had recently escorted a task force of top-tier bubbas on a three-day mission and knew we all dressed alike, if one did not look at the glaring differences in the quality of gear and weapons.

The major had not noticed the difference and was treating me like a top-tier bubba.

Deep down, I think he desperately wanted me to be. It would make for a better story back home.

Oh yeah, I worked with some top-tier guy in-country. All hush-hush stuff, you know, so I can't give details. Look like? Certainly not *a dorky looking kid. He was, umm, eight feet tall and carried a, umm, a rail gun, yeah. Those guys carry them now. And personal teleporters. Swear to God. You don't even know how hi-tech they are now.*

So, for the moment I was Lieutenant Colonel Badass and that suited me just fine. I made no attempt to try to correct the major. His looks of unfounded admiration and respect were far too pleasant compared to the normal contempt the brass usually rained down on us lowly enlisted. I made my best big-boy voice and briefed the major as to the situation he had bumbled into.

"We had no idea," he said, flushing at the thought of looking slightly incompetent in front of such a spectacular specimen of soldiering. I simply stared him square in his fleshy red face as he blustered on about not being kept informed and heads rolling later.

"Well, we have the situation in hand now. We'll be watching the possible IED and neutralizing anyone who tries to recover it."

"Possible IED? You're not sure?"

"They emplaced while hidden behind their truck, so we are not one hundred percent sure but we're operating under the assumption it is live. So, if you'll just turn around …"

"We'll find out if it's live," the major beamed. His fantasy of not only working with but "saving the asses" of some high-level assets had just solidified in his head.

Those cowboys didn't even know if it was live. Thank the gods I was there to take charge and keep 'em safe.

"Corporal Hudgins, get the robot," the major said. Hudgins sped off to the parked convoy and wrestled an enormous green plastic suitcase from the back of one of the trucks. Hudgins slipped the eight plastic buckles around the waterproof container and flipped open the lid. From inside the soft, molded padding he pulled out a souped-up version of the remote-control monster trucks my brother built when we were children. Instead of a cherry red plastic Corvette shell, the robot sported a video camera on a long arm and a pair of pincers.

"This really isn't necessary," I began, but the major was quick to recover his fantasy.

"Nonsense. We need to know what we're dealing with," he said in a tone that brooked no response, his fantasy requiring it.

Yeah, we became fast friends. I won't be surprised if they look me up and ask me to go for a beer the second we are all back Stateside. We made a great team.

The robot was slow and cumbersome, not the speedy, agile remote-control vehicle I had been expecting. It was built for war, sturdy and sparing no expense. I did not want to know the cost, but I knew from the box alone it was worth enough to ruin careers if it was misused or destroyed. How this ragtag reserve unit got their hands on one I could not have guessed.

As soon as Hudgins put all the pieces together and made the robot serviceable, the major snatched the controls from his hands. Corporal Hudgins looked shocked and hurt, his moment of glory after probably hundreds of hours spent practicing with the robot swept away by a man he could not even begin to argue with. Hudgins stepped back away from the major and turned in disgust, pretending to hold security as he gnawed his lip.

The major did not notice and turned his full attention to driving the robot toward the IED. The robot whined as it bucked across the uneven ground, slowly making its way to the spot where we could see churned earth and a corner of the black box.

Ten feet from the IED, the robot lurched on an uneven slope, kicked its right tires off a rock, and rolled onto its back like a helpless turtle, tires spinning and whining helplessly.

"Shit," the major growled. "Hudgins."

Hudgins, who had seen the entire catastrophe from the corner of his eye, hurried to the major's side, eager to hear the apology and be handed the remote as a sign of atonement. Instead, the major simply pointed over at the paralyzed robot with its wheels to the sky, only feet from the explosives.

"Go retrieve the robot, Corporal," the major said quietly. The smug satisfaction drained from Hudgins's face, replaced by a further grimace of righteous indignation. His face shook visibly as he turned from the major to the robot and then back to the major. "Corporal, the robot," the major reminded.

"No, Sir," Corporal Hudgins whispered, trying to keep his voice from becoming a howl.

"Corporal, that's an order," the major growled, eager to regain control of the situation. The idea of losing face in front of an imaginary tier-one asset did not fold in well with the major's fantasy and his face pulled tight, as if he could taste the sourness of the situation.

"I will not retrieve that robot, Sir. That is an illegal order putting one of your men's lives at risk unnecessarily."

"Well, gentlemen, I need to rejoin my team," I said, stepping back away from the two men squaring off between a vulnerable convoy and an IED. "We'll provide overwatch until you …" I paused. "Until you exfil."

I did not stay to hear the conclusion of the argument, but when EOD arrived on the scene an hour later, I knew the corporal had won out. However, I did not want to be in his shoes for any amount of money. The major would never forgive Corporal Hudgins for ruining his story for the VFW† bars back in the States.

"And then the [top-tier] guy laughed at me when I flipped our robot onto the IED" would not give the glorious ending that the major had hoped for.

I arrived back in our camouflaged hide grinning ear to ear, retelling the story to Ballas and Spears, who laughed heartily. The major must have been ordered to cordon and secure the IED site for EOD because two of his vehicles pulled out into the field, giving the black box and robot a wide berth, before parking on the far side so no insurgents could ambush EOD when they went to retrieve the major's upside-down robot.

EOD is one of the most badass and yet completely underrated units in all of the military. Walking up onto explosives knowingly takes more grit then any triggerman will ever know. Who in their right mind signs up to physically wrestle with bombs? That can only end one of two ways, and one of those ways is rather permanent.

---

† VFW stands for "Veterans of Foreign Wars."

Ballas leaned his neck into the hook as higher passed word. EOD had just called in the IED as a "decoy," everything needed but the explosives. At the exact moment as EOD was making their report, many miles away, the insurgents driving the truck had broken under interrogation and admitted to being an emplacement team. They admitted to doing a dry run, practicing their technique for emplacement. Had all gone to plan, they would have returned that night to place the explosives to go along with the black initiation device Ballas had seen and EOD had recovered.

"That didn't take long to break them," Spears quipped.

Ballas shook his head and closed his eyes as he continued to listen to the hook.

"The local judge that Coalition forces lets preside over local-national trials, he just let them go," he relayed.

"Let them go?" I exclaimed.

"Yep. Said without actual explosives, they didn't do anything wrong."

"They said they were emplacing IEDs," Spears seethed.

"I guess he's considering that hearsay."

CHAPTER 31

Checkmate

Sergeant Bronx and Lieutenant Rusher were the cleverest of enemies. While we saw tension in other platoons between the young officers and their veteran enlisted, the two men who led our platoon seemed to work in perfect unison with each other, playing off each other's strengths and weaknesses seamlessly. Once a mission came down from higher, the entire platoon gathered around the table and kicked ideas around once the sergeant and the lieutenant had built the basic framework with which we could work from. Even the junior-most man was listened to with deference and treated with respect, so long as his idea had been flushed out before he opened his mouth. It was as democratic as the military could get.

More than a highbrow theory, it worked.

"We bait 'em," Sergeant Bronx said, looking up from the intelligence briefing I had just finished, bringing us to the point of discussing what to do to improve our chances of killing bad guys and reducing our chances of false positives. The insurgents' modus operandi had begun evolving more rapidly than our ability to counter them. Small, grassroots guerrilla tactics were nimble and fluid and, since the insurgents had no compunction about killing civilians, their tactics were not boxed in by traditional military concerns. Those in a huge organization, even those highly specialized and trained, would always find themselves just a hair's breadth behind when confined by vast hierarchical decision-making processes and the harshest mistress of all: that bitch morality.

"Explain," Lieutenant Rusher said, taking notes as he listened. Sergeant Bronx looked around the room and smiled.

"You're all hard-assed, superhuman fighting machines and that's the problem," Sergeant Bronx said. We laughed and smiled at each other. "I'm kidding. You're all ugly and stupid, but the shitheads don't know that. They think you are superheroes. And that's the problem. We look all snap and pop, making our firm bases super-fortresses with heavy guns sticking out every which way and then they never attack us. They'll wait. They'll let us pass until some other unit, some sickly, weak-looking snoops and smokeys move into our area of operation and they'll attack those guys. Oh, they'll bomb us. They'll bomb the fuck out of us 'cause they don't have to stick around for that, but they won't ever attack us when we're looking so fucking tough."

"So?" Lieutenant Rusher asked patiently, his pen hovering above the notepad just itching to finish the thought.

"So let's not look tough. Should be easy with this bunch of pussies. You or I just won't get out of the Humvee, Sir. That would instantly make us look too tough."

Lieutenant Rusher smiled at the joke and the rest of the platoon chuckled.

"But these pussies," Bronx said pointing at us. "Let them park out somewhere vulnerable, looking like we ain't got any idea what we're doing and let the shitheads come to us."

"And when they do?"

"We fall back," Sergeant Bronx said with a grin.

"Fall back?" Lieutenant Rusher said, suddenly looking up. He cocked his eyebrow. "Fall back?"

"Yes, Sir. We fall back. We fall back like any platoon of little untrained kids would and we fall back fast to a predesignated firm base that we've already secured and have a few men still holding to ensure its virginity."

"And then?"

"And then the shitheads will see us running and chase us. Who doesn't love a good rout? They will follow us blindly as we retreat and run straight into the team waiting to ambush them."

Lieutenant Rusher finished his notes and looked up. "Does anyone see a problem with that plan? Pick it apart."

But for once, no one had any qualms with the plan. We could only grin at the brazen idea.

"No problems with the plan itself? No? Well, then does anyone have any misgivings about being human bait?"

"We're always bait, Sir," Boom said. "Every time we leave the wire. At least this time we get to do it on purpose."

The plan was passed. There was no group vote. It was not a true democracy. The only person whose vote mattered was Lieutenant Rusher, but at least he listened to what his men had to say first.

We circled the Humvees in the middle of a huge field like settlers preparing to bed down for the night after a hard day on the trail west. We kept all our gear inside the trucks, leaving them looking as bare and rarely used as we could. We pulled off two of our five heavy guns, hiding them within arm's reach, but leaving two turrets visibly bare and neglected. Suddenly, we looked like a green unit, just putting boots on the ground for the first time since being flown over, fresh-faced and eager but all too exposed and foolhardy to survive long.

We looked like the perfect target.

It did not take long to make contact. After months of actively searching to find the enemy, it took them only two hours to let them find us.

Or at least start bracketing us.

The first mortar fell slightly shy of our circle, kicking up huge spouts of dirt clods and tufts of sharp grasses. We were not expecting mortars to be employed, and the sudden explosion made us all freeze. The second mortar followed almost immediately, only the slightest of adjustments on the tube being necessary, and it landed directly in the middle of our circle of trucks, a bull's-eye of a shot but failing to hit anything but dirt again.

"Anyone hit?" Sergeant Bronx passed over the net.

Suddenly, Gracie, a more muscular Tyrese with a shaved head and thick, bulging arms, jumped out of one of the trucks, his eyes wide and his nostrils flaring.

"Gracie, get back in the truck," Sergeant Bronx yelled, opening his door.

"You fucking pussies!" Gracie hollered, striding around in a circle like a cage fighter after a bad call by the ref. "This is some bulllll-shit."

Gracie's leg was bleeding. Inside his truck, a door had opened a crack when the second mortar hit and Gracie, standing in the turret, took a piece of shrapnel to the leg.

"Come out and fight, you pussies!" Gracie screamed with righteous indignation. "Of course you had to hit the only black man in this white-bread platoon."

We all tried to stifle our laughter since no one wanted to incur Gracie's ire when he was worked up. His temper was well known and his hand-to-hand combat skills were well honed.

"Come out and fight me man to man," Gracie howled, slapping his chest and striding around the circle. "Course the black man gets hit first, just like in the movies."

"Gracie, get in the truck, we're falling back," Sergeant Bronx yelled again.

Three minutes later we pulled into our pre-established firm base, though to an onlooker it looked as if we had just hastily picked a building at random. It was a lone abandoned one-story cement house in the middle of the field. We were greeted inside by the sniper team, which had been in place since nightfall.

"All clear, Sergeant," they reported.

"Good," he said with a grin. He turned to Gracie, whose pant leg had been cut open and his wound was being looked at. "How is it?"

"Sergeant, this is some bullshit," Gracie growled.

"The bullshit is you needing to see a medic for a scratch like that. A Puerto Rican wouldn't have even made a sound unless his leg was dangling from his knee. Shit, a Puerto Rican would at least have the decency to get his leg blown completely off before even thinking about seeing a medic, and then he would just want to check to make sure his huge dick was still working and not bitch about his boo-boo."

"Now what, Bronx?" Ballas asked when everyone had stopped laughing.

"Now we wait. Get a few guys up on the roof, no heavy guns visible but have them locked and loaded by your feet. It will take a vehicle a long time to hit the house even at top speed but have them ready. Look lax but be vigilant. We want them to think we're weak."

Five minutes after the roof watch was established, we settled in to a game of cheaters' spades on MRE boxes. Spades was our official game of boredom. Anyone could play; if one man was called away another could take his hand without any real difficulty. The problem with spades was that given its simple nature once the cards were dealt and the bids were in, the game was pretty much set in stone as far as strategy. The excitement was suddenly lost and the winner already began to grin despite no cards being thrown yet.

So we cheated.

Cheating added an element to the game that was exciting and often hilarious. The rule was simple: if you ain't cheating, you ain't trying. Occasionally we would try to get one over on the other team. The easiest was kicking a single card over into one of your opponent's piles during their deal. At the end of the hand, they would have an extra card and the game would be an automatic loss due to a misdeal on their part. There were myriad ways to throw the game and ruin the opponents' chances of winning. However, if one was caught cheating, all the points were immediately given to the opponent, who would smirk and make quips the entire rest of the game.

Bronx was a terrific spades player. Not only could he cheat well, he could also boast the entire game without seeming to take a breath. He would throw his cards down as if their very weight smashing against the box could crush any chance of winning for his opponents. His incessant chatter on Puerto Ricans being the master race and how he among them was one of the greatest got into his opponents' heads, driving them mad so they never saw the sleight of hand with which Bronx could turn the game.

"He's going nil," Clark exclaimed, realizing too late Bronx had misdirected us once again, with a story about two coked-up strippers trying to get him into a threesome at the club he had bounced at for spending money when he was younger. With only a few cards left to play, Bronx had cleverly given himself no way to win any of the subsequent hands. He grinned, everyone already knowing the outcome of the game.

"Jesus, finish your story at least," I laughed. There was no time.

The distinct growl of an AK-47 firing off a long burst made everyone freeze. There was a moment's pause and then the familiar chatter of two heavy machine guns responding in kind.

"Roof," Bronx ordered calmly. We ran up to the roof and ducked low, keeping our heads below the cement walls until we got the direction of incoming from the overwatch. Everyone jumped up, and suddenly our seemingly undermanned and undefended firm base was bristling with heavy weapons and men. Everyone waited, keeping their eyes open for any movement in all directions, but all was silent and still. Only a plume of dark, oily smoke rising from behind a copse of trees made the scene look something other than a picturesque day in a quiet farming village.

"We took incoming from that corner of the road," the overwatch who had fired off one of the heavy guns said, pointing his hand for Bronx to follow. "We returned fire, but they were already on the retreat."

"They didn't get far," Bronx said, tilting his head and holding his earpiece to hear what was being passed. After a moment he nodded to himself, as if he had come to a decision, and then took his hand from his ear. "Anyone not on roof watch mount up for a BDA. Pitt's team is reporting all three of the shitheads are down."

I ran down to my assault pack and grabbed an inexpensive digital camera. The platoon had been issued a fancy, bells-and-whistles camera with a lens like a tank cannon and more features than a movie theater, but the overkill had made it our least favorite piece of equipment unless actually doing a clandestine recon and report mission, which were rare in-country. Most often if there was something to report, we would also be acting on it, and the need for a lens that could zoom two miles at one trillion dpi, but that also took up a third of the packing space available, was not high on the priority list. A $30 digital camera could do the job I needed just as well.

We patrolled out a quarter mile from our firm base to the intersection of two paved roads with a thick copse of trees and vegetation that clung to one corner. Spent 7.62 mm shells littered the ground next to the palm tree that stood directly in the crook of the two roads. The insurgent had let off a long burst before retreating.

This was not a professional attempt. It was hurried and without thought. It was three men, most likely the mortar team, whose blood was up seeing the mighty Coalition forces on the retreat. They smelled weakness and their hopes for glory blinded them to the realities of their situation. Bronx had executed the baiting perfectly.

"Fish in a barrel," Pitt said, standing up from his team's hide as Bronx neared their camouflaged position. Pitt had brought his long gun and glanced back at it, a smile playing across his usually stoic face. "Assholes couldn't even stand far enough away to let me take a shot with the scope."

"Sucks," Bronx agreed. As snipers, they both understood the anticipation and desire to line up that perfect shot with one of the most lethal and demoralizing weapons ever created. It was such a rare thing and Pitt was obviously disappointed that, once again, the situation had not allowed him to utilize his skills from one of the military's most difficult schools.

I stood in the hide and began taking photographs with the camera. In the digital age, higher would not just want a written report, but a complete PowerPoint presentation on every single detail of the situation. Insurgents were notorious for using the media to portray any activity against their agents as "attacks by the West on innocent civilians." It worked. Martyrs helped recruiting and the insurgent cause across the globe. Insurgent losses could be turned into political victories simply by changing an armed attacker into an innocent, defenseless husband, father, or son.

I photographed the entire event as Pitt walked Bronx and I through what had happened.

The insurgents had pulled up in a car just shy of the intersection, using the copse of trees to hide their movement from our firm base. They were unaware that one hundred feet away five men were waiting in ambush with a long gun, a heavy machine gun, five M4s, two 40 mm grenade launchers, and enough rounds to back a coup of a small country. Two men had jumped out of the vehicle and ran to the large tree on the corner of the road, while the third waited behind the wheel of the car, ready to beat a hasty exfil as soon as the job was done. One man fired off half a banana clip of 7.62 mm rounds at the firm base, while the other readied himself to exchange places as soon as the first magazine went dry.

What they had not planned on was the two guards with rifles on the roof of the building suddenly becoming four men, each with a heavy weapon, and then suddenly becoming 12. They had not expected return fire, though their proximity to Pitt's team had limited the roof guns. While not actually engaging the insurgents themselves, they did make a deafening noise and kept the enemies' heads down.

"So, then they turned to run back to the car," Pitt said, pointing out their retreat down the side of the road.

"Who did you hit first?" Bronx asked.

"When they were about twenty feet to the car and committed, I took out the driver," Pitt said with a smirk. All three of us looked at the car. It was nothing but a smoldering metal frame, completely burnt to the ground. "Guess the tracers must have started a fire."

"And then?"

"Then we all let loose on the two runners. One went down instantly and is in that ditch, and the other made it as far as the other side of the road. Pretty sure it was just momentum 'cause he was chewed up pretty good."

"Anyone else? Any collateral damage?"

"Nope. Pretty clean," Pitt said, and then chuckled to himself. "I mean, pretty clean for burning their car down to the axles."

"An all-right job, Pitt," Bronx said, looking up and down the road. "All right" was a high compliment from the sergeant, perhaps even worth being put in for a medal. The sergeant was sparse with his compliments and they were hard to detect when they arrived. "Okay, secure a large perimeter. I want nothing getting even remotely near this scene before we have a chance to search and photo everything." Bronx turned to me. "I want pictures of everything and see if you can dig up any intel."

I nodded and the remaining platoon and the sergeant moved out into an enormous circle, finding cover and shade to support what could be a few hours of security.

I stepped over to the first body with our medic. The body was torn to shreds and was lying face down in a dry irrigation ditch. I reached my hand out and grabbed its shoulder. It was my responsibility to take pictures of corpses and collect any intelligence of significance.

I rolled the body over onto its back and stared. Mine was not a look of revulsion or even of secret joy, only the detached look of someone staring at the remains of roadkill. I needed photographic proof for the cause of death, about fifteen 7.62 mm rounds, some tracers, straight through the body from point-blank range.

The leg was severed just below the hip and hung only by a small rope of sinew. Click.

The right shoulder had been completely removed. Click.

There were multiple small entry wounds in the chest that matched up with the softball-sized exit wounds on the back. Click.

The body looked as if it had been chewed up by "Clifford the Big Red Dog" for days and finally left for a newer, more interesting toy. Click.

CHAPTER 32

The Cave: The Constant Daydream

Suddenly, the body's eyes flutter open, full of the most basic instinct in the human body, the fight for survival.

I pick my head up and look around. The medic has disappeared. The platoon and Sergeant Bronx have disappeared. I am all alone for thousands of miles, perhaps in all the world, save for the insurgent.

We are alone.

This is no longer combat. This is not an armed enemy whose life I need to take in order to save mine or my mates'. This is something else entirely.

His eyes focus on me, on my stoic face, and then he looks around for another soul. There is none. We two are the only survivors of this moment, our own personal Armageddon.

I put my camera back into one of the many pouches hanging off my plate carrier. With precise, unhurried movements, I remove a pair of black Nomex gloves from another pouch. Without taking my eyes off his, I begin to pull the gloves down across my fingers, enjoying the tight, compressive hug they give to each digit. I pull them down across my palms and then down to my wrists. I take the time to knit my fingers together and press the material deeper into the webbing of my fingers until the gloves feel as if they are a part of my flesh, as if they always have been. I open and close my hands to test them and squeeze my fists tightly when I am satisfied they are perfect.

I am not happy.

I am not fearful.

I am not overjoyed, depressed, or any discernable emotion at all.

I am simply cold, as if my mind is a barren tundra being scoured by harsh northern winds that whip sharp flakes of snow across it like innumerable razorblades.

This is the darkness, the black cave in my soul where empathy, sympathy, or even hope cannot journey. This is where the monster lives, where sun-bleached bones litter the entrance to the valley I began to walk down in basic training.

I can hear the monster grin, the wet, sucking friction of its lips being drawn across its teeth into a horrible mockery of a smile.

I take a small, measured step toward the man and he wriggles, his wounds all healed but his body unable to respond to his cries to rise and face his enemy.

I take a second step. Then a third and a fourth until I am straddling his hips, looking down at his prone, defenseless body. He struggles to flee but, as if experiencing his own nightmare, he cannot.

Who are you?

The question comes out of the dark, fertile earth like a whisper. It is the question every person must come to terms with on their journey.

Who are you? What are you capable of deep down in your hidden places?

I do not hesitate, inching forward until I am leaning down, straddling the defenseless man's chest. He looks up at me, but his eyes are clouded with confusion. Mine are cold and jet black, like the steel of the rifle strapped to my back. There is no confusion in them, only darkness, only deep, endless shadow.

I slowly kneel, my knees sinking into the rich earth on either side of his armpits. There are sharp rocks digging into my flesh, but I cannot feel them; I only register the dull pressure they are creating in my knees, somewhere far back in my reptilian mind.

He looks up at me and his mouth moves silently, supplicating and looking for the famous mercy of the West. He still does not truly understand. He wants to flee but does not know what from. It has not occurred to him yet.

I sit on his stomach, feeling his bony ribs against my relaxed muscles, and stare down at him silently. I do not pin his arms with my legs. I leave them at his sides, so he may use them, so that he may defend himself if only in a most paltry of ways.

I stare down at him and I reach down into my depths, searching for the answer.

Who are you?

I feel nothing.

No remorse, no sympathy, or pity.

No secret glee, no secret desire, or bloodlust.

Nothing. I feel cold and detached. I feel outside of myself.

I extend my arms exceedingly slowly as I stare into the insurgent's eyes. I want him to watch. I want him to see all of this, to see and understand.

He looks at my open hands moving toward his head and then he snaps his gaze to my face to take measure.

His pupils dilate suddenly. It has finally occurred to him who he should have been fleeing from, who I truly am underneath my sheep's clothing.

I am the monster.

I am the implacable cold of his nightmares.

He looks into the stygian darkness of my eyes as my hands patiently slither around his neck like a snake in the night. Only the flat, cold gaze of a shark is returned. He is not looking up at a man any longer. It is the absence of humanity he witnesses, a cold, hard shell that contains only a bleak, wintry nothingness inside.

His body begins to tremble. His mouth moves in silent pleas.

He knows now. He understands.

I am the monster come forth.

I begin to squeeze my hands around his throat. My thoughts wander to my friends who I watched dancing across the horizon, their bodies completely engulfed in flames as they writhed and screamed, begging for their own deaths. I can see them looking at me, their once pink, young faces burning black as the flames lick them and consume their beauty.

I squeeze harder.

I can feel my friends in my mind, all there standing in a circle around me, watching, their bodies still encircled in terrible gouts of flame but the fire no longer consuming them, only burning endlessly across their charred features. They watch stoically as I begin to crush the insurgent's larynx with my thumbs and feel his spine move underneath my fingertips.

I squeeze harder and the insurgent's arms move up to stop me. He grabs my wrists and tries to pull my hands from his neck. There is a terrible strength there, more terrible still given his right arm had been almost completely disconnected from his torso before the cave, but still he pulls.

This is why I left his arms free. I want him to struggle. I want him to fight.

I want him to fight so he can finally realize all is hopeless. I want him to fight so he knows he has lost.

I want to watch his hope die before his body.

I squeeze harder, staring into his eyes, watching with a cold detachment as they grow bigger still.

His lips begin to move more, whispering pleas and promises. He is close. I can feel the battle within turning as his body begins to shake violently.

His eyes go wide; his pupils consume his entire eyes. He squeezes my wrists one last time, trying to pull them from his throat.

I squeeze harder.

I smile, the coup de grace.

When he sees me smile, he buckles under its malevolent weight. The fight is almost lost.

His soul takes its last breath as the last of his hope disappears.

I feel nothing as his larynx snaps under the pressure of my thumbs.

I feel nothing as his neck grows ever smaller under my touch.

Who are you? What are you capable of?

I squeeze harder.

I feel the life draining from his grip, weakening his body's last attempt to defend itself from the monster perched upon his chest. His lips quicken their movements, trying to hasten his pleas, trying to get out the last prayer.

It is too late. It was too late the moment he showed himself an enemy. Nothing he can say will stop my hands from squeezing with all my strength until my palms touch.

Suddenly, his hands stop fighting me and drop to his chest. His eyes stop focusing on the monster perched on his chest and the spark of defiance, of the human spirit to survive against all odds, is snuffed out.

Who are you? What are you capable of?

I know now. I have found the cold place inside me where neither hate nor love can grow, only the complete detachment from emotion where the monster lives. It is within me.

I can love as a friend. I can hate as an enemy.

But I can kill as a monster.

I know who I am. I know what I am capable of.

The darkness is inside me, I know, and I want to die.

CHAPTER 33

The Cave: Rebirth

"Hey, you okay?" the medic asked, nudging me with his hand. I jumped, startled, the camera almost falling from my hands. I could feel the warm stream of tears tracking down my cheeks as I focused on the dead body laying at our feet. "You kinda blanked out there for a minute, Doe."

"I could do it, Derek," I whispered, looking down at the corpse. "I could have killed him with my bare hands if it came to it." The medic nodded, turning his gaze to the corpse as well.

"That's the question every warrior asks himself," he said. "Could I kill a man? Not with a bullet from far away either, but with a knife, bayonet, or even your hands when you have to watch the life drain out of him. Anyone can shoot a person. The trigger pull is over before the remorse and realization of what you've done has actually set in. When you have to do it up close and personal, when it takes time for them to die, that's when you know if you are capable."

"I could," I whispered, more for myself than his benefit.

I wondered then if I would ever rid myself of that cold detachment that lingered at the recesses of my thoughts.

Once discovered, could it be returned to the darkness?

If I ever found myself in that situation, could I really be so cold?

I knew at that moment I had changed. If ever there was a ritual to celebrate the changing of a boy into a man, that was surely mine. There were no presents or cake, only the knowledge some naive, hopeful part of me died that day and was forever replaced by a cold cave that terrified me when I peered in.

There was only darkness.

CHAPTER 34

Dying with a Brother

Kien was absolutely, without a doubt, out of his mind. Where Ringo, our first attached combat engineer, had been the cool, calm voice of reason and took every precaution to increase his chances of returning to his wife unscathed, Kien had simply resigned himself to whatever fates the gods decreed and acted as if he were completely immune to the dangers of combat.

Standing barely over five feet tall, our scrawny Vietnamese replacement engineer was barely half the size of the warriors he was surrounded by, but what Kien lacked in size, he more than made up for in fearlessness. No warrior in the platoon ever saw Kien show even the least bit of trepidation, no matter what horrible mission he was assigned. It was as if Kien had been to a gypsy fortuneteller and told he would survive the war without a single scratch. He simply knew and so nothing ever disturbed his serene smile.

Kien supported his entire family, those back in the States and those still in Vietnam. Nearly ninety percent of his paycheck went straight home to help support his extended family. He had even taken on a second job on base in the States to help supplement his income.

Once deployed, he had found alternative means of making money in addition to his military paycheck. At least three nights a week Kien would sit down at underground poker games on our base until four or five in the morning. Rarely did he stumble back to his bed with less than five hundred dollars. We did not ask how he smuggled it all back home, but it got there somehow.

No one ever wanted to be assigned as Kien's security. It was Russian roulette to be the security of a diminutive Vietnamese man who seemed way too eager to die most of the time.

Kien needed security because he was assigned one of the worst jobs in the whole of the military. He was handed a cumbersome metal detector, asked to sling his rifle across his back, and then told to try to find improvised explosive devices (IED) on our driving routes before they were detonated. The metal detector was about four feet long so if Kien did happen to find one, he was standing directly on top of it before he knew it. He could not defend himself while he was listening, only put his head down and concentrate on the squealing piglet that must have lived inside the metal detector to make such horrible noises.

The insurgents had stopped taking potshots by then. The risk was not worth the low probability of even the slightest damage being inflicted upon us. Plus, we had been trained to be shot at and take action, shooting back with discipline and overwhelming accuracy. Being shot at made sense to us and, for most, flipped the switch that turned us from laughing, smiling young men and women into cold, dead-eyed killers.

So, they stopped shooting.

And they stopped being around when we were attacked.

Instead, they remotely blew us up every chance they could.

Their tactic was intelligent and psychologically damaging. The threat of IEDs limited our entire unit's mobility to a slow, cautious crawl. We could not just roll up on a target as fast as we could drive our Humvees, hitting with the element of surprise and the shock and awe of armored trucks bristling with enormous weapons suddenly screeching to a halt in perfectly timed and coordinated positions.

Our hands were tied behind our backs and our rifles had been replaced by sharpened sticks complete with a flower tied to the end to tickle information out of bad men. We were rendered virtually ineffective against an enemy who was trying its hardest to avoid a standup fight.

Some say the insurgents are cowards for their ambushes and guerrilla tactics. These same people cheered like hell during the original *Red Dawn* movie. I guess everything in life depends on if you are on the receiving end or not.

The insurgents were making an economic decision to minimize exposure while maximizing casualties. The math worked and the tactics were sound. All we could do was bitch and try to find the IEDs before they went boom.

Where Ringo had only been called out of the trucks to check for a possible cache of weapons, we were forced to push Kien out in front of our convoy on any road that did not have dedicated and constant route clearance. Off the beaten path, we were slowed to the walking pace of a crazy bastard wielding a metal detector bigger than he was.

What should have taken two minutes to drive was ground down into an hour's march. Any element of surprise was lost when our convoy slowed from a speeding bullet train of death into a Veterans Day parade, complete with the turret gunners waving at anyone who stopped to stare, trying to gauge reactions.

Though it was better than the alternative.

Our effectiveness was dwindling and more and more we were relying on the double blinds and leave behinds to maintain any advantage. The insurgents saw us coming into the area of operation and could watch our happy parade move everywhere, even in the dark of night. It was virtually impossible to move five diesel trucks and 20 men at a walking pace without someone noticing and calling our position in.

We were tasked with raiding multiple buildings in a remote village that desperately clung for life to a wide concrete canal. The canal was wide enough to lose a Humvee in, and the only access to the village was the narrow, crumbling road that hugged the canal so tightly our tires were constantly bouncing along the concrete lip, for fear of tumbling off the five-foot abyss on the opposite side.

It could not be any more of a bottleneck if Coca-Cola bought it and paved the road in shiny, narrowing glass. We were exposed and it would only take the most rudimentary ambush to send most of us home on a private flight wrapped in air-tight plastic and a flag.

As always, our team was the first truck in the convoy, suicide vehicle, taking point and navigating the labyrinthine "road" system that crisscrossed and looped around the countryside, as if planned by a small blind child with a crayon. We were the first tires to touch every surface and therefore the most likely to "find" an IED or be targeted by a rocket-propelled grenade to halt the rest of the convoy. We were the lynchpin to any good ambush that was set against us and we had no disillusions about our position.

Whenever I started the big diesel to leave the wire, we would all quietly say goodbye to each other.

"I love you guys," I would say.

"Yeah, love you guys," Spears would say, grinning down from the turret.

"It's been a pleasure," Ballas would reply.

"Love you guys," Boom would say.

"Love you all," Clark would blush.

With our proper goodbyes said, we were ready to die together.

As point vehicle, we were also responsible for our route clearance if EOD was not leading the way. Spears and I jumped out to bodyguard Kien. Boom slid into the driver's seat while Ballas climbed up into the turret for the duration of our midnight stroll.

Spears and I moved out to each side of Kien, keeping as far out to the flanks as we could while staying within sight of the truck and Kien. The terrain often made our separation as little as ten feet from the tiny madman. He sauntered casually while staring down at the ground a few feet ahead of him, completely blithe to the world but for the small patch of potentially lethal dirt just in front of his boots.

Suddenly, without a word of warning, Kien leapt forward and pulled an enormous knife from its sheath on his bouncer. He bounded four steps and began stabbing a pile of debris with his blade in short, swift punches.

"What the fuck?" Spears growled.

"Stop the convoy," I radioed, sharing Spears's sentiments exactly.

Spears ran up to Kien and stood over him with his rifle in the ready, casting his eyes side to side looking for a target. I joined them immediately, each of us sweeping our barrels back and forth across our respective side of the road for whatever ambush had been sprung.

"What's happening, Kien?" Spears asked. "What do you see?"

Kien stood up and pointed the tip of his knife down at the pile of debris and then stepped on the pile to see if it would initiate.

"No IED here," he said triumphantly.

"You thought it might be an IED?" Spears replied, not taking his eyes off his side of the road.

"And then you stabbed it to make sure?" I added, a mix of disbelief and unbelievable anger welling up within me.

"Asshole, you could have got us killed," Spears growled.

"Nah. You were too far to die anyway, just wounded."

There was a horrible moment of silence in which Spears and I looked at where we had been standing and realized Kien was right. Where Kien would have disappeared in a merciful pink mist, never feeling a thing, Spears and I would have been caught by shrapnel, blown away from site, surviving but probably without a few limbs or vital organs for the rest of our lives.

"Shit," I sighed.

Our decision was made.

I radioed in the all-clear and we resumed our slow march. Kien walked the middle of the road and Spears and I walked beside him touching shoulders, watching him as he stabbed random objects of interest and confirming they were not IEDs since they did not instantly explode. After a while we started smiling. The fear was gone. If we blew up, we blew up.

At least we were going to die instead of losing limbs and seeing our organs on the outside.

Luckily, we were safe inside Kien's bubble of serendipity, or divine intervention. No matter how many objects Kien stabbed, we were protected so long as we were standing directly next to him.

CHAPTER 35

The Return Trip Down Guilt Way

Company-size operations were rare for us. To gather that many shooters and support in one combined effort was something of a novelty given the usually clandestine nature of our operations. We could hardly sneak around as a five-man team in the desert without being seen by someone. Multiplying that by a factor of 15 teams was not going to make us any stealthier. We traded in our shroud of darkness for massive, supporting firepower but, given the choice, I think many of us would have kept to the shadows, no matter how overwhelming the weapons and bodies we piled in one place.

We were already running only a 50 percent success rate on our company ops. One had yielded some results, though meager, but the first had left our platoon with five casualties, four of whom earned flags for their mothers. The very idea of massing as a company put a knot in my stomach.

Our team was our family. We could know what each other was thinking without words, and we were fiercely loyal. Our platoon was our extended family, crazy cousins and uncles, with Sergeant Bronx as our capable patriarch who bound us all together. Our company coming together was like an awkward, once-in-a-lifetime family reunion. We knew everyone, but not really. We had seen them in passing. They were family, but the kind you only visit rarely.

For the life of me, I cannot remember the mission of the company when we set out, if we accomplished any of our objectives, or really any distinct moment in which I felt like we were fighting the good fight and not just killing time. I remember reading—a lot. How much? I read *The Stand* over the course of the week while I lay sweating on my gear waiting. Waiting for what, I simply cannot recall.

Regardless of the success or failure of our objectives, we finally packed it in and made ready to head back to base. A company's worth of shooters and all their support were going to drive a convoy from one known position to another known position, with only three major roads to choose from. Chances were one out of three we'd choose wrong.

But that is a silly lie.

Chances were three out of three we were going to choose wrong.

The insurgents were not going to gamble with such a ripe opportunity. All three of the roads would be rigged to blow.

It was not just the initial detonation we were worried about any longer. Tactics had changed. The first blast was to create casualties—screaming, bleeding bait that would lure their mates in for the coup de grace, a secondary explosion based mostly on shrapnel, or just a good old-fashioned ambush with machine guns and a well-placed marksman somewhere out of sight.

It was not good enough just to blow up a truck any longer. The insurgents wanted to cripple the fighting spirit of the Coalition forces until we were too scared to even get out of our armor to help save our own brothers. They were going straight for our hearts.

Sergeant Bronx walked into the main room of the house our company occupied looking especially somber. His normal infectious grin was replaced by a look of utter defeat.

"Gather round," he said, and we all crowded in to hear word. He looked into all of our faces and gave the orders handed down to Lieutenant Rusher. "We leave tonight after dark."

"Finally," someone murmured, and Sergeant Bronx glared for a moment before continuing.

"We are going straight through the village where we hope they'll least expect us. And our platoon has been given the privilege of punching out three vehicles to act as point and locate any IEDs before the rest of the company arrives. We don't want a bottleneck, so these three vehicles will punch out thirty minutes earlier and, if they find something, EOD can be on scene before the rest of the company would even leave. Ballas, your team is going out. Lieutenant Rusher is going to be in the third vehicle, and Derek is going to be in the open back just in case you get into trouble."

"Who's driving for Derek?" Ballas asked.

"Derek can choose whoever he wants," Sergeant Bronx said. Derek, our medic, did not even hesitate but pointed a finger straight at me. "Well, that's settled. Ballas, you good with another driver?"

"I would rather not, but yeah, we'll find someone," Ballas replied, obviously unhappy with Derek's choice.

"Good. You guys roll in sixty. Get your gear on the trucks."

I helped Derek load all of our platoon's medical kit into the open-back Humvee.

"Glad we're on the suicide trip. We'll get to eat at the dining facility before all of those other assholes are even off Main."

"That's fucked up, Derek," I said with a laugh.

"Eh. Either we die or we eat first. It's not the worst trade-off."

When all was prepared, Lieutenant Rusher briefed our route and what to look for. Boom kept looking at me and shaking his head, mouthing "Traitor," and laughing as I shook my head. They had gotten one of the green boys to drive, fresh in-country to replace our losses from the first company op. The Company First Sergeant had been adamant every driver had to be licensed on the Humvee, even at the cost of skill and experience. The military had been in-country long enough the desk jockeys and fobbits had to justify their existence; boatloads of new, unrealistic regulations were pouring down the pipeline.

I took one last look at the rest of the company, who had just begun to prep their trucks for the next convoy that would follow behind us. Everyone was smiling and cheerful, knowing in a couple of hours they would be eating a hot meal and then racking out for some much-needed sleep. Everything seemed to be looking up.

Our three Humvees looked paltry parked next to the massive formation of armored five-ton trucks and myriad weapon systems mounted on the rows of Humvees that would follow behind us. We looked exactly like what we were assigned to be.

We looked like bait.

I climbed in behind the wheel of the open-back Humvee and Derek slid into the passenger seat beside me. He got a comm check and leaned his head back, closing his eyes to catch five minutes of sleep before we were finally cleared by higher to move. I put the rim of my helmet against the steering wheel and closed my own eyes, listening to my own slow, easy breathing as I lulled myself into a cat nap. A follow-on mission could be fragged any second and our night could go from a few more hours without proper sleep to a few more days. The general rule of thumb was catch sleep whenever you could.

"Truck Two's up," Derek said into the hook, the annoyance of being woken from his nap earlier than expected quite clear in his voice. Derek was one of the most senior men in the company and well respected for both his combat and medical expertise. He had been through all the same training all of us shooters had, but he had also gone to what was basically medical school crammed into a year's worth of intense, realistic training. Derek sat up and I rolled my head around my shoulders, taking a deep breath to clear the sleepiness away. We snapped down our night-vision goggles and prepared for movement.

"Oscar Mike," Derek repeated for my benefit, shooting his index finger forward like the barrel of a gun and dropping his thumb like a hammer. I put the truck in gear and we began rolling down the dirt road we had come in on. Luckily, the company had kept eyes on the dirt road all the way until it met up with the pavement about a half mile away from where we had firmed up, otherwise Kieu would have been dismounting from the lead truck and walking his metal detector across every square inch of dirt until we hit pavement. It had been hoped the insurgents would be bold and try to rig up a few mortar shells in the dirt road right underneath the eager eyes of our sniper teams, which had been in place hours before the company rolled by the first time.

I looked at the hazy green bumper of the lead truck, my truck, with a sense of yearning. That was my team, and I should be driving that truck, for better or worse. As flattering as it was that Derek had chosen me above all other drivers, I felt exiled and homesick for the sound of Ballas's voice calling off checkpoints as we navigated the abyss together.

I did not want to die with Derek. He was not my family. He would not know what to say to me as the last faint flicker of life drained from my eyes. His medical training had made him cold and removed from life and death.

He was not a doctor of human beings.

He was a mechanic of highly specialized military equipment.

Our little suicide patrol was punching through one of the village markets with the highest insurgent activity in the entire area. The road cut the village directly in half. The road was lined with shops in varying degrees of decay, some without roofs and some barely more than a stick propping up a piece of corrugated metal to hang a sign from. Beyond the line of shops as far as could be seen were one- and two-story cement houses with high-walled courtyards and beautiful wrought-iron gates, but only a handful of glass windows in the entire village. It looked as if the village had been an elaborate and clever design to facilitate an ambush.

Derek started to tell a story about the old days, which I reveled in.

"We would get done drinking at like three and then up at five for PT. As soon as we were done with PT, we would all stumble into the classroom and hook ourselves up to IVs. There were the few of us, sitting and waiting for our instructor, all hooked up to IVs getting less and less hungover by the second. You always hear about these dumb remedies for a hangover, but I'm telling you, there is nothing to cure a hangover like an IV. You'll be right as rain in ten minutes."

"No one cared?"

"Hell no. The instructors were hooked up to IVs half the time, too. Man, back then the only thing that mattered was how well you did your job when you were on duty. We got in huge bar fights and drank until we couldn't see almost every night, and no one gave a damn so long as we were ready for action when we were supposed to be. We kill people for a living. There was none of this nonsense of corporate values and treating warriors like businessmen. We-fucking-kill-people. That's our job. When did it ever matter if we had tattoos or not, or if our hair was cut just so? Shit, we should all be issued clothing from the *Road Warrior* and wear skull masks. That would really scare the shit out of the enemy, way more than some freshly shaved child with no tattoos shaking behind a rifle, scared shitless that his uniform isn't just so."

I laughed and realized Derek was talking to relax me as we drove through the most probable area for an ambush. Derek did not even blanch, only continued talking as if we were sitting in a coffee shop thousands of miles away in some imaginary place called "home."

"The only thing that we used to get in trouble for was if we showed up on the radar. We could get away with murder so long as it stayed in the staff NCO* realm, one or two grades above us. It was when the brass caught wind that shit had to be punished. I had two friends in training that did just about the worst thing you could do. They got drunk one night and were driving around on base. Dumb to start, but that's not the bad part. The bad part is when they smashed their car into the commanding general's building. Smashed the hell out of the statue out front and totaled the car. When the MPs arrived, they found my buddies both passed out in the car still. There was no coming back from that one. That general burned them at the stake. Drunk driving wasn't the capital offense in the military it is now, but hitting the general's favorite statue certainly was."

"It was a different military back then," Derek added after a moment's silence. "We were too busy training and fighting the bad guys to worry about dumb shit. There were no parents trying to make training easier for their fat little pussies who couldn't hack it. No one used to cry 'hazing' when shown the traditions of their fathers and grandfathers. I used to be a gangbanger before I joined. I mean real bad shit. Now that was some fucking hazing. Basic training? How much easier can you make it before you'll just let anyone in? You think the insurgents have a word for hazing? Think they bitch and moan when their training gets tough? Fuck no. That's why we're dying. People want training and the military to be all soft and cuddly, but then wonder why their overweight, television-addicted little pussy got his arms blown off because he wasn't looking around properly, because he has the attention span of a hummingbird."

We were almost through the village; I could feel my body clenching, ready for the inevitable.

"You want to make America stronger? Stop coddling your fucking kids. Stop telling them that they're always a winner and, no matter what, that they are the best thing since sliced bread. Have the wherewithal to tell your kid, 'Life is tough. Get used to it. Stop crying that shit's unfair, harden up, try really fucking hard, and then, then you just might do some good.' Think about every other nation in the world and what the vast majority of people have to do just to get by day to day. We treat our children as if they are the most fragile and beautiful objects ever to be created. That only has one outcome. They will be fragile, but they won't be so beautiful when the tough and determined beat the absolute shit out of them, because that's human nature. The strong of will survive and the fragile either serve the strong or die under their boots."

---

* NCO stands for "noncommissioned officer."

"We're through," I say, hearing what Derek had been saying but paying attention to every crack and crevice in the pavement. I had put our wheels exactly where the lead truck's wheels had already been. It was statistically safer to follow in the same tracks. Derek exhaled and put his head back on the seat. Our bodies relaxed and we adjusted in our seats.

"Well, that was terrifying," Derek said with a grin.

"Yeah. I thought for sure we were going to get hit," I said, seeing the IR headlights of route clearance on Main only two klicks away. We survived the gauntlet once again.

"Probably waiting for ..."

KA-BOOM.

Ka-Boom?

It did not make sense to my eyes. The truck in front of me, my truck, full of my team, suddenly jumped four feet off the ground and then lurched hard to the left. The doors were all blown open, the sudden overpressure inside the truck simply too great. Like holding a firecracker in a closed fist, the contained blast forced its way outward, snapping the doors open.

Boom was holding on to the top of his door frame, only his feet were left inside the truck as he clung for life. The truck rolled on, no one controlling it any longer.

"Fuck," I whispered.

"Truck One is hit," Derek passed to Lieutenant Rusher.

The lead truck stopped in the middle of the road shortly after the explosion, most of the forward momentum lost to the upward punch of whatever explosives had been smuggled underneath the pavement. Boom let go of the door and fell to the pavement, struggling to get his feet out of the truck. Nothing else moved.

"Probably just waiting for a follow-on ambush," Derek said matter-of-factly, reaching for his door handle.

It did not matter. The entire combined armies of the world could be waiting in an enormous circle with all of their guns trained on the lead truck and we still would not have hesitated. I tore open my door and heard Derek throwing his weight into his.

If I was going to die it would be at my brothers' side.

Besides, the cavalry was already on its way. The moment we were hit, Lieutenant Rusher would have called in our situation report and the company would have been on the move seconds later.

We abandoned our truck, the doors left wide open in our haste as we ran up to where the lead truck had rolled to a stop. We clicked on our red-lens head lamps. Stealth was no longer an issue. We needed to see with our own eyes to give proper medical attention.

And we had just made ourselves giant red bull's-eyes.

Derek looked at the weeds on the side of the road and then back at me as we ran. The road had a shallow canal, only a few inches deep and easily traversed, and the reeds growing up out of it were over six feet high and thick enough that we could not see through them to the bank six feet on the other side. It was the perfect concealment for a triggerman and a machine-gun crew. Crawl deep enough in and one could see out of the reeds without being seen unless under the greatest of scrutiny, which we did not have the luxury of.

Or they could have simply placed antipersonnel mines or IEDs in the reeds. The truck had not rolled too far from the explosion, so a few explosives spaced every 25 or 50 meters could be covering the entire possible kill zone.

I had seen the videos. As the intelligence bubba for the platoon, I had watched 50 of them and selected the appropriate ones to brief the rest of the platoon with so they could avoid situations exactly like this.

Stay in your truck. The insurgents are fishing for first responders to ambush when they are least aware. Wait for a cordon and air support. No sense becoming another causality yourself. Be patient.

Suddenly, I understood. The warriors on the video had gotten the same briefing and had seen the same footage. But when it is your best friends, your blood brothers writhing in the dirt, the idea of staying in the truck and letting them bleed out while you idly watch is the most revolting idea in the entire world. I would rather die with them then have their blood on my hands.

More blood on my hands.

Boom was wandering around outside of the truck, his pupils completely dilated. He constantly shook his head to try to shuffle his thoughts back into an order that made sense. His bell had been thoroughly rung.

Spears pressed himself up and out of the turret, walked down the back of the truck, jumped to the ground, and moved toward Derek. There was a nasty tear in the leg of his flight suit, but his face did not register anything, only a strange stoicism. Two feet in front of Derek, Spears fell back on his ass and looked up, shaking his head as if in disbelief.

Two accounted for.

Nickel, the green driver, spilled out of the driver's seat and slumped on the ground next to the truck.

"Oh my God," he moaned. He kneeled and rolled his forehead back and forth across the ground in disbelief, trying to will the memories of what had just happened to remain unformed and shoo them away forever.

Three accounted for.

I moved to the passenger side, my weapon up and pointed at the reeds. At the slightest noise I was going to drop the entire first magazine and then mount the turret gun, hoping it was still operational.

Kien burst out of the back door and flopped on the ground in front of me. Clark had been chosen to guard the lieutenant in his truck and woe be to them when his switch flipped. Clark was the best of us all and had been equally upset for being traded out for Kien.

"You hit, Kien?"

"Ballas," he replied, his eyes wide and quivering as he tried to focus. A shiver ran through me. Ballas had yet to open his door.

I grabbed the handle and Ballas spilled out onto the ground like a sack of meat as the door swung open. I choked back the bile that ran up in my throat at the sight of so much blood. Under the red light, it was so black that it made my own blood run cold and my stomach begin to revolt, clenching so hard I thought I would implode.

I glanced at the passenger seat where Ballas had been sitting to get an idea of the damage and his possible wounds.

There was no seat left, only fragments of metal and blood.

Blood. So much blood.

Black, shiny blood everywhere.

Blood on everything.

I unclipped my rifle and placed it on the ground beside Ballas, who was staring up into the beautiful night sky, a coal-colored blanket pierced with a million sparkling lights, hinting at the cosmic beauty beyond. His eyes were focused a thousand miles away and I thanked the gods for small miracles. His flight suit was spattered in blood.

I unhooked his plate bouncer and pulled it off his chest. I could not control my hands. They were shaking so hard I feared I might not ever regain control over them. I feared what I was asking them was so horrific they would never want to do anything for me again.

Ballas's eyes began to focus on me as I worked.

"Is it bad?" he whispered, his voice calm and soothing.

He was not worried or afraid. My hands stopped shaking.

"You're fine."

"Don't lie. It's bad, isn't it? I see blood everywhere," he whispered, looking up into my face with a serene look.

I slid a hand underneath him and felt a thousand tiny cigarette burns in his flight suit, but my fingertips could not find the bigger holes I feared. My face began to tighten as I looked off into the distance and concentrated on my sense of touch.

"Can you feel your legs?"

"Yes," Ballas answered.

"Ballas, I'm not finding anything huge. I need to roll you over quick to make sure I am not missing something."

The something huge would be an unseen wound gushing ounces of blood every second, but we left it unnamed. I rolled Ballas onto his side and inspected the back of his flight suit. There was blood everywhere, but no tears in his flight suit bigger than a quarter. I rolled Ballas onto his back.

"How bad is it? Bad?" Ballas asked.

"You're fine," I said, not quite believing it but willing him to. Ballas reached up, grabbed my bouncer, and pulled his face closer to mine.

"Dude," he said loudly, his eyes alight and dancing. "Dude, free college."

The message delivered, Ballas passed out and slumped back to the ground. In his home state, Ohio, a Purple Heart got four years of free tuition to a state college. The prospect thrilled him and then overwhelmed him.

"Hey, check this out," Derek yelled to me. I turned and looked.

Derek had Spears sitting on the ground and the leg of his flight suit cut all the way up to his hip. There was a deep, wide cut in the meat just above Spears' knee. Derek smiled at me and inserted his hand into the wound. Spears was a world-class athlete and had muscular thighs. Derek sunk his fist into the opening until it almost completely disappeared, like some kind of macabre magic trick. Derek grinned ear to ear and looked at me approvingly, like my witnessing such a trick made his day. His whole hand was inside my best friend's flesh.

To this day I cannot get that image out of my head whenever I picture Spears. It haunts me. It taints my every thought of him.

Later, there would be infection when the doctors could not get every single fragment of the shrapnel out.

There would be rotting flesh scooped out to keep the infection from spreading.

There would be pain beyond imagining as the nerves and artery were slowly strangled by the hardening scar tissue.

There would be days Spears would be on so much Oxy that I would cry in my bedroom at the sight of my hero drooling and absently watching television.

Years away there would be an amputation, and I would cry so hard I almost passed out. I would curse the idea of a fair and just God, allowing one of the greatest and most athletic men I have ever met to be struck down in his prime.

There would be tears and there would be anger and guilt.

There would be so much to sift through and deal with for all of us.

But at that moment, I could only stare dumbly at Derek as he grinned and fisted Spears's leg like there was a joke I did not quite understand.

I turned away in disgust and my mood immediately changed to disbelief. I looked at the book-sized piece of shrapnel stuck into the headrest of Kien's seat. I looked down at Kien, who was massaging his right ankle vigorously where he had banged it off something inside the truck.

"Kien, look at this," I said, pointing to the enormous piece of shrapnel. We studied it together for a moment; he suddenly realized what I was showing him.

The piece of shrapnel had shot through the space where any normal warrior's eyes and forehead should have been. It would have decapitated anyone of average height. Kien, who constantly would slump down further in his seat to sleep until duty called, was just short enough that the shrapnel had merely grazed his helmet as it passed above him.

Kien shrugged his shoulders as if unimpressed. He knew he was not going to die yet, so what was the big deal?

KAAAABOOOOOOOM.

We all looked back down the road we had just traveled and knew without a doubt what that explosion meant.

The cavalry was not coming.

"Company was just hit in the village. A truck is in the river," Lieutenant Rusher passed over the radio. "Prepare for immediate medevac, strip the lead truck. We're on our own."

Every piece of gear was stripped from the blown-up truck and distributed between the two remaining Humvees as Derek stabilized Ballas and Spears in the back of the open back. We would be leaving the crippled Humvee, but not with a single piece of our gear on it.

In minutes I was driving the open-back Humvee toward base, speeding along as fast as I could push her. Another IED would have been catastrophic, but we were spared insult to injury. We pulled up to the field hospital 10 minutes later, and they shuffled off my brothers into the warm light beyond the front doors. Derek followed them to debrief the doctors on all that had happened and his methods up to that point.

I drove the Humvee back to our staging area and got out.

Everyone else had somewhere else to be. I was alone; I have never felt so lost.

I looked down at my hands and flight suit. Both were covered in my brothers' blood from moving them into the back of the Humvee.

I shivered and stood motionless for minutes, my mind locked up and frozen with indecision. I felt like my life had come to a most abrupt halt and that I did not know how to get the ball rolling again. I stared into space and then did the only thing I could think of.

I stood alone in our empty platoon room and began cleaning my weapons and serialized gear as I cried. I stripped everything down to its base parts and tried to scrub away the filth so that, when I put them back together, they might work as they should.

I prayed it could work.

I simply did not know what else to do.

CHAPTER 36

Blue Falcons

IEDs were becoming commonplace. Military Intelligence began plotting each one and patterns started emerging as to the frequency of placement in certain areas. It seemed that if the insurgents paid a local national to emplace an IED, it would be done with the least amount of effort possible. They would literally walk out of their front door, go to the road, dig it in, and walk back home. Clusters of emplacements crowded anywhere within walking distance of villages.

Boom, now team leader, placed our team in a sniper observation point in a high-density area of emplacement. The emplacement rate in the area was so high our chances of success bordered on if we could intercede two emplacements in one night. The team, having lost two of its original members, was in great need of something positive. The mood was brooding but with flashes of bloodlust excitement. We needed a win.

Someone was going to die that night. We were damn sure of that.

After the third dummy drop, we hustled out into the darkness to search for a proper position with ample cover and concealment, something of a unicorn in reality. We did our best with outdated maps and a landscape being constantly changed by the whims of low-tech agriculture and irrigation. Where once a grove of palms or a berm had been on the map, we would arrive to discover it had been replaced by a corrugated iron and cinderblock shack in a matter of a week.

Setting in was a crap-shoot.

To our horror, the grove of trees we had planned on hiding in had been logged, nearly half of the trees having been felled but left to rot where they lay. The ground was a hard pan that felt as if it would snap our shovel in half with each ineffective strike we made to dig out a few fist-sized chunks. We could see villages on either side of us that, come morning, would probably have villagers watching us just by peeking out of their iron-barred windows.

Snake eyes. The dice were cold.

We would have to move. Fast. Morning was barreling toward us and we could not afford to be caught out in the open so far from any friendly units. Our leash time was already pushing 20 minutes; a lifetime of horrors could visit us in 20 minutes before the quick-reaction force arrived. We needed to find someplace to hide—and quickly.

The rumble of heavy vehicles and diesel engines carried far on the warm, summer breeze. Boom tilted his head and listened. We all froze and cocked our ears toward the sound. It was growing louder.

"There isn't supposed to be anyone on this section of road tonight," Boom whispered. "We'll never have an emplacement if vehicles are on the road."

"Higher says that they have no knowledge of any unit movement for fifty klicks. They have no idea who it is," Nickel passed, holding the hook to his ear.

"Hide," Boom said, and suddenly we were in a lethal game of hide-and-seek with an unknown unit. We scrambled to get down behind a dead log and the team huddled together. Clark and I shared a look. The rotting tree might stop a pellet gun or hastily lobbed water balloon, but anything more powerful would shred the rotting wood already falling apart in dime-sized pieces. Worse, we would be shredded right along with it.

Clark smiled and nodded.

I nodded back.

Our goodbyes were silently said.

The rumble grew and the waiting seemed to last forever. Boom grabbed the hook from Nickel and quietly discussed our situation with our platoon commander as, somewhere very far away, 10 staff NCOs and officers scrambled to find out who the hell was driving on the highway toward our position. It was a race against time. They would either find a call sign and contact the unit or there was a pretty good chance they would see a bunch of men huddled behind a log and mistake our infra-red flasher for muzzle flash, opening fire out of dread fear of dying themselves in this forsaken country.

Boom snuck a peek above the log and watched the convoy come into view.

"Shit, there are a lot of trucks," he whispered. "Eight, maybe nine, heavy weapons."

Rifles take a good eye and a steady hand to be effective. Hundreds of hours of sending rounds down range need to be spent to make it a truly effective weapon outside a hundred yards.

Heavy weapons, when shot by an expert are almost instantaneously devastating. Heavy weapons shot by a novice are still just as devastating; just give it another 10 to 20 seconds. Heavy weapons took a monkey with a sense of direction that bordered on "somewhere to my front" to be horrifically lethal. They were designed that way. Sure, they might not hit that single man-sized target out at 300 yards on the first few shots, but when you have almost endless canisters of ammunition that can be chewed through in a matter of seconds, the law of probability would say to not bet on your survival.

Or your friends'.

Or anyone in a 45-degree arc given enough time.

"We'll be good, keep your heads down and they'll pass right by," Boom said confidently, sliding down with his back against the log until he was seated. The hook was dreadfully silent. Higher was not having any luck finding who was leading the goat rope of a convoy slowly rolling 100 meters from our position. Boom smiled to himself and closed his eyes, falling into the restful "waiting" state that seemed to occupy much of our time. There was nothing to do but wait for them to pass us by.

Almost directly in front of our position, the convoy came to a screeching halt. Boom opened his eyes.

"Fuck," he exhaled.

The IED mapping was shared across all units and branches. Everyone knew where the IEDs were emplaced with frequency. The reason we were sitting in our current position to interdict an emplacement was the exact same reason the convoy came to a stop in front of us. There was a damn-good chance there was an IED and they were not taking any chances. They would stop, throw out sweepers, and crawl the next half mile to ensure no truck ended up flipped over on the side of the road and *Taps* being played in four or five different small towns across the country a week later.

"Fuck. Fuck, fuck, fuck," Boom whispered, peeking over the log.

The gunners would be on high alert and be able to focus on strange objects now that the landscape was not a green, night-vision blur flying past them under the false security of speed. They were a sitting target and they knew it. Their heart rates increased, their mental functioning sped up, and they all suddenly wanted to piss very badly. They were suddenly in a very bad place and would kill without thought to defend each other.

And now we were in a worse place.

The convoy rumbled and crawled forward a few feet. It stopped for a minute, lurched forward, stopping again only a few more feet down the road. Morning was not far off, and by the time the convoy finally passed us, dawn would be breaking, and we would be out in the open only a stone's throw from two villages known to at least actively help the Insurgency, if not be their strongholds.

"We can't stay like this," Boom said and picked up the hook. He ordered immediate extraction by the QRF and checked his watch. The cavalry would not arrive for at least twenty minutes; any second some nervous heavy gunner could open fire on the suspicious movement only a hundred yards away in an area known for nightly IED emplacement.

Boom reached in his pack and retrieved a red flare.

"Well, this could suck," he said and stood up. He left his rifle on the ground next to me and began walking toward the road with outstretched arms. Events were now in motion that could not be changed. Boom walked diagonally away from our position, hoping that if the situation went south and he was killed, at least the team would not be directly behind him in the line of fire.

Boom was sacrificing himself for the sake of the team.

Halfway across the distance, one of the gunners yelled something and Boom froze. Slowly, he brought the red flare in front of his body and popped it.

"RPG, RPG!" the gunners in the convoy yelled, and what sounded like a hundred weapons were thrown off safe and spun around to target the smoking back-trail of the red "RPG" that was so horribly aimed at the convoy it had been fired directly up in the air, as if it was some kind of signal flare.

"Friendly!" Boom screamed, holding his arms out and dropping the empty flare tube. "FRIENDLY!"

Deja vu.

Searchlights came on and zeroed on Boom, who continued to scream at the top of his lungs as he stood defenseless in an open field waiting to be gunned down by his own military.

Silence from the convoy. The brass inside the convoy must have been discussing options and creating PowerPoints to deal with this new, unknown threat. It felt like being pulled over by the state police when they sit in their car for 40 minutes and you can only wonder what in the hell could take so long. Boom's arms were shaking from being held out so straight for so long.

Finally, doors opened along vehicles and a small force slowly moved toward Boom. After a short talk, Boom stomped back to our position.

"Pack your shit. We are extracting as soon as the QRF gets here."

"What happened?"

"Unknown. They did not contact anyone about their movement. Heads are going to roll. That captain just may be a lieutenant by dawn."

"Where the fuck were they going? This isn't even their area of operation."

"If they knew, they didn't say."

"Now what?" I asked.

"We go back, we clean our shit, and we get ready to go back out tomorrow somewhere new. As far away from these idiots as possible. I am pretty sure there is a better chance we're going to die from blue on blue rather than actual combat. Shit, we could have stayed in the States, killed each other back there, and at least had weekends off. We didn't have to come all the way to this shithole to get killed by our own people."

CHAPTER 37

Tent in the Middle of Nowhere

Life clings to water.

The cement dwellings and archaic farms hug the verdant banks of the Euphrates tightly underneath the shade of the tall, majestic palm trees. Standing at the edge of the river, one might think they were in a lush jungle, full of life and endless opportunity but, only a short walk away, the desert waits, timeless and without mercy.

Driving away from the high, green grasses and the hand-irrigated fields of the river felt like leaving the world behind. We watched from the windows and tops of the turrets as the palm trees grew ever smaller and the sand grew ever finer underneath our tires. The sand began to seep into everything.

We had been tasked with a new area of operation, some forsaken oasis in the middle of the desert far from the rivers. It had once been the vacation spot for the rich and the connected, Hussein's own private island palace, right smack in the middle of the small lake the rest of the cement mansions surrounded. They were all ruins now, crumbling, forgotten tombs held together only by exposed rebar, like huge, ancient skeletons of dread beasts scoured by the sun and sand.

They were the perfect spider-holes for the Insurgency and all at once every special operations asset of every branch descended on the area the size of a small New England village.

The landscape was alien, hard-baked earth broken only by flowing dunes that seemed alive, changing and writhing before our very eyes in the hot, constant breeze. There was only a single, unbroken color of sand for as far as we could see. We drove for hours across the desert as if stuck in a single, timeless moment.

And, suddenly, as we rounded a dune, there was a beautiful, colorful tent. It was long and slender, standing shoulder height at its tallest. The indigenous standing at the entrance could be described in exactly the same way. Their smiles were bright and curious.

They did not know there was a war on.

We were invited in for chia tea and to share what little food they had. It was clean and comfortable inside, and the elderly patriarch sprawled lazily, propping his chest up on a small pillow. We made small talk and drank three-quarters of the tea in our cups, bowing gratefully as we waved off refills.

Finally, someone asked the burning question.

"Why live here?"

"Because we have always lived here, as far back as my family can remember."

I was more curious how, but we did not want to overstay our welcome. We left cases of water and bags of candy for the children. They smiled and waved, and the children danced as we drove away.

They were a brave and beautiful people who lived in the tent in the middle of nowhere.

CHAPTER 38

Blowing in the Doors of Opportunity

There were three pounds of plastic explosive strapped to my chest. The detonator was safely hidden in a pouch on my left side, easily accessed by my left hand while my right was free to remain on the trigger, ready to respond to any threat to my mission. I was a walking bomb, a man saddled with a "suicide" vest that could take out every human being inside a 15-meter blast radius should the explosives detonate.

I kept mumbling prayers to the gods like a shotgun blast, trying to hit any and all I could think of, in case one happened to be listening. The idea of being turned into a pink mist was less than attractive, especially in the middle of our battalion compound.

I pulled out all of the explosives contained in the large pouch on my chest and laid them back down on the workbench in front of me. They had all fit in the enormous pouch. I was pleased and touched the explosives tenderly, like a father stroking his children as they slept.

Sergeant Bronx had alluded to checking on my breaching charges we had built, to make sure I would have everything I needed should a mission require it. He had been my breacher mentor, and I was his apt pupil, back in the States. We had continued that relationship whenever we could find time and acquire the supplies. While he watched and critiqued, I had designed and built a good amount of breaching charges that could deal with almost any type of door we would come across that needed to be opened in a hurry. We had talked about creating some "ghost charges" designed to breach cinderblock walls, but their bulk and the slim chances of needing them had put them on the back burner. Still, I looked at the vast quantity of charges I did have and smiled idiotically.

I was finally going to get that dancing gopher ruining the golf course.

I could only hope Sergeant Bronx was not toying with me.

Shortly after, we piled into the intimate briefing room and took our seats around the long table. When everyone had settled in and opened their notebooks, Lieutenant Rusher nodded for me to begin the intelligence briefing.

The briefing I gave before each mission had changed vastly over the course of the six months we had been in-country. What had begun as a cultural briefing and a tourism guide through the mission's area of operation had turned into something of a nightly news broadcast of all the horrors visited on Coalition forces since the last briefing. There were many. IEDs had become a daily occurrence and at least one of our small unit's 40 trucks was being hit every other day, usually only to the detriment of a tire or some gear, but each time was Russian roulette, and we had already lost so many good men to the game.

The insurgents were getting even more clever. I stood and briefed about two new tactics that had come up on the radar. The first was that they had begun rigging the overpasses and road signs that hung out over the pavement so the shrapnel would rain down onto the only unprotected part of the Humvee, the open top of the turret. The turret gunner would be shredded, and the convoy would be left one heavy gun short if attacked simultaneously. The platoon grimaced at the prospect.

Worse, there had been a recent instance where a team of warriors on patrol were told that another warrior had been hit by a vehicle a few blocks away. They ran to see what had happened and found another warrior trapped under the front wheels of a vehicle. Only it was not a warrior. It was a pair of stolen camouflage utilities loaded up with high explosives like a scarecrow and staged to look like an injured warrior. It was the tar-baby from *Br'er Rabbit* and the warriors walked right up to it unknowingly.

Finished with my scary bedtime tale, I sat and Lieutenant Rusher stood up. He flipped the PowerPoint to the next slide and, as if he had posted a picture of erotic nature, every warrior in the room got an erection.

"Helo Raid" was all the slide said.

I stared and grinned. Sandstorms and lack of proper support had led to little in the way of air assets but there it was, in tall black-and-white letters on the giant screen in front of us.

Lieutenant Rusher smiled and basked in the suddenly high morale of his men. There had been too many losses and too many missions that yielded only a greater sense of disillusionment. With two little words, we were joking and smirking again, ready to fight the good fight, as we had been the first day we had set foot in-country. We had been given back our hope.

There was a high-value target known to be hiding out in a large family compound comprised of a dozen buildings all within a hundred meters of each other. Everyone on target was suspect and to be treated as a potential threat: zip-tied, fingerprinted, and guarded closely when found. This was a very bad man and his family would defend him with their lives.

"Higher has cleared us hot to breach every door given the likelihood of resistance," Lieutenant Rusher said. "I want those doors blown off the hinges and everyone inside those buildings so disorientated from the overpressure that they aren't able to fight back. Do we have enough charges to do this?" Lieutenant Rusher looked at Sergeant Bronx, who looked at me.

"Yes, Sir, we do," I said with a wave of discernable pleasure that swept over the briefing room. The mission was getting better and better. An airborne raid and blowing doors in with high explosives—it seemed like our luck was finally turning around.

In a few hours, 20 men were standing at the edge of a dirt landing pad while the helicopters underwent their final preflight checks. There was still a good chance our helicopter insert would be canceled. It seemed every time we stepped near a helicopter for any reason, the weather would turn sour, or some loose bolt would ground the thing for days. So, we stood on the edge of the landing pad eyeing the helicopters warily, watching for any wisp of black smoke from the engine or for someone to run out of the control tower waving off the pilots to shut it down. We cringed as the minutes ticked by. Our hopes were too high, and we waited silently for the other shoe to drop.

Suddenly, we were clamoring aboard and strapping in. We looked around at each other and grinned underneath our goggles. It was finally happening. After months of canceled missions and failed missions and friends dying on missions, we were about to take off for a direct-action mission that might actually have an effect on the war, if the briefing had not been exaggerated. Bad men could be replaced but it took a while and the chaos in the interim would create even more opportunities and missions. We hoped it was a house of cards, though the insurgents were proving more resilient than anyone had previously given them credit for. They were more like a well-funded hydra creature of myth.

The helicopters took to the sky and my stomach lurched. I had never become comfortable inside moving vehicles; driving around in-country had done nothing to assuage my fears. Watching your best friends' trucks constantly get blown up did not inspire confidence in our methods of transportation.

It was worse when I was not driving. There was a loss of control that made me sick to my stomach. A thousand things could go wrong mechanically and another thousand could go wrong with those who were driving or flying; I could do nothing about those problems. I could only sit there and wait for "Hold on, we're going down." In a helicopter crash, "holding on" is a joke. Wile E. Coyote always "held on" to the giant rock that flipped over on top of him as he fell. Lot of good that did him.

I was only comfortable patrolling with my boots in the dirt, where I was in full control. We had spent endless months practicing our craft on foot back in the States only to be tossed into vehicles for every mission. Our patrolling and navigation skills had been relegated to walking short distances on flat terrain where the objective could usually be seen a mile off in the distance.

Still, the view from above was amazing.

From such great heights, the land was transformed. All the abrasive details of poverty and suffering fell away as we climbed; all that was left was the vague notion of small clusters of families hugging the edges of the waterways and fertile fields. High up, it could have been a view of the Midwest or any farming community around the world. Only the brightly lit windows gave signs of life, twinkling in the absolute darkness like a faux night sky.

It was breathtaking.

For a moment, the fear and adrenaline melted away as we all stared off into the endless beauty rolling away from us as far as we could see in any direction. It was one of the few moments in which I felt human again.

And all at once, every single light as far as we could see blinked out. The world was plunged into utter darkness in a single breath. For the first time in months, I smiled genuinely. It was as if an entire country had blinked out of existence.

"What happened?" someone yelled.

"They only get a few hours of power a day. Their time was up."

Without any moon in the sky, I stared out at the darkness without reference to height or distance. It was the closest thing I have ever experienced to complete disorientation. We were simply suspended in the inky blackness. I shivered.

"Two mikes out," Sergeant Bronx shouted, and we all repeated the time until we hit the target. I closed my eyes and began breathing deeply as I pictured the process of breaching the first door.

"One out," Sergeant Bronx shouted. I kept my eyes shut and tried to concentrate. The raid would all come down to me placing the first charge quickly and perfectly, hooking up the detonator, and blowing that door so we could clear the house our target was in without delay. Any hesitation, any mistake, and the men around me could die.

A few days before, another platoon had been led into an ambush by an elderly woman, who had lured them into the doorway of a house with promises of information. Inside the house was a machine gun aimed directly at the front door. The machine-gun crew did not even wait for the old woman to get clear. They simply mowed her down along with some of my brothers.

It had to go right. The door had to be breached quickly or the first men through the door would be riddled with AK-47 rounds or worse. I felt my knees trembling. The adrenaline was coursing through me now; I took one last deep breath before opening my eyes.

Sergeant Bronx yelled one final time and before I could take another breath we were pouring out of the helicopter as it landed and moving toward the objective. The helicopters took to the sky and were suddenly only a distant noise as we made our approach. Our objective loomed huge and green in our night-vision goggles. I could hear my heartbeat over my footfall and I grinned.

I had never felt so alive and I never would again. Behind every door was the possibility of death; the body rewarded such boldness with a cocktail of chemicals that made us feel invincible. Everything was surreal, hyper-real, and every sense seemed to open full throttle like none of us had ever experienced.

There was only here, now; everything else faded to black.

We neared the first objective and the warriors around me fell into their place, holding security on the windows and the roof while I moved toward the door.

It was like a present from the universe. I was going to be able to put all my training to use and blow a whole bunch of doors in, so my team and the rest of my platoon would be safe. I would protect them. I was going to be able to put the wrong things that had happened right. I would not let any of them slip through my fingers. I could not stop picturing the Humvee flipping slowly inside the column of flame.

I would protect them.

I would keep them all safe.

I would not fail them again.

I moved up to the door and almost froze. My mind went into absolute chaos and it was all I could do to stifle that scream of absolute horror and rage welling up in my throat.

The door was unlocked.

Not locked and not barricaded. Not welded shut or being held closed by a desperate enemy who had seen our approach.

Hells, it was not even closed.

It hung half open, swinging back inside the building a foot; I could not imagine more of a feeling of such utter worthlessness.

I passed by the door, took up a position on the opposite side of the doorframe, and gave the signal to stack up. No one had any idea what was going on and there was no time to explain. I removed a flash bang, held it up for them to see, and waited for all three men stacked up to nod. I kicked open the door and slid in the heavy metal canister. An enormous blinding light and slight over-pressure filled the building, and I followed the three men inside.

The next three minutes were a blur of close-quarter combat tactics, a lot of flash bangs, and even more swearing. The platoon moved beautifully, like water pouring into each building from the doorways, checking for gunmen in every room before moving down the hallways until the entire objective was secure.

Dry hole. Not a single person of interest on site. The helicopters reported no one running from the site before or after the raid got underway.

We did not miss our target. He had never been there at all.

We were quiet on the flight back to base. No one admired the beauty of the countryside. No one contemplated the insignificance of our existence when in the context of the vast blackness of our universe. We put our heads down and wished for nothing but sleep.

CHAPTER 39

Black Hawk Downer

Turned out our target had never gone to the house we had raided. He had talked about it over an unsecured cell phone with dates and times, but he had never actually followed through. The information was good. Our target was probably just one of those shitty friends who made plans and then flaked at the last second because he wanted to watch some movie on television that had come on, even though he owned the DVD and could watch it anytime.

Or so the intelligence guys told us, trying to convince those in the briefing room that the intel squad was not at fault for such a vast waste of resources. The good news was we were going to get a second chance, they added. Our intended target had been sporadically using his unsecured cell phone to make plans for another visit to the area; we would hit him as soon as he stopped moving and turned on his cell phone, for triangulation.

The bad news was we would not be receiving air support for whatever reason. We would be driving right into the heart of where the insurgents were believed to be strongest. On the only road. In loud diesel trucks. Possibly in the middle of the day.

Great.

If our target was not tipped off that we were coming, then his early warning network was either deaf or asleep on the job. Either way, we knew we were going to be driving into an empty hole, arriving hours after he fled, or into an ambush.

For two days, we sat 25 feet from our trucks on a five-minute leash. In five minutes from the call coming in that our target had turned on his cell phone and been triangulated, we would be wheels up. Our food was delivered to the little room we sat in, fully geared, and the boredom became almost unbearable.

For two days, we sat and argued and laughed and slept in our flight suits with our gear tucked up beside us. It would be worth it, we told each other. When the call finally came in, we would roll out and all the waiting and boredom would have been a paltry price to pay for rolling up such a high-value target. It would be a magnificent story to tell our grandchildren as they ignored us and played with their smart phones and rolled their eyes.

Lieutenant Rusher swept into the room in full battle gear, helmet nestled in the crook between his elbow and his thin, muscular body, his eyes alight and a grin tugging at the corners of his usually stoic face.

"Five minutes starts now. Everyone on the trucks."

It took less than five minutes. We had prestaged everything and rotated out a "fire watch" on the trucks so the only thing that needed to be done was a final communications check with each truck, which had also been done by the watch every two hours, and then the communication check with higher.

It was dusk and the sun had not quite set on the horizon, casting its last warm tendrils of light before dipping deep and taking the temperature with it. It was not an ideal time to drive, too light for night vision but not quite light enough to be comfortable spotting an IED before it was too late, but the call had come and there was no delaying.

Wheels up, we sped toward the gate of the base, Lieutenant Rusher calling every frequency he needed so our egress was not held up by a lackadaisical gate guard who had not checked his logbook. Rusher had personally gone out to the gate earlier, putting a note in gigantic letters informing them of our mission and our needs, so we could slip out of the base without any of the normal time-intensive safety measures of leaving base.

One hundred feet from the gate and sirens blared from behind us. I checked my mirror and noticed a white SUV with blue-and-red lights flashing speeding up behind us.

Boom radioed for orders and after a moment Lieutenant Rusher ordered us to pull over but leave the trucks running.

The warrant officer stepped out of his police vehicle, pad of paper in hand, ready to take down our unit and smugly run our speeding violation up the chain of command until the president himself was informed. Lieutenant Rusher bounded from the passenger seat of his truck and ran toward the warrant officer.

"You know you were speeding," the warrant officer said in the slow drawl of the southern police officers in the television dramas.

And before our eyes, our always composed commanding officer finally snapped. Rusher screamed at the top of his lungs, pointing his finger at the warrant officer, telling him to get back in his truck and call his higher, who should have informed him of our movement, though far more colorfully and loudly. The warrant officer, not used to being talked to in such a way, blustered and began to retort, but Lieutenant Rusher turned crimson and the cords of his neck tightened until they looked like they were going to snap.

"We're leaving. If you want, follow us, and give us a ticket after we complete our mission. We're wheels up in ten seconds," Lieutenant Rusher said into his headset. He turned and the warrant officer stood dumfounded, his pad of paper still held up as if he was about to write down our names and ranks.

"Punch it," Lieutenant Rusher passed over the net as he closed his door. We made it 20 feet before the roar of close air support drowned out the rest of the world. We looked up.

Five MH-6 Little Birds, keeping low to the deck, screamed overhead and then continued on in the exact direction we were headed. When we got to the gate, the guard seemed confused by who we were and why we were expecting a hurried version of the normal checkout. Boom leaned over toward my open door and repeated our unit and how our lieutenant had checked in not six hours earlier to ensure this very situation would not happen. The E-3 checked his log book and then shook his head.

"Yep, you're right. Says right here that …"

"We need to go now," Boom growled, and I slammed the door. Our five-truck convoy shot from the gate and we continued to pick up speed. We grinned at our proximity to the moment of our raid.

"No, no, no, no," Boom growled, holding the hook to his ear. "Bullshit, no."

"What is it?" I asked, but I already knew the answer.

"Stop," Boom sighed. "Stop and turn around. The top tier just did the hit. It's all done. They got him."

Silently, I turned the truck around and the convoy followed in a big horseshoe before heading back into the gate.

We unpacked our gear and cleaned all our weapons without more than the necessary words needed to get our work done. We trudged off back to our beds and closed our eyes, hoping that by some miracle our horizontal time machine would take us up to the moment when it would be time to go back to the States.

CHAPTER 40

No Going Home

American outposts and firm bases were hard, sturdy places bristling with gun emplacements manned by even harder, sturdier men with flat, cold gazes scanning the horizons, who were never more than an arm's length from their rifles; not during chow, not during sleep, not during defecation or masturbation, both of which were done in the same sad, sweaty port-o-johns. There was a sense of scarcely contained violence, like a mousetrap that was just waiting for a feather's touch to release the spring and break spines. The slightest provocation and those hard men would jubilantly release every type of gunpowder retribution at their disposal. To approach an American outpost was to feel the hairs on the back of your neck stand and quiver even though you were on the same team.

The Iraqi "base" we approached looked like a child's fort, with dark, whip-lean men lounging about, smoking cigarettes, and talking excitedly with large, sweeping gestures. The only thing missing was a giant sign that read "No Girlz Aloud" and a stack of Ziploc-wrapped sandwiches their mothers had made them for lunch. No one seemed to be watching the approach or manning the heavy guns aimed down the two main avenues. Only the 20-foot-high sand berm around the base that American combat engineers had pushed up indicated anything defensive about the position.

Our company orders had been to co-locate with the Iraqi Army and run missions with them out of their forward operating base, which would have been state-of-the-art somewhere between the Bronze Age and the Iron Age. We all expected to see piles of stones and boiling pots of oil by the entrance, as we passed through one of the two catty-cornered gaps in the berm. The sentries all but abandoned their posts as we rolled through, with enthusiastic shouts and much arm waving at our arrival because with the American military came all of the modern luxuries such as bottled water and dual-purpose port-o-johns. Plus, while the enemy never hesitated to attack the hardly defended Iraqi Army positions and checkpoints, the enemy rarely attacked when the Americans were standing beside them.

It was like a sibling relationship. We were the strong older brother standing with our hands on our hips defiantly, while our sickly, younger brother peered out from behind us and blew raspberries at the bullies, until the moment we had somewhere else to be. Then they just got their asses kicked and blamed us for not being there to protect them.

The moment our Humvees stopped, Sergeant Bronx jumped into the dust cloud we had kicked up and called a platoon meeting. We hustled over to make a hasty circle around him and get our orders. Due to the rush Sergeant Bronx seemed to be in, we were hopeful some type of time-sensitive raid had just come down from higher and we would be punching out soon to go surprise some bad men.

"All right, snoops, the Iraqi Army passed that they got security and for us to just relax." Sergeant Bronx let that sink in for a moment. "Well, fuck that. You all saw the state of security when we drove in. There ain't any. Not one serpentine, not one barrier to stop a vehicle riding on its axles with explosives. It would take the shitheads about thirty seconds to roll in here with a dump truck full of PE4 to turn all you smokeys and stupids to pink mist. Now, who here thinks it's a good idea to let them hold security?"

It was a rhetorical question and we knew where our silence would take us.

"None of you? Good. Team leaders, start a rotation—we are putting two guys on each corner. One from us and one from another platoon."

And just like that, we took over security for the Iraqi firm base. The men on security were not put out, nor was their pride hurt in the least when we showed up. They celebrated the sudden reduction in the actual work they had to do and ran off when we trudged our own heavy guns up to the berm and parked our Humvees across the gaps, creating a gate of sorts.

Ten minutes later a short, mustached Iraqi, swimming in his oversized fatigues and wearing the rank of major, was shouting and herding the group of soldiers who had fled their security detail back toward the berm. He screamed and pointed back to our now heavily fortified security positions. It seemed that Iraqi officer's pride was far easier wounded than his men. He kicked dirt and screamed as the soldiers ran back to their posts to take up security beside the American warriors. The major stood for a full 10 minutes longer, watching every post, to make sure his men did not sully the good name of the Iraqi Army any further than they already had. He mumbled, kicked dirt with a shout, and then disappeared back into a large, well-kept command tent, never to be seen again.

When we were not running missions, the security details took up almost all our time. During some shifts, when the combination of men on post together was just wrong, the hours went so slowly one would begin to wonder if time would eventually come to a complete stop. We were all warriors, but our backgrounds were vast, diverse things, and our one common thread was thin and did not always bridge the gap between men. Some shifts were passed in slow silence, without a word passed between the men besides the compulsory exchange of initial pleasantries, duties, and fields of fire.

And then some shifts could not last long enough, when the conversation was interesting and the stories so unbelievable our laughter could be heard over the diesel generators. Corporal Nantucket was quite possibly the most entertaining person I had ever had the pleasure of sharing a security detail with. His smile was indestructible, forever slapped upon his cherub face despite whatever was going on around him.

"Right before we left I was walking on the upper deck of the barracks at like three a.m. and someone had left their door a crack open," Nantucket said smiling. "I kinda glanced inside as I walked passed and two of our guys were having a threesome with this beautiful girl. I mean, she was hot."

"Did you keep watching?" I asked.

"Fuck no, I'm not a pervert," he said, his tone one of genuine surprise and hurt. "I wouldn't just stand there on the catwalk and watch. That's weird."

"So what did you do?" I asked.

"I took off all my clothes, left them on the catwalk, and went inside," he said matter-of-factly, like it was the only obvious choice. I started laughing, one of those deep unexpected laughs that catches you off guard and seems to erupt like a volcano.

"You went inside?" I laughed.

"Well, yeah. We were shipping out in two days and it's not like this guy [he motioned to his own person] is going to be finding any action without paying for it on such a deadline. So, I slipped inside hoping everyone was really confused, and I was in luck. They each thought that the other guy had invited me. So, I got my turn, said I had to go the bathroom, and left."

I was in tears, trying to compose myself enough that I would not bring down Sergeant Bronx's discontent. Without a pause, Nantucket continued.

"I had this girlfriend who I really liked. I mean, I really liked her. I think I might have loved her."

"Oh yeah?" I replied, wiping the cloudy tears from my cheeks where they had left pink trails down through the dust.

"Yeah, but I thought she was eventually going to cheat on me. Drove me nuts and I had to know. I asked my best friend to try and sleep with her. One night I was purposefully really mean to her, and my friend came in and was nice to her, telling me to leave. I left and that bitch slept with him. I couldn't believe it. I guess I was right," he said and took a single breath.

"And then this one time I was walking home from a friend's house after a party at like ten at night. I had to go through a small patch of forest to get to my housing development from the party. All of a sudden, I see this bright light and a full day later I woke up in a ditch. I had lost an entire day."

"Oh yeah?" My line in his dialogue.

"Yeah. It was aliens."

"Aliens?"

"You don't believe me either? I swear it, man. Aliens. I got abducted. How else would you explain my missing an entire day? Aliens, man. Aliens."

Stories were exchanged and tweaked, told over and over to every new man until they were perfect in their delivery. Some nights were like going to a comedy show and some men were sought out to share security detail with to hear the stories firsthand. Everyone had a story to tell, though not all the stories elicited laughter and smiles.

On one particularly moonlit night when the world was bathed in a warm, white light that made everything seem to glow and pop, I put on my full battle gear and trudged out under the stars to my security post for the next six hours. I caught up to Sergeant Whithers, my complement from the other platoon, and we walked in silence up to our post, relieving our two brothers and exchanging any pertinent information, of which there was none.

Still just desert for miles and miles.

Sergeant Whithers looked ten years my senior even though I was almost two years older than him. Whereas I had moved straight into our unit from the start of my military career, Sergeant Whithers had done two tours with the regular infantry before taking the Indoc. He was a quiet man, saying only enough to get the job done, though he smiled with his mouth often enough. His eyes though, they never seemed to smile.

Our Iraqi Army security guard grinned at us and gave us a thumbs-up, something he had most likely seen in old 1980s movies. Michael Jackson's *Thriller* album was just getting wildly popular in the area and cassette tapes were a hot commodity. Oddly, for all of their technological and cultural sluggishness, every single one of the Iraqis we met had a nicer cell phone than I had back in the States. As if cued, the Iraqi soldier pulled out his cellphone and hit a button. Terribly distorted music blared from the tiny speaker and he shuffled his feet in dance.

This was to be a dance-party shift.

"Put that fucking thing away," Whithers growled, pointing at the cellphone and then miming putting it in his pocket. The Iraqi soldier stopped dancing and frowned. He looked at Whithers like a child might when pleading for their parents to reverse a decision that did not go in the child's favor. Whithers's scowl remained and eventually the Iraqi put the phone away, slinking away down the berm and leaving his rifle leaned up against the sandbags we stood behind.

"Fucking savages," Whithers growled to himself. For such a mild-mannered and patient man, his reaction to the Iraqi surprised me. I chalked it up to lack of sleep and having to stare at the desert for six hours in the middle of the night. Together we checked on the heavy gun that had been brought up and settled in.

Twenty minutes later, like a dog that has been chastised, our Iraqi soldier slunk back into our peripheral vision, taking a step closer, watching our reaction, and then gaining confidence, stepping a little bit closer. After three minutes of watching him from the corner of our eyes, he shuffled back in front of us, his chin tucked and his proverbial tail between his legs. We said nothing and, after another minute of silence, his face suddenly brightened. He jammed his thin brown hand in his pocket, flourishing his cellphone suddenly as if something of great importance was contained inside.

"Please no more 'music,'" I groaned. My plea was rewarded. With a few taps of his finger, he did not bring up music. The noise was hard to place at first, but then the soldier turned his screen so that we could see it.

There, on the tiny cell-phone screen, was the most pixelated and low-fidelity version of pornography I had ever seen. It looked as if Mario had defeated Bowser in the castle and decided to make an old-school Nintendo porn with the princess. Whithers and I squinted and turned our heads. The sound was not even synced so the entire debacle was moving blurs of color smashing into other blurs of color with the soundtrack of a goat being slapped repeatedly in the flanks as it bleated.

I had always been turned on by most anything—an elegant neck, a cute-sounding sneeze ... hell, even a warm breeze—but even I could not find the least bit of eroticism in what we were viewing. The Iraqi, however, seemed to find the video extremely sensual and swayed his hips back and forth as he pointed out a dark blur and grinned, nodding his head "Yes," as if we needed prompting since our faces remained somewhat quizzical.

"Never thought I would be watching porn with an Iraqi," Whithers said dryly.

And then the trouble began.

The Iraqi, hearing Whithers speak, must have taken that as a sign we were indeed taken in by such licentious acts of, well, whatever the hell it was he thought he was showing us. The Iraqi continued to grin and then pointed to the screen, saying something that I did not quite catch. Then he pointed to Whithers and nodded. Then, holding his cellphone with his ring and pinky finger, he began rubbing his two index fingers together at Whithers.

"Fiki-fiki," the Iraqi said hopefully. He pointed at Whithers again and then repeated the gesture.

Whithers stood, took two steps forward, and then got right in the soldier's face.

"Get the fuck out of here," Whithers growled, pointing down the berm back toward the Iraqi tents. There was enough ferocity behind his words that even my stomach tightened. The Iraqi froze, his index fingers still touching. Whithers leaned in even further until his nose was almost touching the soldier's forehead and the soldier could see the minute shaking of every fiber in Whithers's jaw and the veins throbbing on his forehead.

"Get the fuck out of here or I will throw you off this fucking berm," Whithers seethed, his voice soft but the violence contained within it enough to make my bowels shake. To his credit, the Iraqi did not hesitate. He grabbed his rifle and then jumped down the berm in a few bounds, bolting for his tent as soon as he hit level ground. We watched him go and I began to laugh.

"What was that about?" I asked. At the sound of my laughter and the sight of the soldier running for his life, the hard exterior of Whithers's face began to crack and, after another moment, all the tension bled away and he even managed a chuckle.

"Fucking savage wanted to fuck me. Or me fuck him. Whatever," he said, shaking his head but smiling.

"Really?"

"Yeah. I think he showed us the porn to get us worked up and then fuck. The two fingers rubbing thing, yeah, there was a reason it wasn't a finger going inside the okay sign."

"Whithers, you old Iraqi-slayer. Not an hour on post and already getting sex thrown at you," I laughed.

"I would have done it," Whithers said suddenly, his smile fading. "I would have thrown him off this berm. I can't stand them. I can't stand any of them. We come over here to help them and they won't even help themselves. Their fucking army and police forces just up and quit the first time they are asked to do anything. They love the pay and the food, but ask them to put themselves in danger to help themselves and suddenly they all disappear back to their tiny three-field-and-a-hut world. Fuck them. We die trying to help these people and they just resign themselves to cowering."

There was a tremble in his voice that begged for no reply. This was not a conversation, but a monologue that had been rolling around inside his head for years.

"Back when I first came over, I thought we were fighting the good fight, you know? I thought we were the conquering heroes and that we were doing some good. But after a few patrols I realized that there was nothing to conquer, there was no good to be done. They couldn't give a shit if we're here or not. They don't want freedom because they don't even know what it is. A thousand years of being subject to the whims of kings and tyrants, and it's in their DNA now."

"And those assholes," Whithers said aiming his index finger toward the Iraqi Army tents. "Most are here for a paycheck and because we're here. We pull out and they'll desert if they think there will even be a chance of them getting a paper cut. I can't blame them really. They don't know what Iraq is. They don't want to know. They got their brothers and sisters, their cousins and grandparents, and that's it. That's life to them. There's no broader ideals or flags to lay down their lives for. So long as it doesn't impact their tiny little universe of one square mile, then it don't matter, and fuck whatever is happening to anyone else. They don't want to know us, don't want us here, and we are left dying for strangers."

The finality of his last sentence felt heavy on my shoulders; I let the conversation dwindle to the sound of Whithers's heavy breathing and the faint clacking of his teeth as he worked his jaw angrily in private thought. After a few minutes, I thought I would start a new topic, one that was almost always a crowd pleaser with the enlisted men—a question that usually brightened eyes and showed the determined hope of those who flirted with death almost daily.

"So, what are you going to do when you get out?"

Whithers flinched as if I had slapped him across the face with the question. There was a pain and sadness left behind when the grimace receded; Whithers gently shook his head.

"Before I got here, I was in a line company. The good ol' infantry, you know. Those were some rough and tumble boys, good as they come. Had to be, really. They would throw missions at us that in this unit would be laughed out of the briefing room. Take a squad of thirteen guys and go march down main-street Fallujah in broad daylight, and oh, by the way, there is still a heavy enemy presence, and they probably have RPGs, and sniper rifles, and oh, maybe a tank or eight. But here is a single grenade to share between your guys. Make sure it's a good throw.

"But we did as we were told. Always the good fucking warriors, you know. Never a word of protest when the boot lieutenant passed the word of what we were doing—not to him anyway. My boys would piss and bitch at me like I had any say in anything we did, like some fucking lowly sergeant is going to change the way we do shit in the infantry because 'Hey, Sir, that sounds kinda dangerous; pretty sure there is a better way,' but that's not how the infantry does things. We assault, and we never stop assaulting. Push, push, push, kill, kill, kill.

"Only, it wasn't usually us doing the killing. We may get a few shitheads here and there but fuck, man, it's their city, where they know every rat hole and choke point like the back of their hands. So, we go out and fewer of us came back each time. For what? They called them presence patrols, like we were the fucking police trying to stave off a riot after a championship football game. Should've called them 'fish in a barrel' patrols for all the good it did and how dangerous they were."

Whithers, who had slowly worked himself up until his chest heaved, suddenly became silent and peered off into the distance as if watching something I could not see. I waited.

"So, one morning my lieutenant grabs me and briefs me on this really important mission that we gets tasked with. We were to walk around underneath the tall buildings and scare the shitheads away with our scowls and protect the innocent if we saw any bad things happening, like the superheroes we were. The usual patrol for us. I spin my guys up and we head out.

"Rogers, my best friend, is my radioman and the only reason I could even stand these patrols. Just one of those real funny kids, you know. Everything that came out of his mouth made me laugh and he kept me grounded when shit got heavy. I really don't think anything ever got to him. Always grinning and making everyone else feel better with a joke or good word. Couldn't fuck with Rogers—kid was real deal.

"Well, halfway through our patrol Rogers says comms are getting screwy and we need to firm up for a second so he can kick his radio. I halt the squad and I turn to ask Rogers how much time he needs. One second, I am looking my best friend in the face, the next second his head explodes in a pink mist. Just a broken eggshell with blood and brains splattered everywhere. Fucking sniper took him the moment we stopped. That's how they worked. Hit the guy with the radio and the squad is fucked unless they can raise help on their short-distance comms. Before I even have time to yell 'Ambush,' a grenade comes sailing over a cement wall and boom." Whithers snapped his fingers. "Half my squad is deaf and bleeding. We don't even have time to react. AK fire everywhere and half my guys can't even hear it.

"We try to pull back, those who can return fire, and we make for this little courtyard with a high, thick wall—good cover. By the time we drag Rogers's body back with the radio and firm up, almost all of my squad is bleeding or dead. We radioed for help, but it was too late—they had already sprung their ambush—and just as fast as it happened, everything went quiet. So, I kneeled there holding security in the blood of all my men as they moaned, unable to hear their own cries, trying not to keep staring at Rogers's missing face and get us all killed because I couldn't stop looking. I didn't want to look; I just couldn't stop, you know.

"The quick-reaction force finds us, and we get evac-ed. Almost all of the guys in my squad are bleeding from somewhere, or so fucked up from the blast that they get pulled from the line for evaluation. Not me. I'm not bleeding or deaf, or dead. A couple of days later, I get handed a brand-new squad and told that there is this really important mission that they need me to do."

I realize Whithers is crying. It is faint at first, a gentle hum in the background, but growing with every labored breath. As he finishes his story his chest begins to shudder and, despite his effort to keep composure, he begins to sob.

"Sorry, just don't like thinking about it," he tries to explain.

"It's okay," I say, but it sounds weak and clumsy.

"There is no getting out for me," Whithers says quietly. "What the fuck am I going to do after this? The only thing that keeps me functioning is knowing that our lives depend on me burying this shit deep and completing the mission. Do what you got to do, you know? What the fuck would I do after this? I can't go back to the real world now. This is it, this is all I am good for now, killing and war. There is no getting out now. I'm broken and there is no place in the real world for guys like me."

My chest tightened hearing his conclusion. The hope, that last vestige of emotion that we all clung to, like a piece of driftwood in an endless ocean after the shipwreck of war, had left him.

"Hey, man," Whithers says, his voice suddenly fearful. "Please don't tell anyone about me crying. Please? They wouldn't understand, you know. They just wouldn't understand."

We were doomed. Caught between our deep, hidden needs and our masculine pride to stand tall and never be seen as weak, we were doomed. The vicious circle of crumbling emotional states and self-loathing for seeing ourselves as weak for "cracking" was waiting for us.

Deployments had to end sometime.

CHAPTER 41

The One-Square-Mile City

Our unit was being relieved. After months of anger and the feeling of deep loss, it was time to go home.

Without clear battle lines or a uniformed enemy, there could never be a sense of accomplishment. It felt like trying to keep water out of a hole dug at the beach. No matter how fast we scooped out the saltwater filling the hole, more would just seep in and take its place eventually. There was no definitive "win" scenario. We were not fighting an army with a general and a flag. We were fighting naked aggression and hate for the Western world. Still, we had scooped the water as fast as we could and had done our best to live up to the fearsome reputation of our unit with what little support we had been given.

I could not imagine what hell the basic infantry companies had found themselves in, thrown out into the middle of a hostile country, told to secure a house and then live there for their entire deployment. I moan and whimper, but those men, those brave, hard warriors had it a hundred times worse.

Whithers, one of the team leaders in another platoon, had been one of those basic infantry warriors. He had watched his entire team, including his best friend, ambushed and slaughtered in the streets during a daylight patrol of a city block. He alone had walked away, unscathed. The constant look in his eyes told you he would never be okay. He had fought and kicked to try out for our unit so he would not have to walk in broad daylight ever again.

There was nothing wrong with our commanders and the commanders above them all the way up the chain of command. They were hard, competent men, some of whom had cut their teeth in previous "conflicts" and had run into the same exact problems they were facing now. There was no "enemy," not until that civilian with all the rights inherent in that title picked up a rifle and shot someone, or pushed a button and blew up a truck full of Coalition forces. We were simply fighting conventionally in an unconventional war. Not one but both hands were tied behind our backs in the fight; we could only wait for the unseen knife in our stomach before we could try to kick their shin in return.

I had wished to experience war and killing, to see firsthand what others had written about. I had had my fill and then my cup had run over, pouring from the lip in a great deluge I could not stop no matter how hard I tried. I could only wish the stains on my hands were wine.

Pandora and her box is not the story of how streaming music gets to a smart phone. Careful what you wish for.

Still, we were going home.

Soon.

But first we had one last mission.

Some of our higher and the higher of those companies replacing us, needed a meet-and-greet with someone higher still, who was in charge of a vast area of operation out of which we ran the majority of our missions. They were all meeting to allay the fears of a single town's mayor. It was all above our pay grade, but we were tasked with accompanying them, which was odd since they all had their own personal security detachments, a small platoon of basic infantrymen pulled from the line companies. It was not until the mission briefing that we understood why.

First slide.

The meet-and-greet was taking place in a strange city that was exactly one mile by one mile and surrounded by an enormous cement wall, which made the entire city look like something from an era when battering rams were cutting-edge technology. It stood out among the poverty and desolation as an island of wealth and luxury, or had been at one time. It was a private city, run by an elected mayor. It was a wrought-iron gated community, populated by the rich business owners from the surrounding areas. Before the conflict, it had been something of a wonder, a verdant paradise in defiance of the harsh environment.

The pictures of the city preconflict were gorgeous and seemed like a vacation destination.

Next slide.

Not surprisingly, the city had become a target for the Insurgency. Two months earlier, the insurgents had rolled a ZPU, a four-barrel Soviet antiaircraft gun, up to the hill that overlooked the city, jacked the back of the weapon up so the barrels did not point to the sky but at the city itself, and let loose for about five minutes, firing thousands of rounds at the police station. The insurgents had also taken up springing random vehicle checkpoints along the only road leading to the city and kidnapping anyone believed to be of any importance.

Next slide.

The big concern, however, was that, two days prior to our briefing, a U.S. warrior had been shot and killed inside the city walls. He had only been exposed for a few seconds out of the top of his armored troop carrier; the single shot had hit him directly in the neck, one of the very few places not protected by Kevlar. It seemed there was a sniper running around the one-mile city, and the higher-ups did not like the idea of holding a meet-and-greet in the crosshairs of a sniper rifle.

Our mission was to rout out the sniper while also protecting the brass from being shot in the neck or armpit as they shook hands.

Next slide.

Oh, real quick, there was also a vehicle driving around the city believed to be packed with enough explosives to level a city block or two and everyone in it. Make and model unknown. Driver unknown. It could literally be any of the hundreds of cars inside the city.

Next slide.

Questions?

There were no questions. The city suddenly felt more like a gladiatorial arena than a mission. We were being pitted against a sniper and a suicide bomber who was using enough explosives to wipe out our entire platoon in the blink of an eye.

It seemed the military always saved the best for last.

The one benefit of being tasked with protecting brass of a high level is suddenly, as if by magic, we had all of the support we could have asked for. Rotary and fast movers would be in the air on station the entire time the brass was inside the city and we had artillery and tracks with the big barrels at our beck and call.

For almost ten hours, 60 warriors from three platoons ran around the city kicking in every door to any apartment that overlooked the appointed park for the meeting, and every rooftop was topped with a sniper and spotter covering every window and possible shooting position. Those not kicking in doors were running around establishing a moving cordon around the brass, and were checking any vehicle that showed any signs of being weighed down by anything heavier than a feather.

To see it, one might think the president of the United States was making a fundraiser appearance in a derelict park for all of the security and firepower being put to work in the one-mile city, only the president is usually not escorted by 60 overt gunmen, rotary and fixed-wing air assets, EOD, bomb dogs, and tanks for what ended up being a 30-minute visit.

Thirty minutes and the meet-and-greet was done. Good feelings all around complete with smiles, handshakes, and photographs. The mayor seemed elated that he deserved such Byzantine security measures.

The sniper had been clever enough to have moved on after his last kill, or to break down his rifle, hide it, and clap and cheer as Coalition forces passed by.

If there had been a vehicle-borne IED, then it had been abandoned at the first sign of any moving vehicles being checked. It would be easier to wait for Coalition forces to leave and then drive it directly into the front doors of the police station at morning muster.

Our final mission was a stunning success, according to the brass. We had proven ourselves warriors of the highest caliber, etc., etc., etc. They were still alive and overjoyed about it. Medals all around.

Still, it left a dirty taste in our mouths. We had accomplished nothing. Again.

There was no forward movement, only none of us dying, and it left us hollow and unfulfilled.

We mounted up and began our quiet convoy back to base.

"Holy shit," Boom suddenly exclaimed, holding the hook to his ear. "Air just spotted an IED emplacement about a mile up the road trying to hit this convoy and they followed him back to his house. They have eyes on. We're about to make a hard hit."

And just like that, we were speeding down the road at full tilt, grinning ear to ear and our bodies shaking with the sudden surge of adrenaline.

There was no game plan, no briefing, and no tape house mock-ups. We were going in blind, testing our constant training in adaptability and free-flow through dynamic situations. It was if the gods had suddenly, and finally, smiled upon us.

"We are lead vehicle and will hit the target first. Punch in deep and get that turret in a position to cover the front door," Boom said calmly. "When you stop the truck, everyone out but the turret gunner. We need every gun until the cavalry arrives."

For the first time it paid to be the suicide truck in the convoy.

Air directed us right up to the house and informed us of the seven men by the front door. I drove into the yard and slammed the brakes, the truck sliding to a halt 20 feet from the men. Before the truck had completely stopped, Boom was out the door, rifle up, shouting in a foreign tongue to put their hands behind their heads and kneel down. The rest of the team followed, and we glided up to the seven men like serpents, our scopes and red-dots never wavering from their chests. A second truck pulled up, and as soon as their guns were enough to cover the seven men, we poured into the house, clearing the rooms.

By the time, Sergeant Bronx and Lieutenant Rusher had gotten out of their vehicles, the area was secured and all the men of the house were under security. Sergeant Bronx grinned and nodded at Boom.

"That was average." This was the closest thing Bronx gave to praise.

"Search 'em," he said as the lieutenant used the radio to call in our exact position to higher.

The first object that was moved, a plush red pillow that had been next to one of the men, revealed a loaded AK-47. Suddenly everyone tensed. More pillows and blankets were removed. Rifles and pistols were exposed.

"Holy shit, mother lode," Boom said with a laugh.

"I want this whole fucking place turned upside down," Sergeant Bronx said, his voice gruff and deadly serious.

"RPG launcher over here," someone yelled, pulling the launcher from its clever hiding place in a hedge.

"Explosives and det cord here," someone else yelled, pouring out a tool kit and a bag full of plastic explosives.

"Mortars."

"Fuck-ton of ammo here."

The list of contraband kept growing with every piece of furniture inspected.

"Sir, you better call this in now," Sergeant Bronx said. "I think higher will want to bring in specialists for this."

Lieutenant Rusher began reporting our findings and we were informed a much bigger fish—much higher on the rank ladder—was inbound with a forensics team. This had suddenly gone far above us and the smile on Sergeant Bronx's face suggested we had reason to be very proud.

The stack of weapons and explosives was enough to support a small army and the hard faces of the men in custody gave us hope we had stumbled upon a large cell of insurgents, the taking down of whom would have an enormous impact on the surrounding battlefield for many months. The follow-on missions from their interrogations alone would supply our replacements with countless nights of raids.

Finally, after seven months, we had done something tangible. We had captured seven insurgents and their stockpile of weapons. We had made a difference.

A second convoy converged on the house; a large security detachment hustled off the trucks and made a cordon. Out of the middle truck, a large, well-fed man with a pale neck and red cheeks stepped out. He sported a gold star in the middle of his vest.

A much bigger fish indeed.

"Good work, gentlemen," the man said with a politician's smile. "Good work."

He walked over to the stock of weapons and surveyed the pile for a moment before looking at the seven men who glared at him with pure hate in their eyes.

"Excellent work, gentlemen. Now, unbind them."

For a moment nobody moved. Everyone simply stared at the heavy-jowled man. Finally, Lieutenant Rusher spoke.

"Can you repeat that, Sir?"

"I was just informed by a sheikh very important to public relations that some of these men are his family and he has vouched for them. So, unbind them and give them their rifles back."

Still, no one moved.

"With all due respect, Sir, they just emplaced an IED meant for my men and were found with all of these weapons, none of which they are supposed to have beyond the one rifle per household," Lieutenant Rusher said, waving his hand toward the cartoonish pile of weapons and explosives. "They were caught in the middle of an act of aggression toward Coalition forces."

The general's smile faded and his wobbly cheeks darkened.

"Be that as it may, Lieutenant, I have the sheikh's word that these men are not a threat. So, unbind them and give them their weapons back as ordered. Your platoon is relieved of their duty. We'll take it from here."

The threat was punctuated by two more higher-ranking officers flanking the general and glaring at Lieutenant Rusher, obviously waiting for the general to step away before they publicly reprimanded Rusher for even daring to question the general's orders.

"Yes, of course, Sir," Lieutenant Rusher quietly replied. "Get the men on the trucks, Sergeant."

"Mount up," Sergeant Bronx passed over the coms.

We got back on our trucks and watched as the seven men were cut loose and handed back their weapons with apologies.

A minute down the road, we all lost it.

"Fuck," Boom howled, slamming his fist into the roof of the Humvee. "Fuck, fuck, fuck, fuuuuuuuuck."

Fat tears burned down my cheeks as I gripped the steering wheel so tightly I thought the tiny bones in my hands would finally shatter. I cried so hard I could hardly see the road. My anger choked me until I gasped and screamed as the men seated around me dealt with the anger in their own way.

I prayed in earnest for death and for death to every man, woman, and child in that godforsaken place. It had taken everything from my brothers and I, leaving us hollow and cold.

We had not made a difference. We had not done anything but traveled thousands of miles to sacrifice our warrior brothers to a battle that could not be won.

CHAPTER 42

Pink Mist

Despite our engineer Kien's complete and utter death wish, or complete belief he was immortal, he survived his tour of duty and was whisked away from our unit, back into the foggy haze of "everything else that does not have to do with our missions." We wished him luck, knowing he would do well in life wherever he went. Where most warriors sent home letters complaining of the heat or daily gripes from deployment, Kien had been more enterprising and sent home some many thousands of dollars he had won in underground poker games to help his family.

While we thought Kien had been an outlier in his complete disregard for his own safety and mortality, his replacements were quick to prove us wrong and made us wonder if there was something they were putting in the water at the engineering school that had made them selfless martyrs.

Bosne and Nants attached to our unit with only three weeks left to our deployment. They would attach to our replacements and were slated to spend most of their deployment with them, but the engineer brass thought it would be a good idea for the experienced, veteran unit to spin them up before the green unit took over. If they were expecting us to be jovial warriors celebrating their martial prowess minute by minute and matching their own excitement and thirst for combat, they were sadly mistaken. What they attached to instead was a tired and jaded group of men who were ready to be done and hand off the daily fear of being maimed or dying to someone else. We were still professional in our actions but our hearts, when not pumping adrenaline, were no longer in it.

Our company was tasked with setting up a vehicle checkpoint along a solitary road that cut through the center of a vast tract of desert. The checkpoint would be obvious and made to look hasty, easily seen from a distance when oncoming vehicles crested one of the gently rolling dunes. Every vehicle would then be faced with a simple decision; take part in the vehicle check or turn around and make a run for it. While the checkpoint seemed rather straightforward, it was the hidden elements that were our true purpose. Any vehicle that turned around would be intercepted by one of the other platoons, hidden out in the desert and ready to chase down any vehicle that resisted the checkpoint. Those vehicles that did move toward the checkpoint were in the scopes of our sniper teams from the moment they appeared on the horizon. If they saw the checkpoint as a soft target of opportunity and stopped to rig up explosives, their vehicle would be torn to fiery shreds by our Barrett M82 .50-caliber SASR rifles.

When a vehicle did continue to the checkpoint, they were stopped 200 meters short of our vehicles and two lucky warriors got to take the long and possibly last walk out to them. The warriors would get the occupants out of the vehicle, do a body search, separate them, and then one would check the vehicle while the other held security. The vehicle was far enough away from the rest of the platoon that if there was an IED, even an enormous driving bomb like they had seen in the cities, it would only kill the two warriors doing the check.

An entire day in the blazing sun and the most dangerous thing we ran into was an old man with terrible halitosis, who made us take a step back when he opened his cracked lips.

At dusk, we pulled out into the desert and set up a harbor site to eat and rest until first light, when we would set back up. We posted our security and settled in, though no one was tired yet. Boom got a bundle of red chem-lights from the truck and cracked them all, arranging them into a pyramid surrounded by a ring of MREs to look like rocks. He sat back admiring the perfect campfire he had created, and we joined him around it, trying to recreate some semblance of normalcy. We told stories and jokes, laughing so hard at points that Sergeant Bronx got on the platoon radio frequency and told us to quiet down.

As night drew on and the talk became more sporadic, we tried to involve Bosne and Nants, asking them questions about their training and experiences. Both were straight out of combat engineering school and full of enthusiasm for their first deployment.

"So, how long were you in your unit before you deployed?" Boom asked, leaning back against the Humvee tire.

"A few weeks," Nants replied. "We got out of school and went straight to our unit—didn't get to use any of our leave time before we deployed even. Said the battalion had already taken predeployment leave and we had too much to do. I got something of a long weekend with my family, but then we were working like ants to get everything ready for the deployment. Then we got here. Why? How long do you guys get?"

"We were training together for almost a year before we deployed," Clark said, the mention of "we" drawing a quiet sigh from me. Ballas and Spears were gone, and our team's "we" was down by almost half.

"That's cool," Nants said. "I wish we got that much time, but we were both pretty excited to get over here as fast as we could."

"Excited?" Boom asked.

"Yeah, get over into the shit, see some real combat. All they ever did was talk about it in school, talking about how important our job was to the infantry and without us the infantry would be crippled."

"What is your job exactly then?" Clark asked.

"We are here to lay down our lives for you guys," Bosne said matter-of-factly.

"Wait, what?" Boom said, perking up.

"Yeah, it's the engineer's job to go before the infantry and clear the lanes so you can close with the enemy. We go first, checking for mines and IEDs, and make sure you guys can do your jobs. We die so you guys can kill the enemy."

"That is so fucked up," Boom said, the horror clear on his face.

"It's true. I would gladly die for you guys," Nants chimed in.

"Jesus, don't say that," Clark said. "You don't have to die for us. Jesus, don't say things like that."

"But it's true," Bosne retorted. "If we die so you guys can do your job then we didn't die in vain."

"Fuck, no one has to die for anyone here," Boom said. "I don't want your deaths on my hands so stop saying you want to die for us. We can all live, and everyone can just go the fuck home when this is done."

"Just saying," Nants said quietly.

"Well stop fucking saying," Boom replied. "It gives me the creeps. You two will be fine and we are going home alive. Everyone stop talking about dying now."

The mood around the campfire had soured; Boom packed the chem-lights into an empty MRE package, casting us back into a beautiful, starlit darkness that only the desert could seem to cultivate. No one spoke a word the rest of the night except to wake up the next warrior on security. The engineers had touched something raw in us and we shut down, not wanting to dwell on the possibilities. The end was too close. We were almost there.

We had all seen too many movies where the partner dies just before retirement.

After three days of checkpoints and nothing to show for them, we packed up and headed back to base. We pulled into the battalion motor pool and instantly felt the quiet weight that had settled over everything. We began pulling our heavy guns off the trucks, when I saw Stitch, my best friend from the Holding Tank and the Schoolhouse, walking up to our trucks. I didn't notice how swollen and bloodshot his eyes were until he was standing in front of me.

"Zimm is dead," he said quietly. I closed my eyes. Zimm had been with us from the beginning and had even painted our class flag at the Schoolhouse.

"How?"

"Ambush. They were hunting down a mortar team, Zimm out front as always, and they got ambushed from the reeds. They returned fire and when everything stopped, Zimm was dead. Shot in the face."

"Oh," I said numbly. I would cry, long and hard, but not until later. Right then, I could not feel anything, only the cold emptiness of my brain protecting me, hiding the hurt until it would be safe to feel it, though with considerable interest due. The engineers, so eager and enthusiastic two days prior, did not know what to say as Boom and Clark squeezed my shoulder and then continued to unload the truck.

Two weeks later, after turning over our missions to our replacement battalion, one of my left coast brothers I had gone to the Schoolhouse with walked up to me as we made our final gear check to leave the base and start our journey home.

"Hey, did you guys know Nants or Bosne?" Slant asked. The two engineers had been attached to Slant's company and I thought he must be inquiring about my thoughts on their performance in the short time they had been with us.

"Yes, good guys. Really gung-ho, but good guys."

"Yeah, they're dead," Slant said. This time, I could not reply. Slant waited but then continued when he saw I was unable to form the question. "We went out, all sneaky-pete, and went after some shithead down in the Nutsack. Ended up a dry hole, but it took so fucking long that the captain thought it would be a good idea to throw out the engineers to sweep the return route since, well, you know, there is only one way in or out. Nants and Bosne jump out ahead and start the sweep, side by side, sweeping every inch of that shitty road.

"One second I am looking at them through the nods and the next second, boom, pink mist, the both of them. Nothing left. Huge IED. Would have killed everyone in a Humvee."

"Oh."

"They didn't feel a thing, man. Pink mist. That's the way I want to go if I'm going," Slant said thoughtfully.

"Yeah," I replied, unable to formulate anything of conversational value.

"Well, have fun back at home, man. Hope we get to catch up some time," Slant said smiling, sticking out his hand. I shook it and tried to muster a smile, though I fear it may have fallen short.

"Stay safe," I said. *Stay alive.*

Slant nodded and sauntered back toward the battalion area they had taken over. I stood there for a minute longer, staring off at the horizon.

They didn't feel a thing, man. Pink mist.

Pink mist.

CHAPTER 43

Finale

In the present, it was just announced on the news that some major Iraqi cities many warriors had died to capture and hold were just taken over by the Insurgency after we "withdrew." We conquered, men giving their blood and their souls for the victory that was asked of them, only for politicians to abandon their ghosts and forget their great sacrifice. My brothers are among those ghosts, now only forgotten statistics.

They will always remain beautiful memories of men, to those who raised them or served beside them. Those that did not die there left a piece of themselves that can never be replaced or heal.

Not that you can hear me. Not that it matters now.

I am sorry, Mr. Hemingway.

I am sorry, Mr. Heller.

I am sorry, Mr. Vonnegut.

General Sherman, I did not listen.

Afterword

Thank you, thank you, thank you.

I hope you enjoyed the book, that it took you away for a moment or two. If you did enjoy it, please give me a review, as that is the best way to help authors. A five-star rating is worth a bar of gold when your name is unknown.

I wrote this book purposefully vague, with respect to my unit and branch, because I believe my experience was something of an unfortunate universal across all the respective spec ops units at that time. I am proud as hell I was a Recon Marine and everything I accomplished during my service.

But I'm not special, so "John Doe" stood in my place in an unnamed branch so you could focus on the stories.

If you like my writing, please check out *Company of Bones*, Book One of the Pendulum Series, available on Amazon. It was my catharsis when Covid shuttered my business for four months and I found myself back in that cold, dark cave.

Thank you, thank you, thank you.